THE
EIGER
OBSESSION

John Harlin III is editor of the *American Alpine Journal* and contributing editor for *Backpacker*. A former cohost of PBS's *Anyplace Wild*, Harlin is a frequent contributor to numerous publications, including *Outside* magazine. He lives in Hood River, Oregon, and Oaxaca, Mexico, with his wife, Adele Hammond and their daughter, Siena. *The Eiger Obsession* was the winner of the Banff Mountaineering History Award 2007 and was shortlisted for the Boardman Tasker Prize 2008.

THE
EIGER
OBSESSION
JOHN HARLIN III

Facing the Mountain that Killed My Father

arrow books

Published by Arrow Books 2009

5 7 9 10 8 6 4

Copyright © John Harlin III 2008

The right of John Harlin III to be identified as the author of this work has
been asserted by him in accordance with the Copyright,
Designs and Patents Act, 1988

Published by arrangement with Simon & Schuster Inc., New York, USA

First published in the United Kingdom in 2008 by Hutchinson

Arrow Books
The Random House Group Limited
20 Vauxhall Bridge Road, London, SW1V 2SA

www.penguin.co.uk

Addresses for companies within The Random House Group Limited can be
found at: www.randomhouse.co.uk/offices.htm

The Random House Group Limited Reg. No. 954009

A CIP catalogue record for this book
is available from the British Library

ISBN 9780099525141

Penguin Random House is committed to a sustainable future for
our business, our readers and our planet. This book is made from
Forest Stewardship Council® certified paper.

Printed and bound in Great Britain by Clays Ltd, Elcograf S.p.A.

CONTENTS

CONTENTS

THE EIGER
OBSESSION

Grandes Jorasses

Mont Blanc

Bernkastel-Kues

Dru

Fou

■ Mer de Glace

■ Biolet Campground

Chamonix

Looking Southeast

Luzern

S W I T Z E R

Interlaken ●

Grindelwald ●

Lauterbrunnen ● ▲

Eiger

Lake Geneva

● Leysin

● Geneva

Chamonix ●

FRANCE

▲ *Mont Blanc*

ITALY

● Grenoble

0   10   20 miles

0   10 20   30 kilometers

GERMANY

Munich•

•Zurich

AUSTRIA

LIECHTENSTEIN

L A N D

ITALY

•Trento

Eiger *Mönch* *Jungfrau*

Kleine Scheidegg ■

■ Grindelwald

Lauterbrunnen ■

Looking Southeast

THE EIGER
OBSESSION

ONE

THE SHATTERED PILLAR

———————————————

WHEN I was a kid it always bothered me that Dad hadn't been able to survive most of his 4,000-foot fall. He would have wanted to savor the event: his "ultimate experience," the one he had been looking forward to, even though he wanted it to come later. My mother made sure that the film in his movie camera was developed, because he would have filmed the whole thing if possible. That's just how he was, and it would have been strange if he'd changed at the last minute.

Or maybe he would have. Changed, that is. Another minute of life might have been enough time for him to reflect on his children, ages eight and nine, and to realize how selfish it was to die when they needed him. Or maybe he would have learned that the opportunity to watch his children grow up, to participate in their lives, is a much greater adventure than dying. And what about his parents? Did he think about how he was hurting them? No, I don't think he did. But if he'd had that minute to think, perhaps he would have. Maybe it's best he didn't. It was too late, anyway.

But who am I to criticize? My own nine-year-old daughter is watching me through the telescope as I climb past where Dad came down. I didn't want her to be watching; that's just how it worked out. I'm here, climbing up the Eiger, headed toward the place where Dad's rope broke almost forty years ago.

When I was young I believed the final sentences of Dad's biography: "Johnny has decided that, when he is grown, he wants to be a naturalist and forest ranger, with plenty of skiing on the side, and some mountaineering as well. Not on the Eiger, though; the Eiger is his father's. His own eye is on the Matterhorn." That had been true when Dad died, when I was nine and he had promised to take me up the Matterhorn as soon as I turned fourteen. It did not stay true after I became obsessed with climbing and turned my eye on the Eiger.

This morning, when I tied into the rope, I was in the grips of destiny. I knew I'd be here someday. I could have changed my fate, except that this is the fate I chose. My only fear was whether I would measure up to the challenge. For me, death isn't the ultimate adventure; it's the ultimate failure. And while I can find no evidence that Dad ever wrote about needing his children, I write about my daughter all the time. It would be hard to find two people more different than my father and myself.

And yet a few years ago I was in a hut on the Italian side of the Matterhorn, perched on a sharp ridge at 12,000 feet, overhanging thousand-foot drops on both sides. A storm raged outside, and every so often the door would fling open and otherwordly apparitions appeared, clad in crampons, roped together, and coated in wind-driven snow. The door would slam shut and the climbers would shake off their snow-encrusted clothing. At an adjacent table an older man kept staring at me as my partner and I prepared our dinner. He was lean and weathered, maybe sixty, and reflected forty years of mountaineering past, with at least another decade left to go. His friends were all speaking in Czech, but this man was quietly staring at me. Finally he urged his young friend, who spoke English, to approach my table.

"My friend wants to know," he said, "are you John Harlin?"

The older man didn't even know I existed. But he'd been

climbing in the 1960s, back when everyone knew about Dad, whose name was also John Harlin, and he'd seen my father's pictures. The next morning he and everyone else in the hut went down, scared off by the storm's aftermath: ice-coated rock. My partner and I continued to the summit and over to the Swiss side of the mountain. We were on our way to the Eiger, but fresh storms got in the way and we didn't climb it.

It's always been the same. I can't go climbing without Dad's shadow hanging over me. And I love that shadow as much as it appalls me.

I don't believe in ghosts, but that's not keeping me from looking for them here on the Eiger. Dad was the twenty-eighth person to die on this wall, and the toll has now grown to the mid-forties. Protection is now better, skills are higher, clothing has vastly improved, but above all we have helicopters to thank. Now when someone gets in trouble, at the first break in the weather a helicopter goes in with a rescuer dangling from the end of a long-line winch, and the would-be victim is plucked to safety. It's a different world today, a safer world, though gravity still makes missiles out of falling stones, and a flux in temperatures still glazes smooth rock with thin ice. Someone died here just two weeks ago. But they're not dying at the rate they used to. Eight people died on this climb before it was even a route, before anyone made it more than halfway to the summit. The first three people to try climbing this wall solo—without a partner—also fell to their deaths. Dad used to say, "Death is a part of it all." I say it's the ugly part. But it's why I'm here, why Eiger climbers come. We come because they died, and by dying they created this legend, and we want to be a part of the legend, without dying.

Until the 1930s, the north face of the Eiger was just a tourist attraction: a gigantic shadowed wall of rock, ice, and storms, the biggest in the Alps. It's hard for me to see this 6,000-foot near-vertical face simply as a piece of Alpine decoration, but that's all it used to be. Not that it didn't already have stories. The Eiger, with its great brooding wall rising to a 13,022-foot summit, is the left-most and smallest of three stunning peaks. The Jungfrau, meaning "young lady" or "maiden" in German, is the tallest and fairest, at 13,445 feet. In between rises the 13,368-foot Mönch. The story goes that the tempestuous Eiger—which is often translated as "ogre," though others deny the term—wants to put his lascivious mitts on the Jungfrau, but is kept away by the jolly Mönch, or Monk. You can buy old cartoonish paintings and more recent postcards attesting to this relationship in the Alpine village of Grindelwald, which rests in the valley bottom almost directly underneath the Eiger. In Grindelwald, you have to crane your neck to see the Eiger's summit 10,000 vertical feet above you. You can see a bit of the Mönch from there as well, but none of the Jungfrau. To see those peaks you need to take the cog railway up to a little cluster of hotels and restaurants at Kleine Scheidegg. At 6,760 feet, Kleine Scheidegg is well above tree line and far too high for a village, but it makes a spectacular setting for ski hotels, summer sightseeing, and Eiger gazing.

It's impossible to understand the Alps without understanding relative elevations. On the published page, elevations are just a bunch of numbers, but in real life these differences define the scale of things, and this scale supplies a Wagner-sized dose of melodrama. Absolute altitudes are as nothing before these relative numbers. The higher Mönch and Jungfrau, for example, hold no wall even close to matching the Eiger's—nor does any other mountain in all the Alps, nor for that matter in either North or South America. You have to travel to the Himalaya to find such imposing verticality for so great a height.

When a climber today speaks of the Eiger, we assume he means its north face. Nineteenth-century mountaineers, however, ignored the north face—to them it didn't look remotely climbable. At first all that mattered to mountaineers was the summit, and the Eiger's had been reached way back in 1858 when an Irishman was quoted a cheaper price by Swiss guides for climbing the Eiger than the Matterhorn, which at the time was also virgin.

4

The Irishman and his guide went up a ridge on the west side. Over the following years other ridges were climbed as well. Strangely enough, the north face wasn't left entirely alone. At the turn of the twentieth century, Swiss engineers put a tunnel through it. They were on their way to the summit of the Jungfrau and put a switch-back inside the Eiger, but after twelve years of blasting and picking through the Eiger and the Mönch, they finally called it quits inside a rock pinnacle on the pass between the Mönch and the Jungfrau, where they built a restaurant. The goal was simply to entertain tourists, giving them a cog-driven ride to Europe's highest and most spectacular rail-served observation deck. I suspect it is the most amazing feat of tourist tunneling in the world.

Maidens, monks, ogres, ski lodges, and cog railways are not the reasons Dad and I came here. Our Eiger story begins in 1935 when a new breed of climbers from the Eastern Alps—Germany and Austria—brought their fresh vision to Switzerland in order to climb the biggest wall of all. Their new vision was that nothing was impossible. Every summit in the Alps had long ago been reached, and most of the ridges and easy faces had been climbed more recently. Now their goal was to climb the biggest and steep-est of the faces, the ones that had been dismissed as ridiculous in earlier decades. Usually these faced north, where glaciers of old carved deepest and today's ice and snow freeze longest. To accom-plish their goals they did three things: they learned how to climb better than anyone else, they used pitons as artificial aids to help them get up what they couldn't climb with hands and feet alone, and they risked their lives as no one had before. In short, they rose to the challenge. By 1935 all the great north faces in the Alps had been climbed. Except one.

The first two emissaries from the East arrived here in August of 1935. Max Sedlmayer and Karl Mehringer hiked to the base of the Eiger's wall and in two days climbed halfway to the top, dis-playing the boldest, most technically proficient climbing ever seen in the Western Alps. They then froze to death in a storm. The site of their final ordeal has been known as Death Bivouac ever since, and Mehringer's body sat there entombed in snow and ice until it was discovered in 1962.

Four more Germans and Austrians came the following summer, in two pairs of two. They met and joined up on the mountain, and in a brilliant display of navigation, they discovered a line of weakness on the lower face, which is somewhat easier than the route followed by Sedlmayer and Mehringer. The four made it almost as high as Death Bivouac when they turned back. The throng of journalists and other spectators at Kleine Scheidegg speculated that one climber had been injured by a falling stone. This had happened two days earlier, but they'd climbed on nonetheless until apparently the injured man was too weak to continue upward. All four were climbing down, slowly and carefully, when disaster struck. Below them was a section of rock on which they had used a special trick: the leader had traversed across smooth rock using tension from the rope. Now they had to reverse the tension traverse—but there was no place to fix the rope in this direction. As they searched for a solution, one of them slipped, plunging to his death. Another was pulled up to the piton, where he froze. A third strangled in the rope. Toni Kurz was still alive, trapped on the overhanging rock.

By one of those twists of Eiger fate, these events occurred within earshot of a tunnel window leading to the cog railway inside the face. Minutes before the accident, a workman had leaned out the window and shouted for them, since everyone knew there were climbers on the wall. A climber had yelled back a cheery "All's well!" When the worker heard this, he put a pot of tea on the stove to warm his arriving guests. But an hour or two later they still had not shown up. According to Heinrich Harrer's *The White Spider,* the worker's mood grew sour from impatience and he walked back to the window to find out what was delaying them. He yelled out into space, where wind-whipped clouds raced by. A desperate voice called back, "Help! Help! The others are all dead. I am the only one alive. Help!"

The worker ran back into the tunnel and telephoned for help. Soon after, two Swiss mountain-rescue guides climbed onto the cog railway to investigate. At the tunnel window, the men crawled onto the ice-glazed face and slowly approached the unseen voice. Eventually they came to within 300 feet of Kurz and learned his plight. But it was impossible to reach him and darkness was falling. He pleaded with them, saying that he couldn't survive the night; they shouted they'd be back in the morning.

The next day four Swiss guides made it to within 130 feet of Kurz. They found him hanging from the rope, one hand and arm frozen solid, and eight-inch icicles dripping from the crampon points on his feet. But his voice was strong. The guides told him he had to somehow climb down to his dead partner, use his ice axe to cut the body free from the rope, climb back up as high as he could get, then split the rope he'd recovered into its major strands, tie these together, and lower the cord to the rescuers so that they could attach a stronger rope that he could then pull up and lower himself on. It was asking a lot of a hypothermic climber with a frozen arm and hand, but eventually Kurz managed every step. To separate the strands he used his teeth and one good hand. This took him five hours and gained him a cord just long enough to reach his rescuers. They attached a strong rope, and slowly Kurz pulled it up with his teeth and one hand. But the rescue rope wasn't long enough, so the guides tied on another. Eventually Kurz pulled the first rope up, and somehow he managed to attach his carabiner rappeling system, another Eastern innovation. Slowly he crept down the free-hanging rope until he reached the knot between the rescue ropes. And there the carabiner jammed. He fought and fought while his strength was running out; he even tried to chew the knot into suppleness, his teeth chattering against the metal carabiner. A guide climbed onto the shoulders of another guide and was able to touch Kurz's crampons with his ice axe. And then Kurz said quite clearly, "I can do no more," and slumped over dead.

I hate that story.

But that's where I'll be early tomorrow morning, at the Hinterstoisser Traverse, named for the Bavarian climber who pioneered the irreversible crossing. Today I'll be climbing past where two Italians fell in the summer of 1938, bringing the total death count up to eight even before the face was climbed.

Down in Kleine Scheidegg, Eiger-watching on the telescope had turned into a vulture's pastime. From 1935 onward newspaper headlines had been trumpeting "The battle with the Eiger Wall" and punning "Nordwand" (German for "north wall") into "Mordwand" ("death wall"). Meanwhile, old-guard climbers had been going ballistic. To many conservatives, the new techniques and attitudes being developed in the Eastern Alps perverted their beloved sport, perverted even the structure of society. The Swiss journal *Sport* editorialized that the Eastern influence was "evil," and of Kurz and friends, they wrote, "If they had reached the top it would have been merely degradation inflicted on one of our great peaks. . . ."

Over in England at the Alpine Club, whose members had essentially invented climbing as sport just a few generations earlier, their *Alpine Journal* declared that climbing the north face would be "ninety percent luck," where "a fanatical disregard of death, staying power and bodily toughness are details of mere secondary importance." Climbing on this face was nothing short of "a degenerate form of the Children's Crusade of the Middle Ages." The club's president added in 1938: "The Eigerwand continues to be an obsession for the mentally deranged of almost every nation. He who first succeeds may rest assured that he has accomplished the most imbecile variant since mountaineering first began."

All these quoted words are reprinted in Heinrich Harrer's definitive Eiger history, *The White Spider.* Harrer's personal response included, "Climbing is the most royal irrationality out of which Man, in his creative imagination, has been able to fashion the highest personal values. Those personal values, which we gain from our approach to the mountains, are great enough to enrich our life. Is not the irrationality of its very lack of purpose the deepest argument for climbing?" Shortly after the Italians died in 1938, Harrer himself made the first ascent of the Eiger's north face. He was perhaps the least experienced climber in what started as two rival teams of Austrians and Germans and merged into one rope of four. Anderl Heckmair emerged as their leader, and together they climbed brilliantly up the face in four days, the last two of which were spent in storm.

A year after their success, Hitler blitzed into Poland and the British captured Harrer as a POW in India, where he had been scouting for a future attempt on Nanga Parbat, the ninth-highest peak in the world. In 1943 he escaped from prison and spent two years traveling overland as a fugitive to forbidden Lhasa, where he befriended and tutored the young Dalai Lama. Harrer chronicled his epic journey in *Seven Years in Tibet.* I met him after a Washington, D.C., lecture in 1990 in which he had praised my father highly, explaining how Dad had been the first American to climb Harrer's own route on the Eiger's north face. But more importantly, he told how in 1966 the "John Harlin Route" became only the second line up the massive wall, and how Dad's route had been the biggest climb of its era, just as Harrer's ascent in 1938 had been the greatest of its own era. Heinrich Harrer had been one of my father's heroes, and Dad had always wanted to meet him, though he never did. I felt like a bridge between two great men who should have known each other.

In the introduction to *Seven Years in Tibet,* Harrer famously wrote, "All our dreams begin in youth." The Eiger had been one of my biggest dreams, appearing when I was twenty and was reentering the climbing world for the first time since my father's death. I wanted to climb all of Dad's big routes and launch into new ones of my own. Then tragedy struck, and publicly I vowed not to climb dangerous walls. Still, the Eiger's tentacles never let me go. In the secret recesses of my soul, immune from the pressures of responsibility, I always felt that of all the mountains in the world, there is only one I have to climb.

And finally, here I am.

My partners, Robert and Daniela Jasper from Germany, are on the rope in front of me. We've been waiting two weeks for conditions to finally get right, and now we think they are. Above I can make out many of the named features of this, the 1938 Route: to my left the Shattered Pillar reclines precariously against the wall; above, the Hinterstoisser Traverse holds the memory of its infamous tragedy; the three numbered icefields follow, famously peppered with falling rocks; then we'll reach Death Bivouac, where Dad spent most of the last two weeks of his life; the Ramp will try to block us with its notorious Waterfall Chimney and Ice Bulge pitches; the Traverse of the Gods leading to the Spider will allow me to look down on where Dad's rope broke; we'll climb the Exit Cracks to reach the summit two days from now, if all goes well.

The rope comes tight and my eyes return to the immediacy of climbing. Eiger rock feels cold to my bare hands. There is a long, long way to go.

TWO

CASTLES AND CRAGS

I **WISH** I knew my father. All my life people have asked me how much I remember him, and the answer is that I really don't know. My knowledge of him is a hybrid of what I've been told, what I've read, and what I actually remember. Where does a true memory end and a planted one begin? And which is truer, the first-hand impressions a son gathers on his own, replete with the baggage of that relationship, or the secondhand stories that are filtered through the luggage of friends, family, and biographers?

I've met so many people who thought they knew Dad, and so much has been written about him, and I've seen so many photos, that keeping those separate from my personal memories is pretty much impossible. Family and friends, of course, wanted me to know the good stuff. By the age of thirteen, my reading about Dad had been limited to the short text in *Life* magazine accompanying his double-page color portrait and the headline: "I'd have thought the Eiger would break before John." Also a profile in the *Weekend Telegraph* magazine that eulogized him under the title: "John Harlin: The Man Who Had to Excel." Accompanying pictures showed Grandpa John (labeled "Rear Admiral") in his two-star navy uniform straightening Dad's air force tie, Dad standing in front of his

F-100 fighter jet, and a family portrait in our home in Leysin, Switzerland, with Dad's pipe in mouth and a proud smile on his face.

The blurb at the top of the article summarized what was to come:

> He climbed the North Face of the Matterhorn at 20 and worked for Balmain as a dress designer. He graduated as top pilot of his class in the U.S. Air Force and flew in the USAF formation flying team. He played for the All-American Services football team and at 30 could still run 100 yards in 9.7 seconds. What drove John Harlin to excel at everything he did? What drove him to the Eiger? "He was searching for something," said one of his companions, "something that he thought he could find through climbing."

That was the father I knew. Or thought I knew. Dad died just before I turned ten, and left me with one perspective. His biography, *Straight Up: John Harlin: The Life and Death of a Mountaineer,* by James Ramsey Ullman, came out when I was twelve and I read it at thirteen, leaving me with another perspective. It turns out that Dad didn't climb the Matterhorn at all, let alone by its notorious north face; instead he'd had an ignominious debacle and never admitted the truth. He didn't work for Pierre Balmain, as he'd led some people to believe, though he had spent a weekend at the designer's house, where he was told he wasn't cut out to be a dress designer. He was indeed the top pilot in his air force class, but they didn't take him into their formation flying team. He played on the Hahn Air Base football team in Germany, but not the All-American Services team. *Straight Up* doesn't speak to how fast he ran one hundred yards in the last year of his life, so one item in the *Weekend Telegraph*'s brief list of "facts" might have been true. The worst of it is that in all likelihood, each of the partial truths was told to the reporter by my father himself.

So I have to wonder: would I really have known Dad better if he'd stayed alive?

In many ways it was James Ramsey Ullman who gave me my father. Not to be nurtured by him, but to understand him, or at least to begin the understanding process. Jim didn't arrive in our house in Leysin until the summer after my father's death. He had been following Dad's career from a distance, as I don't think they ever met in life, though Jim probably saw Dad give his speech at the American Alpine Club's annual meeting in 1964, two years earlier. Ullman was a prolific writer of popular novels and nonfiction, and his climbing books made him likely the most widely read mountain writer in the English language. In Dad's life and death Ullman saw the ideals from his novels played out in real life. The trajectory of Dad's life—and his death in the pursuit of a great dream following years of intense effort—was the stuff of fiction. You'd expect the hero to have character flaws, even a hero popularly known as "the Blond God," as Dad was often called. Ullman swooped in for the story. And because of him I had a fuller portrait of my father.

Dad was heavily in the process of becoming himself when death cut the journey short. I still cry sometimes when I describe his death—not so much because it was unfair to me, but because it was unfair to him, unfair to the life he could have led, to the contributions he could have made, to the mature person he nearly was in the end. Mom cried from joy when I turned thirty-one, and had thus outlived my father by a year.

My father used to tell Mom that she would make a pretty widow, as she wore black well. He told her that again the winter he died. It infuriated her, as did his bragging about close calls. So he didn't talk about those much, but the widow comment was too tempting. Her anger came because he seemed not to value our feelings, and because she felt it would be a waste of a good mind and body. He countered that her concern was for her own feelings and that this was selfishness—and that what he did with his mind and body was his own business. So she wore to the funeral the very dress that had prompted his comment. It was one she had bought to stuff in a backpack: it didn't take up much space or weight, it could be washed in a glacier stream, and when they went to dinner in the valley, it would not look as if she had come directly from a base camp or a pack trip.

I don't believe that Dad actually had any desire to die. But he was perfectly willing to take death as the consequence of a life worth living, which to him was always at the edge. In his unpublished essay "The Web: An Entanglement in Interpretation," he wrote:

> A man strains for a handhold and drives a piton that secures him to the mountain that is god-like in its permanence. But he clings between permanence and a space without limits. It is then that the profession of mountaineering becomes an illusion, a falsity eroded by the acid of man's own transience and the brevity of his instant of time. As the warmth of life rushes out, his body reacts in a spasm of the animal's desperation to live. When the web hangs on the rock and we have survived, an awe emerges for the simplicity required to endure.

Of a moonlit solo climb in the Calanques of France's Mediterranean coast, Dad wrote, "I knew that if I climbed on, it would be to prove something. It would be a performance, and I would not be satisfied until I killed myself. . . . If I were killing myself I must not push that far yet, I must be careful. Later, maybe, later. Then I knew how much I yearned for that ultimate experience—and how fear had masked it. By piercing that mask, that shell of a body, I wanted to physically transcend the personal with a perspective reality—to find a vivid moment of truth. But not quite yet."

Those are some of the lessons I learned from Dad: be strong, love beauty, endure all, and if it turns out you've bitten off too much or the stars are misaligned, revel in every moment of life's ultimate adventure: dying.

●　●　●

NOT LONG after Dad's death, his own father, John Harlin, Sr., reminisced: "He was born in Kansas City, but he was conceived in La Paz, Bolivia. La Paz is 13,000 feet up. About the same as the Eiger. Sometimes I almost think that's how it got into his blood." Grandpa John had been flying for a mining company in the Amazon during a period when his erstwhile employer, Transcontinental and Western Air, later known as TWA, was in bankruptcy from having lost the U.S. government postal contract. They regained the contract by the time Dad was born, hence his flatland birthplace at TWA's headquarters in Missouri, in 1935.

His Andean conception may not have influenced his direction in life, but his birth into a flying family certainly did. Dad grew up around planes the way I did around mountains. Before TWA, his father had pioneered air routes on the Atlantic coast of South America in a "flying boat" and flown bombers from an aircraft carrier between the World Wars. After Dad's birth Grandpa flew passenger planes beacon to beacon across North America, then rejoined the navy to spend World War II with the Naval Air Transport Service in Hawaii. Immediately after the war, he set up TWA's Ireland operations before becoming chief of operations for TWA's new international division. They moved to Versailles, outside Paris, when Dad was eleven, where they lived in a chateau built by Louis XVI for his sister Elizabeth. From there they traveled all over Europe and north Africa establishing the renamed Trans World Airlines. A few years later they moved back to the States, and Grandpa John gave up his executive position to return to flying, from which he eventually retired as a captain as well as rear admiral in the Naval Reserve.

Dad's parents wanted him to attend Annapolis Naval Academy. In preparation, they sent him off for a summer at Bullis, a navy prep school. But what Bullis taught my father was that he hated military drills and discipline. He chose Stanford University instead, near his home in Redwood City, just south of San Francisco. In compensation to his parents and in the hope of flying, he signed up for Navy ROTC at Stanford. Eventually the navy tested his urine and decided there was too much sugar in it (a risk for diabetes) so they couldn't accept him; with military logic, the air force took him instead. It was one of those strange twists of fate with enormous repercussions down the years: the navy doesn't station fliers near the Alps.

Marilyn Miler, my future mother, and Dad met in 1954, in the Stanford Alpine Club when he was a nineteen-year-old sophomore and she a twenty-year-old junior. She fell in love with his sensitivity to beauty and art, combined with his athletic power and intellectual breadth, a combination she didn't see in others. Where most climbers would march up the trail to reach their routes, Dad would pause to appreciate the gnarled form of a dead tree, and to remark on it. Both of Mom's parents were college educated, but they had chosen a reclusive, simple, Thoreauvian lifestyle in the woods of Washington state where they, too, reveled in nature. Mom was at Stanford on a scholarship, and a scholar she was. Her thinking was rational and meticulous, like the botany professor she would eventually become. She was enjoying her youthful brush with climbing, but felt no attraction to hard physical adventure, especially not the risky kind. In the spring of 1955 the young lovers were seriously discussing marriage. When my dad-to-be flew off to Europe for the summer (he could fly free standby on TWA) she drove to the Hopkins Marine Station in Monterey, on the California coast, southwest of Stanford.

While there she started having second thoughts about the maturity of her twenty-year-old fiancé. Among his troubling attitudes was his reaction to the death of their good friend, Ann Pottinger, who had succumbed to exhaustion while attempting Higher Cathedral Spire in Yosemite. Mom wrote to her parents that "John has eternal admiration for Ann, because she *forced* herself." By contrast, Mom had turned back on the same climb the weekend before Ann's death because the heat and strain were too much for her. Dad had been furious at her weakness. After Ann died, Mom pointed out the obvious wisdom of her own action. Dad blew up at that, scolding her with, *"At least she tried!"*

While Mom was in Monterey, Dad was trying to climb in the Alps and to find work in Parisian haute couture, having recently declared his college major to be art and dress design. During a practice climb for the Matterhorn, he took an eighty-foot fall (according to him) on the steep side of the Riffelhorn. The next day he and his partner got lost in the dark trying to find the bottom of the north face of the Matterhorn. When it seemed they wouldn't have time to climb that face after all, they switched back to the Hörnli Ridge (the standard route), but ran out of time and turned back before reaching the summit. Afterward, Dad took a train to Paris, where the only top-flight interview he could secure was with Pierre Balmain. Balmain wrote later that my father was "completely off-type for a designer," but this intrigued him enough to invite him to his country home for the weekend. Dad was shown his room and, Balmain continued, "a few minutes later he appeared on the lawn wearing only the briefest of red shorts. He was walking so naturally in the sun that the three of us greatly admired both his physique and his nonchalance at displaying it." At nearly six feet in stature, endowed with large muscles naturally sculpted (he didn't lift weights), and with yellow hair topping what was often called a movie-star face, he already inhabited the nickname he'd later be given, "the Blond God."

Dad's spin on the Matterhorn and Paris stories would haunt him beyond the rest of his life. His Matterhorn fiasco in some tellings became an ascent of the north face, and the Balmain visit became an apprenticeship. While it wasn't the first nor would it be the last time he would inflate achievements to suit the way he wished things had gone rather than the way they actually had, these are the two examples I see repeatedly mentioned in print and in climbers' private letters. Charitable friends say that he wanted these successes so badly that he probably came to believe in them himself. I didn't used to think such self-deception was possible, but I'm now learning that it is. Some things are clear: Dad had supreme faith in his ability to achieve his goals; only the highest goals were worth striving for; and failure simply didn't register—it couldn't be accepted.

The final twist of 1955, with the longest-running consequences, came shortly after. Dad stormed back from Europe in a fit of jealousy, having heard an untrue rumor that Mom had been too friendly with another man. They passionately made up for uncommitted sins, and the planted seed became me. When I started making myself known, the marriage was hastily set for October. I was born seven months later as my mother was on her way to a parasitology lab; instead she made a hasty detour to the school hospital.

My mother somehow managed to wrap up her undergraduate degree a month after I was born and an accelerated master's degree the following year (plus associate membership in Sigma Xi, a national honorary scientific society), while helping Dad to pass his courses so he could move on to the air force and earn a living for his family. Meanwhile Dad spent much of my first two summers climbing in the Canadian Rockies, and in the school year between he was president of the Stanford Alpine Club. I've grown up with stories of being carried to almost 10,000 feet on Mount Rainier, of Mom climbing Mount Saint Helens with a breast pump while I was crawling the floor at her parents' home, of hiking to the top of Yosemite Falls, where my parents endured their friends' criticism while I toddled outside the tent in a gentle rain. In 1950s America, these things just weren't done. Mom only had to see the huge smiles on my face to know that I was in my element outside.

With one child born, it was time to add the other so that they would grow up together, and so my sister Andréa arrived on schedule early in 1958. Mom's coveted Ph.D. would have to wait. A few months later Grandpa George helped to drive us from Washington state to Florida, where my father was stationed, and then Dad's ordeal began: trying to balance work and family while craving his youthful freedom above all else. We moved, not always in sync, from Florida to Oklahoma to Arizona. When we reached Arizona he spent nearly every weekend on desert crags. His air force motto was "A flier yes, a soldier no." In his Vance Air Force Base class yearbook, under "Likes" he listed "mountain climbing," and under "Dislikes" he listed "Air Force."

Dad reveled in freedom, and reacted like a snared animal when he felt fettered. Children were links in the chain. He wrote Mom to that effect during one of the out-of-sync base moves:

> When I'm away from the kids, my desire for you, my sex appetite, my personality, everything, changes. With them I have a trapped feeling, and I lose interest in myself, you, even life. I just become a slob. . . . But away, I become a romantic. My whole body starts enjoying life—a breeze—the taste of a drink—the sounds that are all around—music. I become very sensitive, careful of how I speak; more graceful in movement—more interested in sports (and better at them)—just a different person. This person is more me, and it's the way I want to be.

And he was that better person when he was in his element. When flying, he wrote:

> Sometimes the clouds, especially cirrus, would reach nearly 40,000 feet. On climbing out, the bird would be heavy with fuel. And as I approached the tops, the rate of climb would sink to less than one thousand feet per minute. I could see the sun straight above, but I could never seem to free myself from that heavy mist.
>
> Thirty-six thousand feet, 37,000 feet, 38,000 feet.
>
> Minutes would stretch infinitely. And always that sun was saying: "I'm here. I'm here. Can't you reach me?"
>
> Then all at once there I am in that world of color and dimension, the clouds actually below me, their forms sculp-

tured by the light. I want to shout for joy, for being alive in
the sun!

Flying and climbing at the limits of his abilities were but two
paths to the same world: nature, adventure, introspection, and
freedom—above everything else, freedom. Freedom from rules: he
even talked the air force into letting him fly in mountaineering
boots rather than military shoes. Freedom from home: his wife
would take care of those burdensome chores. Freedom from the
mundane of every sort, free to feel "life effervesce within me," as it
only could in high places. He wrote of "the sheer joy of freedom
and movement. The aircraft is my body and the sky the dimension
of my youth. Whether flying or climbing, the sky has become
more than a playground. It is my life."

At home Dad would not tolerate talk of household chores, especially not any that he should have been doing, nor did he want to
hear what the children were up to. Home was the place to entertain
his climbing friends and to prepare for his next trip to the mountains, to work on big projects that would replace the air force, or to
read and talk philosophy with friends and his wife. The last thing
he could tolerate about home was anything domestic.

In 1959 the air force stationed Dad at the Hahn Air Base in
Germany, and our home became a two-level house at the edge of
the vineyards in Bernkastel-Kues, an ancient pair of towns along
the Mosel River, joined by bridges. We lived on the Kues side,
while Bernkastel's medieval town center—with its tight streets
lined by overhanging Tudor-style buildings—justly gets all the
fame. But from our side of the river we could see the old castle on
the hill, which had been destroyed when Louis XIV plundered the
area in the 1680s (the French revolutionary army also sacked the
area in the 1790s, as did Napoleon in 1806). The main turret still
rose one hundred feet or so.

We could live off the military base because in theory Dad
could reach Hahn in the required fifteen minutes. The theory re-

quired no traffic and squealing his tires around every bend, but the air force didn't know this. It was Mom who most wanted to live with Germans, as Dad had not yet completely forgiven them for World War II. He idolized Europe, or rather the idea of international rather than American citizenship, but not until he began building close friendships with some Germans did he overcome his prejudice. When we moved there, he certainly did not go out of his way to woo the community, not even our downstairs neighbors, the Hoffmans. On the contrary, when Mom told him that he was causing trouble by roaring his engine up the hill and under the Hoffmans' bedroom window at all hours of the night, refusing to speak German, and not dampening his hi-fi with the hours, he bitterly told off Frau Hoffman. Repeatedly Mom had to stand as a buffer between the community and Dad.

My mother was fascinated by the community. She wasn't interested in the flying scene, nor in most military people, and instead she pursued her own interests in natural history, European history, learning the German language, and participating in German women's groups. Only occasionally did she go to the base, mostly for medical services or to stock up on groceries and supplies to balance the limited goods in local shops. My primary memory of the base is the PX—the military grocery/department store—with its shelves upon shelves of tasty and tempting goods unavailable in the real Germany, where we lived.

Meanwhile my sister and I were thoroughly immersed in German culture. The Hoffmans had children our age, and they along with another air force family living off-base became our primary playmates. We'd live with them when my parents traveled without us, and I learned to shovel coal into the furnace with Herr Hoffman. First I, and then Andréa and I together, would walk a mile or so through the vineyards to a German kindergarten. My principal memories of that are of how much fun it was to use the vineyard as a toilet, and how impossible it was to take a nap with my classmates. As a toddler my parents had nicknamed me Sputnik, after the Russian satellite that had just been launched, because I was constantly in motion. By the time I started first grade in the local school, German was more my language than English, and you wouldn't know my sister or me from Germans by listening to us.

Dad once put me in the pilot's seat of his F-100 fighter bomber. It was on the ground, of course, and the instruments overwhelmed me. I couldn't possibly imagine the power that Dad experienced as he blasted through the sound barrier over the deserts of Algeria, or dueled with his flight instructors in Arizona and once even with a Soviet MiG along the border between East and West Germany. Though Dad loved his plane, he hated its mission. What he loved was hot-rodding in his jet, dogfighting with his instructors and later his students, bringing home wounded planes in bad weather—all these were sport, challenge, joy. What he hated was that his plane, the most advanced in the American arsenal at the time, was not just a fighter, but a fighter-bomber, and it carried nuclear weapons. In the event of war, each pilot had a preassigned target to destroy. In Dad's case, the target was Prague, Czechoslovakia. The exquisitely beautiful city had been Dad's favorite when he lived in Europe as a kid, in large part because it had escaped Allied bombing. Now his job, if the Cold War turned hot, was to annihilate it. A year after we moved to Germany, Dad went on official record as being morally opposed to nuclear weapons; he wanted to be relieved of his duties as a bomber. The air force complied because they couldn't have a pilot who refused to drop his payload. Dad was demoted to instructor and assistant flight safety officer.

Dad's new duties did at least allow more time for mountains, where he was spending a vast number of weekends and every week of vacation time he could squeeze out of the air force. He would leave the base on Friday after work, drive four to eight hours depending on whether his goal was the Eastern or Western Alps, climb all weekend, and drive home on Sunday night in time to catch a few hours of sleep before reporting to duty on Monday morning. Mom accompanied him on one such trip as a passenger, not a climber, and later wrote to her parents, "I am utterly exhausted and do not know how John can keep up the pace weekend after weekend. His answer is, life is short. Lost days will never come back."

Our Bernkastel years would have been comfortable had it not been such a period of frustration for Dad, and therefore for the rest of us, especially my mother. She didn't like the influence the air force had on him, and she didn't think he was nearly as free of it as he thought he was. He spent a lot of time and much of his emotional energy sifting pressures from the military and its society against his own values and ambitions. We all suffered from his inability to resolve the conflicts. Combine this with the shackles of home, and Dad's demands became impossible.

"All John wanted of a wife," wrote Mom in a letter, "was that she be a Balmain model, an Eiger climber and a perfect housekeeper, have shining hair (without curlers), get a Ph.D. (in her spare time), be a devoted mother (with invisible children), plus a reader, mixer, camp director, secretary-treasurer, and (also in her spare time) do anything else she wants."

There were fights at home, and Mom (and later I) was always at a disadvantage with him, as he was convinced of his invincibility and he could always shout louder. Dad would not tolerate tears. Tears came easily to Mom, and so this was perhaps their biggest source of friction. Dad would scream at her that tears were her play for sympathy. He had learned this from his mother, who also teared up easily. He insisted that she and women in general used tears to get their way. Occasionally he'd lose control so badly that he'd actually hit Mom. Later he would apologize and insist he didn't mean what he said or did. Once Mom tried to get out of something *she* had said by using "I didn't mean it" as an excuse. But Dad countered with "Oh, yes you did; you don't say things you don't mean." Since she always meant what she said, he wouldn't accept her apology. Because reasoning with Dad during a heated argument didn't work, Mom sometimes tried saving her logic for after he'd calmed down. But then he'd get mad that she was ruining the congenial mood by reigniting a storm that had long since blown over in his own mind.

Most of these subtleties were lost on me at the time, but the fury was not. And since I'd inherited my mother's sense of reason and relative emotional control, the injustices of his outbursts came to haunt me more and more as the years went by. I would come increasingly into Mom's position, both through empathy for her and because that's how I worked, too.

My parents' long-awaited honeymoon in the Alps was finally realized in February 1960, when they drove to see the Eiger. Dad phoned Kleine Scheidegg, which unfortunately was full, so instead they found L'Hôtel Ermitage in French Switzerland between Interlaken and Leysin. That stretch of road always stayed in their minds as extraordinarily beautiful, and they dreamed of someday living there. When they reached Geneva the next day, they searched for ways to work in the French part of Switzerland someday after the air force. Dad spoke with the Swiss Air people, who told him they gave priority to Swiss nationals. Dad immediately determined to become one, though it would take twelve years, as Mom remembers. She also remembers that this was one of the rare times they were ever alone together. When they were alone—absolutely alone—they got on marvelously. She knew that on her own merits without children to make him desperate or friends whom he wanted her to impress, she could compete with any woman.

A year later Grandma Miler—Grandmommy we called her—came to visit, and all except Dad took a seven-week carcamping holiday through Italy. My memories are limited to carving hip-holes in the ground for my grandmother's comfort at night, and exploring a huge sea cave near Naples. I don't actually remember that Dad flew down in a T-33 trainer jet to meet us in Sorrento, Italy, at the home of friends. But Mom recounts that after settling Grandmommy and us kids, she and Dad hiked to the sea, where they swam in the nude and rolled in the sand until four in the morning. The beach and the sea were empty but for them. My mother remembers the night as typical of Dad's spontaneity. We all said good-bye when daylight returned, but that afternoon he was back. His plane had caught on fire and he brought it back to Naples after jettisoning his fuel tanks into the Mediterranean. It was another frustration due to a conflict of values. He craved the opportunity to jump from his plane, but he hated to throw away so much government money when there was a chance he could land the plane in a recoverable condition. And he reveled in the act of pitting his skill against the plane's fragility. At least twice this happened to him, where he was justified in ejecting but instead chose to bring the ailing plane to ground, even when it was in flames. Hahn sent a plane to Naples to pick him up.

Even in her lowest times with Dad, my mother loved him deeply. She would lose patience with his antics, but always respected his ability to think (when not in a tirade) and admired his passionate mind. "John has always wanted to write," she wrote her parents from Kues. "He can, too, when he tries. He can do almost anything he wants to. He has overwhelming unused talent." She could see through to better times when he would be free of the military and when he would grow up, as he increasingly showed evidence of doing. Or, if it came to it someday, when she would strike off on her own with the kids. She still had every intention of getting her Ph.D. and entering—or reentering—a life of science when the time finally came. She wrote a friend: "So many wonderful places exist in this world. Oh to have several lives, simultaneously or consecutively!" And she's always said, about being with Dad, "Whatever happened, life was always an adventure."

THREE

AN ALPINE
APPRENTICESHIP

THE WORLD Dad loved best was built of stone and
sheathed in ice. And if there was anyone who rubbed Dad's nose in
the lowland trappings of family, it was Gary Hemming, a charis-
matic wanderer who would later receive his own biography, *The
Beatnik of the Alps.* The relationship between Gary and Dad was as
stormy as the mountains they shared, and as enduring as most mar-
riages—an institution Gary despised.

They had first met in 1954, about the same time as my parents began dating. They were climbing independently in Yosemite
when they both responded to an accident on Lower Cathedral Rock
and helped to bring the injured climber down. Over the next years
they climbed together across the western U.S. and Canada, typically bickering like a quarreling couple as they competed in their
attempts to correct each other's faults and show their own superi-
ority, and yet inevitably they would join forces at the next opportunity. Gary roamed America as one of its earliest climbing bums,
living the vagabond lifestyle that most climbers aspire to, especially during that passionate, idealistic stage of life. Gary wandered freely where he chose to and couldn't understand how Dad
had exchanged his youthful freedom for the shackles of domestic-

ity, a fact he would repeatedly point out to Dad, even with my mother present.

One morning in the spring of 1961, Frau Hoffman opened the door of our shared house in Kues and found Gary asleep in the stairway, bearded and unkempt. He moved in for some weeks, and then returned regularly from France, where he was attending the University of Grenoble. He and Dad stayed up long hours planning climbs for the coming summer and then outlining a project they dreamed up called the High Altitude Space Laboratory, or HASL for short. The idea was for the U.S. Air Force to establish a laboratory in the Karakoram Range in Pakistan, home to the world's second-highest mountain, K2, which had not yet been climbed by an American. Dad and Gary would launch the project the next year with an expedition to climb K2 itself while laying the foundations for a research laboratory to be used by the budding space program.

Despite some high-level contacts arranged in part by Dad's father, funding never materialized and HASL died on the vine. But their climbing did somewhat better. The previous year Dad had organized his month of leave to make a series of increasingly difficult climbs with Jerry Robertson, mostly in the Chamonix area, finally climaxing with the Eiger. It turned out to be a bad year for weather, and many of their climbs were stormed out, while others didn't go as well as they should have for a number of reasons. By the time they reached the Eiger, the weather pattern was two days of storm followed by one day of clearing. As it turned out, due to bad weather, no one got up the Eiger's north face that summer. So in 1961 Gary and Dad decided to reverse the sequence, beginning with the Eiger and moving on to the Mont Blanc Massif (a.k.a. the Chamonix area).

In late June the Eiger was still full of loose snow. Especially at that warm time of year, fresh snow melts fast, carrying with it loose rocks that make the Eiger's face something akin to a shrapnel-plagued war zone. Gary and Dad assessed the situation and returned to their homes (Grenoble for Gary). The next weekend they were in the Mont Blanc region, doing various ascents interspersed with occasional returns to the home front.

Later that summer, Dad and Gary hunkered in their tent near the valley village of Courmayeur, on the Italian side of Mont Blanc, the Alps' highest mountain. This peak isn't just tall, it's vast and complex. The south, or Italian, side is arguably the wildest region in all the Alps. Massive ridges begin in the valley floor at about 5,000 feet and rise to the broad shoulders of the 15,780-foot summit. Difficult granite faces *begin* at around 13,000 feet in altitude, and no lifts or trails provide shortcuts through its guardian glaciers and buttresses.

Dad and Gary had recently climbed the Col de Peuterey and the Brenva Ridge on Mont Blanc. Now they were waiting out interminable rain in the valley, looking at the wet underbelly of a beastly storm. Sleeping in the tent next to theirs was the distraught girlfriend of a Swiss climber who had not returned from a subsidiary peak on the Peuterey Ridge. The Swiss, Henri Briquet, and his German partner, Konrad Kirch, were days overdue. Despite the woman's pleas, no one else seemed to be paying any attention, in large part because it would be so difficult to reach the climbers: Henri and Konrad's intended summit, Punta Gugliermina, rises roughly 9,000 vertical feet above the campground, and the complicated terrain is difficult enough to manage in sunshine, let alone storm. This is seriously big country, with 1,000-plus-foot granite walls stretching for miles alongside plunging glaciers with massive crevasses. Crest a ridge and another glacier tumbles endlessly down the other side. One boom after another thumps the sky, either from a cascade of falling rocks, a serac collapsing over a cliff, or maybe a new crevasse cracking open. You want to see where you're going.

Gary and Dad hiked up into the clouds looking for Henri and Konrad, cursing the fact that no one else would come. As it turned out, help of a sort arrived not long after Gary and Dad reached the

Gamba Hut (the Gamba was later destroyed and resurrected as the Monzino Hut). Henri and Konrad were merely two of nine who had been caught by the storm, and some of the others were the heroes of Italian and French alpinism, including already legendary Walter Bonatti—the master alpinist of his generation—and the rising star Pierre Mazeaud, who would go on to become a regular partner of Dad's, the first Frenchman to climb Everest, and an important political figure.

In mid-July, 1961, all nine were fighting for their lives. A party of four Frenchmen including Mazeaud had headed toward the greatest unclimbed feature on Mont Blanc—and indeed in the entire Alps—the Central Pillar of Frêney, which lords over the Frêney Face. As so often happens, others had the same idea at the same time, and soon three Italians led by Bonatti were kicking their boots into midnight snow holes punched by the Frenchmen just ahead. Both teams had made earlier attempts, and neither wanted to be beaten to the prize.

The next day the teams joined forces, and a day later—July 11—they had already overcome most of the route's difficulties, including a wild pillar of smooth vertical granite that tops out at 15,500 feet. Mazeaud and his partner were fixing ropes on the top pitches of the great pillar when they were struck by a violent thunderstorm. Fighting the wind and rain, they made it down to where the French and the Italians were preparing separate bivouac ledges. Then a bolt of lightning hit Mazeaud's partner in the ear, paralyzing him. During the night the storm raged into a full blizzard at 15,000 feet, where the climbers were huddled.

When the storm first struck—as Mazeaud was climbing the great pillar—Konrad and Henri were at the top of the difficulties on the Punta Gugliermina, at about 12,500 feet in elevation. They bivouacked in the blizzard, and the next day fought their way higher, aiming for the tiny Craveri bivouac hut that would be their only hope for survival. At 2 p.m. they reached the summit of Gugliermina, and Henri groaned to Konrad, "The race is a long ways from being finished." Darkness fell, and they had to rappel to find the hut. While pulling down their ropes for another rappel, one got stuck. They yanked and pulled and cursed and screamed until finally there was nothing to do but cut off what could be salvaged. Three or four blows with a stone severed the rope so that they could continue with what remained. Henri craved rest from their continuous fight for survival; he insisted on bivouacking in the open. Konrad was convinced the hut was nearby and headed on alone with a headlamp. He finally found the tiny hut and went back to fetch Henri.

The little bivouac hut shook all the next day from the violence of the storm. But at least Konrad and Henri had shelter, even if they were out of food and water. Over on the nearby Frêney Pillar, the French and Italian climbers were huddled in the open, growing steadily weaker from fighting the altitude, their exertions and hunger, and the storm. Bonatti decided they must descend at all costs to avoid freezing to death. At 6 a.m. on July 14 they started rappeling into the storm's renewed fury.

That night on the Frêney Glacier was the worst of all, and all seven shook violently from the cold. They had descended to 13,000 feet, but were still being whipped by ferocious winds and their wet clothing was freezing, as were they. They divided the last of the tiny amount of food they'd saved, while snow continued falling by the foot. In the morning they crawled through deep powder toward another set of rappels, but when Bonatti reached the bottom of the first rappel, he waited an hour for someone to follow. No one did. All but Mazeaud were stumbling, crying, and already dying from exhaustion and hypothermia. At that time they heard a voice crying out from the Col de l'Innominata, a voice lost in the maelstrom but unmistakably human. They cried back but were not heard through the wind.

Konrad and Henri had also decided to fight their way down rather than wait indefinitely as their hunger deepened. While threading past monstrous crevasses on the Frêney Glacier in knee-deep snow, they, too, heard voices coming from the Col de l'In-nominata. The sound whipped and spun like the swirling snowflakes that beat into their faces, but it was unmistakably a human crying out. Konrad and Henri screamed back into the wind that they were on their way, but there was no indication the voices had understood them. Suddenly all was quiet except for the howl of the wind.

While the climbers were battling the storm, Dad and Gary's frustration with their colleagues at the Gamba Hut turned to anger. The professional rescuers seemed poorly equipped, at least in Dad and Gary's estimation, and seemed to take their rescue mission far too casually. Making matters worse, the guides—notorious for their cliquishness—lived up to stereotype by dismissing the amateur efforts of then-unknowns Gary and Dad, who were made to feel completely unwelcome. In the morning five guides headed up one direction for Bonatti, Mazeaud, and friends, while three guides headed down to a viewspot where they might spy Konrad and Henri with binoculars if the weather briefly cleared. None of the guides hiked up to help Konrad and Henri.

Furious, Gary and Dad raced off on their own, trying to reach the Craveri bivouac hut, the only place that they figured Konrad and Henri could have survived. After hours of steep scrambling through the blizzard, Gary and Dad drew close to Col de l'Innom-inata. Of that day, Gary later wrote:

> The last hundred and fifty feet are nearly impossible. The snow is either waist and shoulder depth or it treacherously covers the rotten rock of the ever-narrowing couloir which we are ascending. The wind is increasing now, and the snow is falling steadily and heavily. With only 60 feet left to reach the col we very nearly turn back. But John forces a way up a passage that was quite beyond my abilities to lead, and on reaching the crest of the col yells "Off belay" to me. Here he gets two answers: one from me and another from behind him,

somewhere out in the fog! For thirty minutes we yell and call out questions in French, German, and English as to their whereabouts and condition. Nothing comes back but an occasional OOOOHH-AAAAHH groan-like response, sometimes near, sometimes far, depending on the wind.

Hearing the pitiful groans they figured that Konrad and Henri were near death. But in these conditions Gary and Dad felt it was too dangerous to continue on to the glacier on their own. If one of them were to fall into a hidden crevasse, the other would have no chance to pull him out. So they descended to fetch more rescuers. They left a fixed rope in the couloir to facilitate their return.

When they reached the Gamba Hut in the midafternoon they found all the guides already settled, and none willing to head back up. Further efforts would have to wait until the next day; now, they said, it was time to eat and rest. Gary and Dad burned with anger, and stepped outside to discuss what to do. That's when Dad saw two figures following their footsteps down the mountain. It was Konrad and Henri, who had not been so far away after all, and had used Gary and Dad's rope to escape the col.

The hut being full and Henri's girlfriend being anxious, Konrad and Henri continued down to the valley floor after warming themselves and eating a meal. Additional professional rescuers had by now arrived, and they made it clear that Gary and Dad had no role to play here, and besides, the bunks were full. Gary and Dad decided to descend as well, and the hut keeper presented them with an itemized bill for the previous night's stay and the food they'd eaten. They stormed downward in tempers to match the weather.

Later they would learn that just hours after they departed, Bonatti burst into the hut with a partner. Mazeaud, he said, was tending to the others, who were dying of exposure and exhaustion. Bonatti and partner had managed to make it down in part because of a rope they'd found fixed in the Col de l'Innominata, but the others had been too weak to move, other than Mazeaud. The guides burst into action, but by the time they found the climbers, Mazeaud was suffering from severe frostbite and the rest were dead.

These events would go down as one of the great tragic episodes in Alpine climbing history, where strong climbers perished slowly in a storm that wouldn't let up. Most accounts would credit the heroic rescuers, who risked life and limb. But these accounts always focus on the Central Pillar of Frêney climbers, ignoring Henri Briquet and Konrad Kirch. And ignoring Gary and Dad, who felt the rescue operation had been bungled. Five years later Gary would lead French guides on a celebrated rescue on the west face of the Dru, another Mont Blanc range peak, and by then both he and Dad would have famous new routes. The heavily publicized rescue made Gary a media darling and for a while one of the best-known people in all of France. But in 1961 he and Dad brooded over their humiliating dismissal as mere amateur Americans out of their league among Alpine professionals.

Gary and Dad went on to more climbs in that summer and a body recovery on one of the Mont Blanc glaciers when a French military pilot flew through gondola cables, killing six and injuring more. At the end of their summer campaign they drove back to Switzerland, hoping to find adequate conditions on the Eiger. Their chance never came, as once again the summer's weather had prevented anyone from getting up. They did explore the lower reaches, though not much higher than Dad had gone with Tenzing Norgay or Jerry Robertson in years before. (Ironically, in September, not long after Dad returned to Hahn Air Base after running out of vacation time, the weather finally cleared and sixteen climbers from Switzerland, Germany, Austria, Czechoslovakia, and Poland made it up. Someone also tried to make the first solo ascent, but he fell to his death.)

Gary and Dad ended their "year to *romp!*" (as Gary had put it) unhappily, not merely because of the weather, but because they'd argued more than even they could swallow. Among the bitter pills were that Dad criticized Gary sarcastically for his inexperience and excess caution on snow and ice, while Gary spat back at Dad's confusion while rock climbing on the Grand Capucin. Later Gary wrote Dad, "Let me tell you, and very seriously, how sorry I am about last summer. Looking back, I can see how badly I let you down. Certainly, if there was ever anyone ready for the big climbs, it was you . . . if you had only had a seasoned partner." I don't have record of Dad's response, but the squabbling couple resumed its troubled partnership that winter.

In the winter of 1961–62, Dad regularly flew or drove down to Munich, where Konrad lived, and they continued south to the limestone peaks of Austria and Italy for their weekends. In March Dad organized an international team including Konrad, Gary, and a Yugoslavian, Aleš Kunaver, to attempt the first winter ascent of the Walker Spur on the Grandes Jorasses, one of the massive north faces near Mont Blanc. They were shut down by storms after 1,000 feet of climbing, and suffered a similar fate compounded by heavy rockfall and frostbite in Dad's toes four months later. In between came yet more climbing in Austria and at least one trip to the Calanques. It's no wonder that when I asked my mother about things I did with my father during that period, she said, "I have little recollection of you and Dad together, as he was either flying or climbing or preparing for projects."

But I also discovered an old letter from my mother to Ullman in which she said, "John [Dad] told me when I started Johnny skiing at Grenoble winter 61–62 that he was not interested in seeing him until J. III could keep up with him on skis. I was nearly in tears because I wanted him to show some support, to care enough to come look. But no. So I worked with J. two years. Then he kept up. Then he outskied his father."

I never realized that Dad wasn't interested in my learning curve; I simply assumed he wasn't around, as usual. But thanks to

Mom, for the next decade skiing felt like the most important thing in my life. My first ski memories—from those days in Grenoble—are of a line of us long-footed ducklings following our teacher around on the snow, and then our whoops and hollers as one by one we pointed our tips downhill and zoomed between her legs by sitting on the tails of our skis. I remember the sense of my skis sliding forward, faster, faster, and somehow willing them to move toward the teacher and finding that I could make the boards take me there. Thrill, under my control. It was a great feeling, love at first glide.

Snow was a rare and precious commodity in Bernkastel-Kues, but now that I could ski we'd head up to a hill just above our local vineyard whenever Jack Frost indulged us. Lines of grown-ups sidestepped up on their skis, and even though their legs were much longer than mine, they didn't move nearly fast enough for my taste. As soon as we reached the top, we'd point the boards downhill and zoom to the bottom. My skis didn't have metal edges, but few of us could steer well enough to do much turning anyway. This pathetic little slope was just enough to keep my soul on fire after returning from Grenoble. Dad's comings and goings didn't leave much of an impact on my young mind. Discovering the snowy gates to heaven most certainly did.

Dad's own soul was now thoroughly focused on the Eiger. He'd first had his eye on climbing the north face way back in 1954, when he was just nineteen years old and ridiculously inexperienced for such an ascent. While in the Alps that summer he met Tenzing Norgay, who was in Europe during his victory lap after making the first ascent of Everest. Despite his minimal mountain experience, Dad wanted to be the first American to climb the infamous Nordwand, the most revered wall in the world. What a double coup it would have been to pull this off with Tenzing of Everest! He talked Tenzing into climbing the standard, easy route on the nearby Jungfrau together, but after exploratory jaunts on the Eiger's west ridge and the lower reaches of the north face, Tenzing realized that the Eiger was an entirely different sort of mountain from Everest, requiring a lot more technical skill than he had learned on Himalayan peaks. He was twice Dad's age, and far too wise to get in over his head. They never did make an attempt.

Then there was Dad's visit in 1960 with Jerry Robertson. Even assuming he and Dad had the skills for the Eiger (they certainly didn't have as much experience as they should have had), the weather patterns never gave them a chance. And there were the two trips in 1961 with Hemming, not to mention endless aborted desires. By 1962, as Dad put it, "the mountain had become a pinnacle of frustration and a goal that had to be accomplished." In Konrad he had finally found the right partner.

FOUR

THE FIRST AMERICAN ASCENT OF THE EIGER, 1962

FOR WEEKS Dad had been telephoning Kleine Schei-
degg for reports on weather and snow conditions on the Eiger, and
recently the answers had gone from bad to better. In dense fog on
the afternoon of August 18th, he and Konrad pitched their little
pup tent on a meadow beneath the wall. They built a small fire,
cooked a pound of liver on skewers, and set the alarm for 11 p.m.

At midnight they crawled out to a half canopy of stars, the
other half cut off by the bold black outline of the Eiger. In an hour
they were at the *bergschrund,* where steep snow had pulled away
from the rock wall revealing a dark throat of emptiness. Dad bal-
anced at the snow's sharp edge, then tilted forward until his hands
fell against the rock. His headlamp caught a cluster of alpine flowers hanging from a ledge. They were so beautiful and incongruous
that it took an impatient yell from Konrad to get him moving
again.

Soon the climbing degenerated into what Konrad called
"dangerous hiking"—just a series of rotten cracks and ledges covered with loose rock and hard black ice over which they scrambled

together. With the arrival of daylight came the soon-to-be-familiar sound of air compressing as a huge stone winged its way over the Rote Flüh, 1,500 feet above. The stone hit behind them, showering fragments toward another climbing party that had appeared below. Rocks started falling more and more regularly, landing all around, but usually behind them.

Traversing to the Difficult Crack, Dad used his hammer to shatter ice off the rock so that he could hold on. He climbed past a rope hanging down the wall, probably left after the recovery of Barry Brewster, an Englishman killed a week before on the Second Icefield.

Konrad was already mumbling that he hated the damned mountain and that he wished he were on the good firm granite of the Walker Spur, their earlier unfinished climb. At least the nearly vertical Difficult Crack itself offered solid rock. The climbers behind had nearly caught up as Konrad finished the long hard pitch when the leader slipped on the ice. His piton held and he didn't fall far, but his guttural curses revealed a nationality: Austrian.

Konrad hauled up his pack and Dad followed with his on his back, for now they had to stay ahead of the other climbers. They scampered up a few pitches of easier climbing, and by the time they crossed the Hinterstoisser Traverse—the great gateway to the vast central wall—the others were well out of sight below. The wall seemed theirs again, the weather looked good, and both Konrad and Dad wore huge smiles. Those vanished when Dad reached the First Icefield. Falling rock and ice chunks blasted continuously into the ground around them, sometimes shattering into a spray of shards. Dad found a stance and brought Konrad up. He took one look, groaned "Oh my God!" in German, and hurried off to find better shelter. He had just disappeared around the corner when a stone caught Dad below his ear. He went numb and his sight dimmed; shell-shocked, he fairly ran to Konrad's belay to recover.

Soon Dad discovered himself on what he called "the most rotten and dangerous bit of climbing I have ever had the misfortune to come across." Two weeks later a German fell into the rope of two of Dad's friends, pulled them from their positions, and continued on to his death. Konrad mastered the rotten, vertical pitch, but not without leaving his pack suspended by a piton in the middle of the difficulties. When Dad's turn came he pulled out the piton with his fingers. Twice he thought he would fall. The Ice Hose itself was also nearly vertical, but the frozen waterfall had formed with enough pockets and bottlenecks that Dad could use them as handholds. Ice axes in those days had straight picks that didn't hold in ice the way today's tools do, and grabbing the sculpted ice with his bare hands felt much more secure than relying on hardware. But just as the ice ended and Dad was delicately pulling himself onto a friction slab, the rope jammed on something below. Konrad had to climb unbelayed to free the rope, leaving both of them unprotected until, rope newly unstuck, Dad could reach a fixed piton and let his breath come back.

They continued up alternating ropelengths in the lead on the frighteningly smooth and unprotected slabs. Dad said Konrad moved "with cautious disdain, like a cat in wet grass." It felt like they were climbing on roller skates, made dangerous because they could find no place for pitons in the crackless rock.

The Second Icefield looked and felt like burnished steel. It swept above them in a smooth sheet almost 1,000 feet tall and half again as wide. To Dad's horror, he discovered that he'd forgotten to sharpen his crampons, and their dull points barely scratched the ice. This forced him to laboriously cut a thousand feet of steps diagonally up toward the other end of the icefield. Along the way the strap on his ice hammer broke. He lunged for it, missed, and nearly came off as he watched the tool slide out of sight. His heart sank with it. Konrad climbed up and took over, discovering that his sharper crampons bit well into the ice, allowing him to dispense with the step cutting.

Finally they reached the rock and could relax, but by now it was time to find a bivouac spot. Night fell as they searched for something, anything. Finally a session of excavation yielded a sitting platform, where they could pull the bivouac sacks over their heads. While digging through a rucksack, Konrad dropped the stove and tea, so now they were reduced to placing an inch-wide "meta" solid-fuel heating tablet on the end of a long, flat ice piton. They lit it with a match and held a cup of snow over the burning tablet. Eventually this brewed a cup of Ovalmaltine. Although the air was well below freezing, they felt snug under their bivouac sacks. They were enjoying the solaces of a hard climb, wrote Dad: "Warm drink and warm feet, with intermittent sleep."

In the early light they called good morning to Hans Hauer and Nik Rafanowitsch, the Austrians who had caught up with them at the end of the icefield and were now bivouacked a hundred meters or so away on a makeshift ledge of their own. The Austrians offered them tea, but instead Konrad and Dad started up toward the Death Bivouac, named in memory of Sedlmayer and Mehringer. On this morning Dad felt as if he'd lost all contact with the ground: "It was as if we were completely and seemingly forever part of an environment of vertical rock, ice, and cloud," he wrote. The mood broke when they spied six climbers moving rapidly up the steps Dad had cut into the Second Icefield. Resting at the Death Bivouac, Konrad and Dad watched the approach of a miniature army.

The Third Icefield sloped at sixty degrees overall and would not take an ice piton well; Dad wrote that he thought a lot about falling during the traverse to the Ramp. He had to bring Konrad up to his stance "protected" by the most precarious ice belay they had experienced so far. Konrad followed with no axe, balancing on the steps Dad had cut into ice so thin that the axe dulled as it repeatedly glanced off buried rock. In places the ice was so hard that Dad could only drive an ice piton a couple of inches deep; instead of using a carabiner, he just draped the rope over the piton.

Suddenly they were in the Ramp. Arching their necks, they

could see a 1,000-foot chimney system cutting diagonally up the vertical rock face, capped by two of the most infamous ropelengths on the route: the Waterfall Pitch and the Ice Bulge.

Five pitches up the Ramp they came to the first of the real difficulties, the overhanging Waterfall Pitch. Only it was all ice. Dad didn't put his crampons on, though he soon wished he had. He had to clear ice from holds with his hammer, and hung from slings on the three fixed pitons that he found. At the top of the overhang he stuffed three of his own pitons into a solution hole, packed chips of ice around them, and looped a sling around the lot. By hanging from this he managed to reach easier ground. But on the next pitch he came face-to-face with the Ice Bulge. A cannonade of rock and ice blasted over the ice, forcing him to the left where he was safe under a rock overhang while rocks whisked harmlessly overhead. Dad managed the overhang, banged in a piton, and brought up Konrad. Three more ropelengths were spent dodging falling rock until they were on the Brittle Ledges. Above them the difficult Brittle Crack connected the Ramp with the Traverse of the Gods, where they bivouacked. A rope looped around a loose block was the best overnight protection they could find.

As night came on Dad listened to Konrad snore, while thirst and the twinkling lights of Grindelwald, visible directly below, kept him awake. Around midnight they looked out the vents in their bivouac sacks to check the weather. A line of storms flashed lightning from one end of the horizon to the other, approaching so fast they could see cloud movement in the light of the flashes. As Konrad went back to sleep, Dad watched the storm advance. Soon he could hear distant thunder and see glow-spots turn into bolts of lightning. Then intricate patterns of brightness laced the bulbous clouds. Cities began to disappear: first Bern, then Thun, the lake, Interlaken, and finally Grindelwald. Then the storm was upon them. But after five hours it had lost its youthful energy. Heavy snow fell, but the electrical discharges were over. Konrad and Dad broke camp early, then carefully negotiated six pitches across the

Traverse of the Gods, a steeply angled "ledge" system with downward-sloping slabs poised at the brink of space.

Konrad led the last length into the Spider. When Dad came around a corner and saw the belay, he felt horrified by the blurred image of tons of snow sliding down the Spider. "Does it ever stop?" he yelled over the roar. Konrad answered simply, "No." Dad felt beaten, "a man without an acceptable alternative." But five minutes later the avalanche did stop. The smaller ones that hissed in its place might not rip a man off the ice, they figured, and Dad headed up.

As his axe bit into the ice, spindrift parted around his body; he breathed as if he were swimming, tilting his mouth away from the flow. His greatest urgency was speed: he'd timed the breaks between major avalanches at two minutes on average, and in that time he had to reach the central ice rib in the Spider. He got there just as the next big one swept past.

While Konrad tended to the rope, hoping to keep it out of the avalanche's main stream, Dad drove in an ice piton. It started snowing hard again as Konrad came up and took the lead, which meant more severe avalanches would start almost immediately. Konrad was about eighty feet above when Dad saw a wave of white spewing down the upper face and falling into the Spider. Konrad saw it, too, and drove an ice piton with furious speed. They clung to their pitons, choking in the powdery snow, until finally the wave passed and Konrad could resume climbing.

Above them three couloirs appeared out of the fog, three nondescript options for the climbers, each funneling fresh snow into the Spider. Below, dark figures materialized out of the fog shouting in Swiss-German and Austrian-accented German. This was the army they had seen on the Second Icefield. At an overhanging bulge Dad placed a long ice piton next to the rock. His crampons clawing at the smooth stone, his hands compressing powdered snow for holds, he managed to pull himself onto firmer ground above. They left the piton for those below, which proved providential for the lead Austrian when he fell shortly after clipping into it. The Swiss and Austrians had all roped together, and now because of the conditions Konrad and Dad decided to pool their efforts as well into one long, unbroken rope, a truly international team of four countries: Germany, Austria, Switzerland, and the United States. It was only noon, and Dad had no doubt that they would reach the summit that day. The only concern was that Hans and Nik had not been seen since the previous night.

Franz, a highly experienced Swiss rock climber, seemed like the perfect choice to lead the Quartz Crack above—a notorious 130-foot chimney/overhang. But Franz had trouble with the ice glazing the rock, and after desperately searching for holds at the crux, he arched into space, intercepting an avalanche plume and clearing his belayer by about five feet.

Dad peered down the wall into an open cauldron so hostile he could hardly imagine Nik and Hans down there somewhere. Life in an environment like this seemed impossible. Dad kept hoping to see a human shape appear, or even to hear a voice from the Traverse of the Gods. But there was nothing, only the storm and the Spider's ever-shifting shape.

After a struggle lasting nearly an hour one of the Austrians climbed the overhang, and with an upper belay the second Austrian and the first Swiss climbed up relatively quickly. But then they made the mistake of pulling the rope through the carabiners in order to haul up a pack. Now the rope from above actually angled far to the side, and the rest of the climbers were left with very poor belays.

The Swiss party was sinking into desperation. One of two climbers named Sepp climbed to just below the crux, where he was directly in the stream of water and wet snow that ran over the ice. He screamed "Zug! Zug!" (Pull! Pull!), but the rope at this angle could do nothing, it could barely even protect him. Sepp panicked, tried to move, and gravity took over; he slammed into the rock thirty feet lower. The same thing happened on his next attempt, and on the third attempt he cried and pleaded to be pulled upward.

Dad called it "an incredible performance, like watching some ghastly and completely burlesqued melodrama of which, somehow, the consequences had a bearing on your own life." At virtually the same place Sepp fell again, but this time the rock was less kind to him. He moaned that his ankle was broken.

The Swiss talked of trying to haul Sepp to the summit. But Dad felt this was madness, for these people couldn't even climb the rock under these conditions *without* an injured man. The only thing to do was to leave him if his ankle truly was broken. He was crumpled not far from the "Corti Bivouac" and could be rescued from the summit with a cable just as Claudio Corti, an Italian alpinist, had been in 1957 after his partner died. Sepp's life and the lives of everyone else seemed to depend on someone reaching the summit and descending soon. Dad and Konrad discussed leaving the group and climbing faster to get help, but they ended up deciding to stay together for now to assist as they could.

Konrad led up the overhang, as the belay from above was useless. He found it difficult as well, at one point pausing to yell down, "God, but I left a part of me back there!" While Dad belayed he felt sorry for what he called "those wretched fellows, their clothing wet and partially frozen, their bodies shaking uncontrollably, and their spirits broken." When he followed Konrad he took the Swiss rope and threaded it through the carabiners as he climbed. That way they could drop one rope to haul directly and use the one threaded through the carabiners to belay the Swiss. With this combination of belays and pulling, the Swiss made it up. It seemed that the broken ankle had mended itself at the prospect of being left on the face.

Darkness was coming soon, but no one wanted to stop. Most of the climbers were already experiencing some frostbite in their toes, and another night of inactivity would only make it worse. "In addition," Dad wrote, "we had begun to have that old feeling of doubt, that slow realization that maybe that road you are on is a one-way street in the wrong direction. No panic, no fear, just the strong oppression of the odds being too high—an unfair twist of luck after winning so much."

Since the Austrians were somewhere above, Dad and Konrad let the Swiss move ahead. Darkness had settled when Dad and Konrad reached the bottom of the final, 300-foot-long exit gully. While the others all stood in slings in the steep groove a full rope-length above, Konrad and Dad excavated a pitiful ledge on which they could sit as long as their heels dug into the snow below. They found no place for safety pitons. All they could risk doing was to loosen the straps of their crampons for improved circulation in their feet; putting on their goose-down socks was out of the question. Avalanches kept hitting the bivouac sack, threatening to knock them off.

Inside, their principal problem was staying awake, for without anchor pitons, falling asleep would mean sliding off their ledge, the next stop 5,000 feet down. One of them would hold a candle with a hand held high near the wick and its reservoir of hot wax. When the candle holder nodded, the candle would tip, and the hot wax would immediately wake him. Toward morning the temperature plunged, indicating a clearing sky.

With daylight they caught up to the others. Frostbite was making the Swiss more and more clumsy. No one spoke, but through sheer determination everyone moved upward.

Bright sun greeted them on the summit ridge, and they could finally see their dream, the summit. Clouds blanketed all the lower landscape, leaving only mountain heights pushing into the sunlit world. Dad wrote in the *American Alpine Journal,* "The snow ridge reaching to the summit cornice had the fantastic brilliance of a jewel lit from within. Chips of ice from axe blows were caught in the air and lit by the sun against an impeccable blue."

Dad spent a week in the Hahn Air Base hospital, where his lightly frostbitten toes recovered. The Austrians and two of the

Swiss had fingers or toes amputated, while two of the Swiss lost both fingers and toes. Hans and Nik spent two more days on the face but completed the ascent just before a massive rescue operation was scheduled to start. They both spent several months in the hospital. In his article, Dad referred to the two Swiss with the same name, "Sepp." The record shows another name that might have sounded like Sepp on the wall, but I've left the misnomer to help with their privacy, whether or not that was Dad's intent.

FIVE

INTERNATIONAL CITIZENS

ACCOMPLISHING his long-held goal didn't even come close to quenching Dad's Eiger obsession. Instead, it merely opened his eyes to the tremendous possibility of this great wall—a possibility that would gnaw at the next four years of his life, and then swallow it.

Just months after his climb with Konrad, Dad confided in Roy Brown, a nonclimbing doctor at Hahn Air Base and a good friend. Roy remembered: "One night in Bernkastel with cold Mosel wine, we found ourselves looking at maps and routes of the Eiger. John described his hopes and calculated his approach for an international team doing the direct route up the Nordwand. I could see passion in his eyes."

At that time there was but a single route on the entire north wall. These days there are two dozen, and the original route, the one Dad had just climbed, is typically called the "Classic Route," though more formally it's the 1938 Route, or the Heckmair Route. More than anything, Dad wanted to be the person to add a second line to this monstrous wall. And it couldn't be just any line; it must be the direct line, the one that tackles every difficulty head-on rather than weaving to and fro across the face looking for weaknesses in the wall. Heckmair had chosen a brilliant route, and there's a very good reason why it's still far and away the most popular on the face: it's the line of least resistance. No one has improved on Heckmair's navigation in all these years. Still, that was 1938. For Dad it was now 1962, and times had changed. He would bring the Eiger into the modern era.

Though Dad's sights remained firmly fixed on the Eiger, and many attempts at the direct would follow, the rest of life nevertheless took up most of his time. He had less than a year remaining on his air force contract; re-upping clearly wasn't an option, nor was moving anywhere but the Alps. The question was what to do professionally.

Dad and Mom had already started laying the groundwork for a new sort of international school. The names and locations for the school went through various permutations, but the most durable seems to have been "The International Institute at Mont Blanc," with headquarters in either Courmayeur or Chamonix. According to a prototype brochure, the school was to have three principal objectives: "1) Thorough academic preparation for discerning universities. 2) Character building through adventure. 3) Understanding the world community."

The first was to take place with highly qualified teachers from diverse countries. The second would feature mountain expeditions that would "give an insight into the individual's character and then build upon it through constructive adventure." And the third would teach students how "to live equitably with those from different national environments, to sympathetically understand different customs, and to be able to communicate with peoples of different nationalities." All of these "are foundations for eventual world citizenship," they wrote. "Without being overly dramatic this goal of our school is so vitally important, one could say that the survival of our present civilization depends on it. For war is now synonymous with annihilation, and life thus becomes dependent upon international understanding and cooperation. Youth is our only hope, and the means is education."

Dad worked on the big picture, the adventure angle, and the finances, while Mom developed the science curriculum and many of the academic details. Unfortunately, financial backers never materialized, and there was objection on the academic side, too. Looking back at their efforts from a twenty-first-century perspective, I think my parents were on an amazing track and merely a decade or two ahead of the financial backers they needed, as well as the teaching experience it would take to impress them. In 1962, however, I was still in kindergarten, and the only thing I might have understood from all this was that I wasn't getting the skiing time I deserved.

The important thing—my ski time—was about to change in the coming winter, when my mother, sister, and I spent Christmas and long weekends in the heart of the Bavarian Alps. Dad had been assigned to the military base near Garmisch so that he could train with the U.S. Armed Forces biathlon ski team for the upcoming CISM—Championnat International Militaire de Ski—in Chamonix. He had precious little skiing experience, having learned with my mother in California just a few years before. Where she had signed up for lessons, he merely aimed for the bottom and relied on strength and reflexes to keep from killing himself. Besides being able to run on skis—a skill he didn't yet have—he needed to shoot quick and straight. That skill he had learned in childhood on safari in Africa with his father (he gave up hunting, but not shooting, after killing a dik-dik antelope and breaking down in tears when he learned she was pregnant). In any case, this biathlon opportunity was like a paid holiday for Dad, and it sent his spirits soaring.

Garmisch was just an hour's drive from Konrad's home in Munich, and it proved an attractive place for a number of Dad's other friends to come visit, including Gary. Best of all, though, was that his ski-training officer proved to be a climber as well, and almost immediately Sandy Bill became one of Dad's closest friends. They discussed the Eiger Direct, of course, and even drove to Switzerland to have a look at the face between training sessions.

And then there was the folk singer Julie Felix, whose enthusiasm and vitality we all fell in love with, especially my sister and I. She performed at the local pub, and Andréa and I would try to get her to sing "I Knew an Old Lady Who Swallowed a Fly" every night we were allowed to stay up (after many verses, the Old Lady swallows a horse to catch all the other animals she's swallowed trying to get the fly; she dies, of course).

But this was all incidental to my life at the time. The essential thing was the skiing. Because I couldn't ride the chairlifts without my mother, most of my skiing was confined to the hill next to the ski lodge. My mother must have been inside, I suppose, keeping an eye on me as needed. This allowed me to ride the T-bar to the top of the steep bump-covered slope. I had no idea how to ski these moguls at first, so I'd wait on top of the hill until a good skier would happen by. Then I'd push off and try to follow him down. My new skis had metal edges—wide steel plates held in with screws—and the skis were so long that I had to jump to touch the tips (this was so that I could grow into them). I suppose they bent with enough pressure, but I was a skinny little kid, and would remain so into teenagehood. My boots were low and soft-leather affairs that were easy to walk in because that's what boots were like back then. I would never inflict that gear on my daughter, but in the winter of 1963 it seemed to work just fine, and somehow as the days went by I could follow faster and faster skiers down that bumpy slope until finally I was prince of the hill.

The chairlift opened a much bigger kingdom. Mom claims that I fell on my first runs, and she even remembers me crying in my tangled skis. But the only memory of distress that stayed in my brain occurred when Mom pulled off her ski glove and the diamond from her engagement ring fell into the snow forever. She was wearing it because Dad's parents were in town, and for their sake she donned his family's heirloom. We spent hours (it seemed) combing through the snow to no avail. To me it was a waste of good ski time.

Dad's race went badly, as the starting gun sounded while he was in the early stages of dysentery. He had to make several side trips into the woods, not always in time, and mildly frostbit his privates. He completed the race unhappily.

Life beyond the race, however, was going well. Mom summed up in a letter:

> John took a milestone in paterfamilias. For the first time he entered family outings positively. Both children could take care of themselves on skis now. After the races we spent a week skiing a quatre—Zugspitz and into Austria. John was very proud when Andréa and Johnny were almost not issued a ticket first time round, but then they appeared at the ticket window for the next run after coming down from the Zugspitz. We picnicked on the slopes and simply relaxed and explored. As he had long ago proclaimed he was waiting until the children were 10, he now reaped the joys of older youngsters unbound by diapers, bottles and papoose.

Mom gushed to her parents: "I am happier than I have ever known myself—fulfilled, re-created, complete—anticipating an exciting future and terribly glad to have what I have. The core of my happiness, of course, is being so very much in love."

It seemed that everything good was coming together at once. Dad was maturing, having reached the ripe age of twenty-seven. He was leaving the air force in June, and despite his love of flying, he wrote to his navy pilot friend Paul Revak: "When you consider the twenty-four hours in a day and 365 days in a year, there appears a question of values. The meadows and mountains of a lifetime clock make pushing throttles a little insignificant." He had climbed his Eiger, and dreamed up an even bigger Eiger project. And his kids were metamorphosing ahead of his time line from dead weights to something verging on interesting beings.

I was the great beneficiary of the new family-friendly Dad. In

February, shortly after Dad's race, we drove to Austria for my first mountain ski tour. At least it felt big to me. To ski uphill you need two things: bindings that let your heels lift while walking, and "skins" that keep your skis from sliding backward when the tips are pointed uphill. Historically skins came from seals, whose fur runs strongly and stiffly in one direction. Early skiers cropped the fur short, oriented it so that one could slide forward and not backward, and lashed it to their boards. In the 1960s "skins" were mohair on cotton, and later would become entirely synthetic, but the original name lives on. Of course they didn't make skins for six-year-olds, so Mom found a sturdy sewing machine and folded a set over and over until they'd shrunk to size. In those days your heel was held down by a cable, which was tensioned by a lever in the front. The cable ran through hooks at the side of the ski, and you only had to unhook the back set in order to let your heel lift for touring.

Our objective in February 1963 was a peak where three countries joined on the summit: Italy, Switzerland, and Austria. The ski ascent wasn't steep, but it was long, and my legs wore down from dragging the skis one step at a time, over and over and over again, in the too-warm sun. Eventually, though, we were on top, surveying white-clad peaks as far as the eye could see in all directions. This was my first true summit, the top of a real mountain, and I was as proud as proud could be, and just as tired.

During the next four decades I would occasionally remember this day, and always wonder if it really could have happened that year. And then I came across a slide in one of Mom's old boxes. A young mother has her arms around a small boy. The label says: "Ski tour Feb. 63. This point: Austria, Switz and Italy come together. Johnny kept up with his father rather well (age 6) & left me behind!"

The next month, Dad took me on my first roped climb. We were camping among the seaside walls and towers of the Calanques, a rugged coastline of white limestone cliffs and turquoise finger inlets stretching from Marseilles to Cassis on the French Mediterranean coast. When storms wouldn't quit in the Alps or Dad just needed a solid dose of sunshine and pleasure, he would pack up the Sunbeam Alpine and drive south to the sea. I remember arriving well after dark following the daylong drive from Bernkastel. The evening cicadas were deafening as we threw our sleeping bags on the dirt next to the car in the parking lot. But dawn came still and quiet, with a salty scent to the air and a brisk coolness that belied the warmth to come. A few miles of sage-banked trail wound across the arid Provençal landscape—such a contrast from the sullen drizzly northland we'd just escaped—until suddenly the land dropped off perhaps a thousand feet to the dappled turquoise and azure waters below. Twisted cypress trees interrupted the otherwise whitewashed verticality of this terrain, unlike anything I'd ever seen. Here the trail began its equally twisted descent to a short strip of sand at the head of the Calanque d'En-Vau, the diamond among jewels.

Tents were strictly prohibited in the heavily protected park, but at that time open-air bivouacs were still allowed, and we slept on the sand listening to the gentle rustle of tiny waves on the slender beach at the head of the inlet. Besides the beauty and the refreshing sunshine, I remember a few vital things from my early trips to the Calanques: the din of those cicadas on the plateau and the quiet down at the beach; the cube of precious margarine that floated out to sea during the night and Dad swimming out to rescue it; Mom's agony while sea urchin spines were being pulled from her feet after she fell on a climbing traverse above the sea; searching for and eventually finding our lost Siamese cat; and the alternating current of terror and exhilaration that I felt as I followed Dad up the Petite Aiguille ("little needle") that towered over our sleeping beach.

Dad tied me in with a bowline around my waist, and thus began my education in knots—and in stomach butterflies, and sewing machine leg. For suddenly the 200-foot pinnacle that looked so attractive became a towering wall of intimidation. Initially the scrambling felt easy, but then a section of rock loomed vertically and below I saw the open space into which it felt like I'd plunge if my hands couldn't hold, or my foot slipped. Gripping the rock with everything I had, my body tensed until my leg started chattering uncontrollably, like a needle going up and down in a machine. It would take me almost two decades to bring that fear-based reaction under control. On the Aiguille a tug on the rope from Dad took care of it, telling me where to go (up!) and that I was secure and must trust the rope. He didn't pull me up, as I was supposed to learn to climb. When I finally topped out on the pinnacle, Dad cut loose a mighty yodel that echoed down the canyon walls and brought cheers from my mother, sister, and various of Dad's climbing friends on the beach and the surrounding cliffs. Dad beamed. I felt ten feet tall, or make that 210 feet tall.

About this time Mom learned of a job teaching high school and college science in the French part of Switzerland. This seemed too good to be true, so she packed Andréa and me in the backseat and drove to Leysin for the interview. When I caught sight of this snow-covered mountain-clinging village perched far above the valley floor, my eyes popped. Mom parked at the switchback next to the Leysin American School and went in to talk to the administration, leaving Andréa and me in the car. Swish, swish came the high school kids, zipping on skis right down the middle of the street next to us and sliding into the entryway, where they could step straight from their skis into the building. Could such a place be real? Here was paradise, and after seeing it with my own eyes, I would have done anything at all to live inside these pearly gates.

Surprisingly, Dad wasn't immediately convinced: Leysin wasn't on any climber's map. Mom brought back postcards showing the twin limestone towers of Tour d'Aï and Tour de Mayen rising spectacularly just above the village, and told him how they appeared to offer rock climbing. She explained that Leysin would put him within two hours' drive of the Eiger and Chamonix (in opposite directions). And there was another matter: she had offered to finance the family for a while to give Dad a break after the air force, and even more importantly, to give him time to write (he now wanted to become a professional writer) and to work further on the International Institute.

The alternative to Leysin was England, where Mom had been offered a job teaching. England was hideous. Somehow my young mind knew that it didn't have snow, and even if the country wasn't as unbearably flat as it must surely be, hills to me were worthless if they didn't turn white in winter. Dad would be staying somewhere in the Alps, at least until something changed financially to allow the rest of us to join him.

Many a day I lay on my stomach on the floor of our house in Kues, an unfolded map of Switzerland in front of me, counting the crosshatched lines that revealed ski lifts. Hours of study burned the lifts and roads and mountain names into my heart, making the alternative seem all the more unbearable. It was the first time I could see a distinct fork in my life, and the consequences of each direction felt vivid and irrevocable.

Finally the job offer came in the mail. Mom could teach biology and chemistry at the Leysin American School and at the American College of Switzerland, located a few hundred feet higher up in the village. We could live in a neighboring chalet, and the small salary was enough to survive on. There was just one catch: she could have the job only if Dad agreed to become sports director of both schools.

This was not what Dad had in mind; he wanted a break from work, and then to start his own school. But he agreed to take the job for a year so that Mom could have hers. When I turned seven and started first grade in Kues, both in May, I knew that my lowland living was drawing to a close, that the English rains had been banished, and that the time for serious skiing was on its way. It would be hard to imagine a happier kid.

The air force contract ended in June, but the American School didn't start until September. In between came freedom. We were moving to Chamonix, where we'd live in a tent while Dad came and went from the peaks above. Dad took the wheel of the Sunbeam Alpine, Gary sat on the console between the front seats, Paul Revak sat in the passenger seat with my mother on his lap, and Andréa and I squished into the luggage compartment. The summer's worth of camping and climbing gear was lashed somewhere. With a final wave to the Hoffman family, we thundered out the driveway.

Dad's excitement must have been beyond measure. Twenty-seven years old, just finishing six years of military confinement (his entire postcollege adult life), he was looking at an entire summer of climbing before moving into a Swiss mountain village. In fact, we were all on cloud nine. How else could we fit into a two-seater? The horn honked, the men whooped, Dad yodeled, and I just grinned from ear to ear.

ing smaller peaks. For the majority of today's climbers the goal is a challenging and beautiful climb rather than to reach the highest summit of the range. Even the summit is optional. All that counts to many of this new breed is the integrity of "the line"—a ridge, a couloir, or a face that ends where the feature merges with a greater feature, such as a couloir into a ridge, or a ridge into a bigger ridge, or a face into a gentle summit slope. Thanks to a network of ski lifts and mountain huts, most of Chamonix's amazingly good granite and Alpine ice routes lie within an hour or two's walk of a gondola or hut door. In all the world, there is no finer climbing, nor more conveniently accessed mountains than Chamonix.

We picked the Biolet campground for our summer home because it sprawled through the forest where the river flowing out of the Mer de Glace glacier meets the Chamonix Valley. The Mer de Glace is well named: "sea of ice." It fills a broad basin with fifteen square miles of ice up to 700 feet thick (and that's not counting the large tributary glaciers). In the 1800s the glacier extended into the Chamonix Valley proper and covered what would become our campsite, but by the 1960s the glacier had melted back far enough that in the valley we only had meltwater to play in. No sooner was the tent up than Andréa and I scampered off to find the scoured boulders and braided stream channels characteristic of fresh glacier rivers that have suddenly flattened from their mountainside tumbles. Because Andréa was only five years old, while I was the mature one at seven, I was in charge of our safety. Mom says that she monitored us at first, but my recollection is of just my sister and me—sometimes with other campground children—hopping from rock to rock in the cold morning dew, in the midday sun, and in the afternoon shadow as Mont Blanc's bulk closed down the day. Walking through the woods on the way back to our tent, we never failed to be disgusted by the "Rings of Poop," as we called them: circles of rocks piled high with feces and toilet paper. We were all shocked by how much litter decorated French trails during that era. Spent rifle shells were a different story: we pretended these were long-lost artifacts.

Closer to camp was an old basement foundation without a house on top. Steel I-beams spanned the pit, and our game was to walk across them, and then as skills progressed, to turn around in midcrossing. I doubt Mom knew of our balancing game; she was too busy trying to teach herself chemistry so that she could in turn teach it to high school students in September. But I thought it was safe enough, as the drop was only eight or ten feet into weeds, not directly onto concrete. Andréa also crossed because, she says, "big brother would never let it be otherwise."

Meanwhile Dad was up in the mountains, battling the weather. His major project that summer was to make the first ascent of the south face of the Aiguille du Fou ("lunatic's needle"). He had first noticed the face two years earlier when he and Gary looked across the Mer de Glace and were stunned by "one of the smoothest, most beautiful granite faces we had ever seen. At that moment we both resolved to climb it: From the bottom of the couloir to the summit block by the most direct route possible." Any other line, he said, "would only taste the face and neither devour it nor savor it."

But a quick study with binoculars made plain that the problems would be greater than any other technical climb in the Mont Blanc Massif. They decided to wait until they had "gathered sufficient experience in the Yosemite artificial climbing technique" and until they had a good-enough supply of the new American chrome-molybdenum pitons, which were unavailable in Europe. This combination finally came together in the summer of 1963.

Of his first attempt that June, shortly after our arrival in the Biolet campground, Dad wrote that just as Konrad touched the snow beside him, a rumble sounded in the couloir above: a mass of falling ice was coming their way. It struck above their heads, showering over them in an arch, and roared on down the gully, setting off smaller avalanches along the way. Dad whistled with relief. After a pause for their nerves, they set off down the couloir, "the backs of our necks prickling and our ears straining for the return of that feared sound."

Within an hour it was snowing, and by the time Konrad and Dad reached the Envers des Aiguilles hut, they were floundering in snow to their waists. Gary and the Scotsman Stewart Fulton, who were to join them on the wall, prepared a hot meal for their return.

Konrad had to drive back to Munich for a law exam, and the rest of us, including Stewart; Gary's girlfriend, Claude Guerre-Genton; and our Siamese cat, Kuzma, all decamped to the Dauphiné Alps, where the weather was better.

In July we returned to Chamonix, where Dad's friend Tom Frost showed up on his return to the States from making the first ascent of Kangtega, a 22,000-foot peak in Nepal. Tom and Dad had been asked to represent the U.S. at the Rassemblement International D'Alpinisme, an annual gathering of elite climbers sent by Alpine clubs of various nations. Tom was keen to join them on the Fou, and they in turn were delighted to have him on board, for he was one of the pioneers of the new era in Yosemite big-wall climbing and had more experience in "the Yosemite artificial climbing technique" than the rest of the crew combined.

While my sister and I played games under the dripping awning of our canvas tent, Dad and friends endlessly waited for good climbing weather. Finally in desperation Stewart and Dad set off in doubtful conditions for another reconnaissance. In the upper couloir they found nearly vertical rock plastered with snow, but continued until they reached the bottom of the face. Six more rope-lengths took them to a better perspective on a huge overhang that blocked their intended route.

They decided it was climbable at about the same time that the threatening storm broke, bombarding them with hail. It became so intense that they had to find shelter under a small overhang during the descent. Finally, with night falling and the hail turning to rain, they again took flight from the vertical world. Avalanches fell and missed. At two in the morning they stumbled exhausted into the refuge, exactly twenty-four hours after leaving it.

A week or so later Gary, Stewart, Tom, and Dad set off for yet another try. They made it over the giant overhang—the haul rope hung thirty feet out from the wall—and after their hammock broke they spent the night standing in slings in the rain. When it was still raining in the morning they slid down their ropes to the comforts of the hut.

On still another attempt the rain came as they were ascending their fixed ropes in the crack, but they decided to push the route anyway. Stewart was leading a long, unprotected layback in the diagonal crack when he slipped, arching down hard on the one good piton he had managed to place. The rain and Stewart's bruised hand forced a retreat.

During short breaks in the weather Mom took us kids up the switchbacking trail to Montenvers, the upper end of the cog railway that led to the flank of the Mer de Glace. Andréa and I surged uphill wasting vast amounts of energy until our shoulders sagged and our lungs exploded. At rest stops we dropped our packs and flew. Leaping off tall trailside boulders, we landed lightly and zoomed up again. The sense of weightlessness from removing the heavy packs felt so real that our young brains half believed we were on the verge of staying airborne.

When Dad came back from his latest stormed-off attempt on the Fou, he promised that he'd bring me to the hut near its base, the Refuge de l'Envers des Aiguilles ("hut behind the needles"). This was the moment I'd been waiting for all summer: the time when I would finally be able to strap on crampons, carry an ice axe, and hike up the crevasse-riddled glacier. Even now, more than forty years later, every time I step on crunchy blue ice I'm transported back to my first hike up the Mer de Glace. It's a magical feeling, one of the strongest and most visceral I have, and it surges through me like a rush of joy.

Because my feet were so small, Dad had to unhook the center stem on a pair of women's crampons and collapse them until they fit my boots. He tied the middle of the rope around my waist (this was before climbing harnesses), put an ice axe in my hand, tied my mother to the far end of the rope, and off we marched onto the wild blue yonder. Ice sparkled in the bright sunshine, and the little crumbly kernels on the surface crunched with every step. With spikes underfoot there was no risk of slipping, only of tripping if you didn't lift each foot carefully. It wasn't long before we were approaching an open gash in the ice, and then I was gingerly leaning over to look down into the sky blue walls of a crevasse. A hundred or so feet down, the walls faded through indigo to black. Cold breezes wafted up from the gash, as did the sound of rushing water, way, way below. It was both terrifying and exhilarating. I imagined what it would be like down there where under-ice rivers inhabit a mostly frozen world of darkness. I'd heard stories about people spit out the snout of this glacier after having fallen into a crevasse a century earlier.

A shiver ran through me, and then Dad was calling:

"Come on, Johnny. We can cross it up here."

We jumped the crevasse at a narrow spot, the first of many such hops. Some were broad jumps for which I'd need a running start with my small legs, but always Dad would belay me for the split seconds when the bowels of the glacier threatened to snatch.

Dad beamed over my enthusiasm about glacier travel. Mom's fear of heights was still in its infancy; she seemed to be enjoying herself as well, though not half as much as I. We'd left Andréa in the campground with friends.

After an hour on the glacier, we angled off to the rock, where steel cables and occasional rungs helped us follow the steep "trail" to the hut. While my little legs were starting to wear under the miles of trail and glacier travel with a pack on my back—having gained nearly 5,000 vertical feet since leaving the campground—each new experience recharged them with fresh energy. Scrambling up the steep trail, grabbing cables and steel rungs, up and evermore upward.

The hut was a kid's fantasy. The big wooden door creaked open to reveal a dining hall and kitchen—the staff was busy preparing the evening meal—and past them were bunkrooms lined with double-decker beds. But the best part of the hut was the big patio with its panoramic view of the Mer de Glace rimmed by sharp-toothed peaks. Climbers sorted their gear on that porch, gear to whet any boy's fancy: coiled up ropes, clanging iron pitons, aluminum carabiners, stepladders, cookstoves, packs, sleeping bags—all the equipment that makes a big climb possible. Voices boomed in more European languages than I could identify: French, German, English (of various accents), Italian, and likely others that still cause me to scratch my head—Catalan? Czech? Slovenian? Whatever the language, by the directed looks I could tell that I was often the focus of attention. Small even for my age, I was the only youth on deck.

I don't know why Dad and Stewart took the next day off from their attempts on the Fou. Maybe they were waiting for Tom and Gary to bring up more food or gear, but in any case Dad and Stewart took me climbing on cliffs behind the hut. We weren't going for the top, only about three ropelengths up, totaling 300 feet or so. It started off fun, too. And ended that way. Along the way I had to relearn, as best I could, how to relax in the face of fear. Somehow, at least until you get used to it, even a rope leading up to your father is less convincing than the primitive part of your brain that equates falling with dying.

"Tension, Daddy!" I yelled with trembling voice, meaning for him to pull the rope tight. But tension is cheating, and Dad wasn't having that.

"Come on, Johnny, use your feet!"

My feet were pumping up and down uncontrollably in another bout of sewing machine leg. What had started as so much fun all of a sudden felt miserable. But then I got over the hump, and suddenly felt that flood of relief again. I look at pictures of myself above the Envers des Aiguilles hut, missing my front teeth and under an oversized helmet, and all I see is a boy in his element. That's how I felt, too, as we headed back to the hut.

When we reached the refuge, Stewart joined Tom and his fiancée, Dorene, and headed up to the Fou, where they'd bivouac. The next morning Dad followed with Mom, Gary, and Claude. I was to stay in the hut that day, which I was delighted to do. Mom would return that evening with a couple of young American men, leaving Claude and Dorene to bivouac and descend the following day. In an article that he published in the *American Alpine Journal,* Dad wrote of his approach with Mom, "The sky was aflame with signs of bad weather." They continued on anyway, figuring that everyone could take care of themselves.

Eleven years later Konrad and his wife, Joëlle, met the Envers des Aiguilles hut *gardienne* (manager) at a party in Chamonix, and she told them with great emotion how I'd gone climbing with Dad one day and then he'd left me at the hut while he headed up with my mother. The *gardienne* said that she had worried about me at the time, and kept a close eye on me all day while I served tea to other climbers, and she was pleased to learn that I'd grown up well after all.

After saying good-bye to girlfriends and wives, the climbers continued up the wall, where Tom led perhaps the most difficult artificial pitch in the Western Alps. Dad was leading above that when darkness forced him to rappel. Just then, the sky tore open and they were pelted by hail and soaked by rain before they could get into their bivouac sacks. Lightning struck the Fou, lacing the darkness with incandescent whiteness, and the storm whipped up into one of the hardest of the summer. Wet in their sacks, they marveled at the electrical display and wondered if the next flash would be marked for them. Dad discovered another unhappy fact: their large canteen had leaked onto his spare clothes.

Down at the hut, I hadn't felt the slightest bit nervous until the wind picked up and dinnertime came and Mom still wasn't back. I remember lightning crashing all around the hut, and booms shaking the walls. I could hear the wind fighting the thunder outside as I tossed in my bunk. Grown-ups told me not to worry, but they weren't doing a good job of covering their own. It didn't make sense that Mom wasn't back unless something had happened to her. If nothing had happened, why hadn't she returned as promised?

The two fellows Dad had assigned Mom to accompany down the glacier were large but inexperienced. She felt honored that he placed so much confidence in her, but worried because she didn't feel safe with such neophytes. Darkness and storm caught them halfway to the hut. In flashes of lightning she spotted a shallow crevasse and told her companions that they needed to hole up there until daylight. She figured that it was better to leave me worrying than to risk stumbling or getting lost. But the guys insisted on moving down the glacier, all on one rope, despite a big drop-off below. The bigger man was in the tail when he slipped and kept accelerating. He would have yanked the others after him if Mom hadn't been able to plunge her ice axe into the snow and arrest his fall, saving them all. From then on, they listened to her and moved one at a time. Alas, there weren't any more shallow crevasses to take shelter in.

I was still tossing in my bunk when the door creaked open and my mother walked into the room. Our mutual relief overwhelmed her exhaustion and my fear.

Dad and his partners finished their route, perhaps the hardest in the Western Alps, and he went on to climb the Hidden Pillar of Frêney with Tom in August, which he called the most difficult route on Mont Blanc. But he wasn't done yet. Now it was time to meet up with Gary and Stewart at the Alpiglen campground at the foot of the Eiger. The goal was the *direttissima:* the most direct line possible from base to summit.

Through the telescope at Kleine Scheidegg, Dad studied a Japanese team on the lower section of what Dad was already calling the Classical Route even though it was still the only route. Above them was a team of Spaniards who were making extremely slow progress. But the Spaniards and Japanese were merely interesting. The ones that counted were Italian: they were attempting the Direct. Ignazio Piussi and Roberto Sorgato forced their way to just below the First Icefield before a storm caused them to abandon the wall. The Japanese team also began retreating. Higher up the Spaniards doggedly pushed on despite the storm. Their image in the telescope was continually streaked by falling rock.

The storm grew more violent in succeeding days, dusting Dad's camp in Alpiglen with the snow of an early winter. They kept a careful watch on the face through the telescope, and whenever the clouds briefly parted, they could see the Spaniards moving ever more slowly. Though the Spaniards never signaled for a rescue, it was obvious they were struggling for their lives. On the fifth day, when Dad saw them on the Traverse of the Gods in a position to be rescued from above, he "gave the general alert," in his words.

Alpine rescue went into motion. Early that night Toni Hiebeler, Sorgato, and two friends of the Spaniards on the face went up the west shoulder with a walkie-talkie and a megaphone to call to the climbers. At about two in the morning Piussi and Dad, heavily burdened with food and equipment, started the ascent to Hiebeler's camp. If Hiebeler found the Spaniards alive, Piussi and Dad would continue to the summit and then descend the Exit Cracks to assist the Spaniards until a cable could be lowered for the final rescue.

"The power of Piussi, this huge simple man from Treviso," Dad wrote, "became evident as we ascended 2,000 feet of completely iced rock in two hours. In our few mutual words of German and Italian we talked of the Direct and each expressed a willingness to join forces." At dawn they hailed the bivouacked crew. While tea was brewing they learned that nothing had been heard from the Spaniards, now presumed dead of exhaustion and exposure in the below-0°F temperatures on the north face. Still, Piussi and Dad continued to the shoulder.

A cold blue sky outlined the quiet north face. By radio they learned that the telescope in Scheidegg had found something in the Spider that resembled a body and a rope. The upper extremity of this rope was hidden, but was assumed to lead to the other climber. Mountain pilot Hermann Geiger's helicopter, summoned from Sion, passed overhead, but difficult air currents kept him away from the wall. The pilot confirmed what was seen through the telescope, but no more. Eventually everyone decided to abandon what would have been an extremely dangerous rescue attempt, now turned into a body recovery.

During all this, Sorgato, Piussi, and Dad agreed to join forces on the *direttissima,* and as they descended the west flank they discussed route possibilities and their different ideas of equipment and food. Low on the west flank Piussi pushed by and jumped into the forty-five-degree ice couloir, glissading at tremendous speeds. Dad and the others carefully glissaded after him, always in a self-arrest position. It seemed to Dad that "Piussi's dramatic burst of daring and skill was this great man's way of throwing off the frustrations we had been through in the past days."

They hoped to start the *direttissima* immediately, but the storms continued and eventually Sorgato and Piussi had to return to Italy. Dad was due in Leysin, where his family and job were waiting.

SEVEN

LEYSIN

JUST EAST of Lake Geneva, where sharp-toothed mountains pinch the broad Rhône River valley, the windows in Leysin can be seen glinting high on a south-facing hillside. There are two ways to get to this village besides foot or helicopter. There's a little cog railway with bucket seats designed to keep you from tumbling into your neighbor as the train climbs the impossibly steep slope. Measured along the railroad track, it's only four kilometers from the valley to the village. The longer way to get there is by automobile. Because cars can't climb like a Swiss railroad, the skinny, vertiginous switchbacking road requires sixteen kilometers to cover the same terrain. In the 1960s the road narrowed to a single lane around cobbled switchbacks, and a stone wall protected cars from the steepest drop-offs. Over the next three years I would revel in pointing out the ragged-edged gaps to newcomers where cars had gone over the edge, dropping into the valley bottom a thousand feet below.

Leysin is a real mountain village. And while it is not always above the clouds (wouldn't want that: no snow), it *is* above the valley fog. Where Chamonix has its Mer de Glace ("sea of ice"), Leysin revels in its view of what residents unofficially call the Mer de Brouillard ("sea of fog"). During much of the winter the valley fills several thousand feet thick with condensation. The view is like looking across a great lake whose surface is the top of a cloud; most people who aren't climbers have only experienced this from the window of an airplane. We usually stood above vaporous waters in a separate world of toothy peaks along our horizon: the Dents du Midi ("teeth of noon"), the Dents de Morcles, Les Diablerets ("devil's horns"), and directly above us, the twin Tour d'Aï and Tour de Mayen ("Morcles," "Aï," and "Mayen" are ancient Celtic names whose meanings have been lost, but the French words "Dent" and "Tour" are clear: tooth and tower). Off to the south, looking small from a distance, are the highest of all: the permanently ice-clad summits above Chamonix. The view from a balcony in Leysin is as spectacular as the view from the best bivouac ledges in the world.

When doctors discovered in the late 1800s that the ultraviolet rays in sunshine help to cure certain types of tuberculosis, the little alpine pasture-town of Leysin sprouted sanitariums like mushrooms. People lived in separate buildings divided by nationality, occupation, and income level. One building held Russian aristocrats while they gambled away their estates before death. Patients would ski wearing nothing but their Skivvies, the better to soak up ultraviolet rays. Unfortunately, the otherwise postcard-perfect village is now marred by a vast collection of sprawling boxy apartment buildings, all of which have a façade of balconies facing the sunshine. Two years before we arrived, one of these boxes had been turned into the Leysin American School (a high school), and another into the American College of Switzerland.

Just past the high school were twin little chalets, one of which was ours. My sister and I leaped out of the car to explore our new mountain home. We were beyond ourselves with excitement, and left Mom to deal with the moving van that wouldn't unload. The driver said he could only accept a man's signature, and Dad was climbing. Finally my mother brought the school's principal over to sign, and we were able to unload our long-lost toys. (Women wouldn't get the vote in Switzerland until 1971, and it was 1990 before the national supreme court forced the final canton to accept female suffrage.)

Every chalet in Switzerland has a name, and ours was Pollux; our twin was Castor. To me, our little chalet had everything. The top floor with sloped ceilings held three little bedrooms, one for my sister and one for me. The main floor held kitchen, living/dining room, bathroom—and the living room opened onto a large balcony that lorded over the plunging hillside below. When the snow built up deeply enough to absorb a ten-foot tumble, I would stand on the railing and somersault into the powder below. Under the balcony was an unheated daylight basement that would hold all Dad's climbing gear and often a climbing partner or two as well.

Below the chalet was nothing but steep meadow yielding to steep forest that sank into the sea of fog. I didn't understand how anyone could stand to live down there. Behind our house directly across the narrow access road was a T-bar ski lift—in winter I would be able to catch a run or two after school. The woods provided trees for forts. A quarter mile toward town was the high school where my parents taught, and in the evenings we fetched dinner from the cafeteria and brought it home to eat. If it hadn't been for my own school, life might have been idyllic.

The first problem with school was the language. Switzerland, a bit smaller than New Hampshire and Vermont combined, has four official languages. Only about 1 percent of the Swiss population speaks Romansh, an ancient Roman language that has survived in pocket populations in isolated valleys; it is treated as an official language and a cultural tradition. Italian is spoken by the segment of Switzerland that borders Italy, at about 6 percent of the population. Most popular of all is German, at 74 percent public use, though real Germans complain that the singsong Swiss accent makes a mockery of their beloved guttural barks. When we moved to Leysin, German was the language I could read and write.

Leysin's language is French, spoken by about 20 percent of

the nation's population. Though it's hard to imagine that an educated person in Switzerland could speak neither German nor English, my teacher at least pretended to be monolingual, much to my distress. A few weeks after starting school I soiled my pants in class because I couldn't communicate to the teacher that I really, really had to go.

Europeans begin grade-years in early summer before the schools' short summer holidays, whereas Leysin American School followed the American pattern of beginning in September. Thus Leysin's first-grade class was well under way by the time I joined it knowing only two languages, both utterly useless. One day I was running to school because I was late (school was over a mile from home, all downhill) when a teacher saw me and offered a ride. As I got out of the car, I told her *"Merci."* Her response, *"De rien"* ("it's nothing"), hurt me deeply. She'd provided me a ride, which was clearly *something,* and then she called it "nothing"? Was she insulting me? Mom explained after school. There were other trials besides language, like fitting in. One day I combed my hair with a front flip like the one Dad was sporting at the time. The teacher called me to the front of the class and patted down the wave, again humiliating me. And somehow the language and cultural learning curve was so steep—or my brain so narrow—that the process of absorbing French squeezed the German right out of me. A year later I was riding the village gondola when a skier spoke to me in German and I couldn't respond. I felt utter bewilderment at being unable to speak; it was like a portion of my brain had been removed. By then, however, my French was almost as good as any village child's.

The good thing about school being downhill from home was that I could ski to class in the morning. The bad thing was that I would have to carry my skis back uphill in the afternoon. Besides that burden, the heavy untracked snow that fell at village level made turning my long stiff boards a challenge. So I didn't often ski to school, but I did join the village ski team. Racing never was my passion, as running gates just didn't offer the joy of free movement that to me was the essence of skiing. Downhill racing (as compared to slalom) was better because at least it offered the thrill of speed, even if my lightweight frame didn't glide as fast as the heavier kids'. Still, for many years to come racing provided opportunities to ski. By training with the team on Saturday mornings I earned a steeply discounted ($18) annual lift pass available only to village team members. And then I could have real fun on Sundays, usually with my mother and sometimes with Dad, an adult friend, or the high school ski team.

The T-bar across the street from our house offered quick after-school entertainment. To reach the main gondola, which served the big runs, we had to hike across town with skis on our shoulders. A four-person gondola would then take us to the top of La Berneuse, far above timberline and across a long span where the wind once blew two gondolas off the cable. I loved to point out to newcomers, especially when the wind was strong, where the little gondola cabins and their occupants must have landed, far below. One day, undoubtedly a couple of years after moving to Leysin and after my skills had developed, my father took me up the big T-bar on the other side of the Berneuse. From the top of that lift we shouldered our skis and hiked to the ridge, then edged our way across a steep slope far out of bounds behind the freezing-cold north face of the Tour d'Aï. Finally we popped into a huge bowl of untracked snow between the Tour d'Aï and the equally vertiginous Tour de Mayen. It seemed like no one ever went back there; the snow felt wild and remote, as did the landscape. My heart nearly burst with excitement: the brilliant sunshine was crisp, cold, sharp, snappy, full of energy—not lazy heat energy, but the cold energy that demands action. So we plunged down the slope, carving giant warp-speed figure-eight turns, crisscrossing each other in a blur of flying snow, rolling our edges in the fall line, and zipping back the other direction. We crossed again and again, being careful not to slam into each other. It remains one of the great runs of my life, perhaps the greatest.

While my new world orbited around the ski lifts, for my parents—especially Mom—the immediate focus was the schools that had hired them. The students lived in the building on different floors from the classrooms. Although some of the high school students were from Europe or had grown up in the States, many had parents living in Africa and Asia—places where college preparatory schools were not available while the parents worked for the World Health Organization, on engineering projects, at embassies, for the United Nations, or for multinational corporations. In those days most of the kids were American by birth or parentage; today LAS advertises that its 330 students come from some fifty different nations.

Though Dad took the work as sports director for LAS and the American College mostly so that Mom could have her own job and we could live together in Switzerland, he knew how to make the most of his confinement. The mountains became the schools' gym, and students ran, climbed, and skied for their physical education. I could tag along sometimes even though my head barely rose above their waists. But I wasn't there when Dad led a pack of students he was training for the Haute Route down a steep ridge outside the ski area. The Haute Route is a multiday hut-to-hut traverse across rugged terrain between Chamonix and Zermatt, and so the training needed to be on similarly difficult terrain. Dad's students were making hop turns down the ridge when one student lost control and dropped off a double set of cliffs on the wrong side of the ridge. The landing was steep and the snow soft, two prerequisites for surviving big drops unscathed. But there was no returning to the ridge. So Dad sent the rest of the students back by the safest route with instructions to send a car around the mountain. Then he pushed off the edge himself and escorted the wayward student several thousand feet down to a village where the car could pick them up.

Dad was of the persuasion that the best trial is by fire, and what doesn't kill you makes you stronger. His education program wasn't to everyone's liking, but it worked for a number of the boys. "Guess he figured to make us all real men," recalled Bruce Bordett, one of his students. "Some of the kids really took to it, became great climbers, ski teamers, and princes among men. Some of us just were happy to survive."

On a website devoted to Leysin's expat community, someone recently posted that he was returning for a visit and looking forward to seeing old places, and he reflected: "John Harlin was without a doubt my favorite teacher during my years in Leysin." Another posting read, "I knew John Harlin II. I was in school at Leysin when he was the PE teacher there. The force of his character was amazing—he brought the best out of all of us. He taught me never to surrender." Another: "He taught us to climb, and to extend our personal limits like no one I ever met before or since." And yet another: "He was regarded as the Blond God. He taught me what No Fear really means. He taught us what the brotherhood of the rope really means. I will never forget what he taught us and how it carries forward to my kids and theirs. Be aware. Persist. Look inside for the strength you need. Above all, trust in yourself."

Mom recalled a student whose energy, intelligence, and leadership got him into trouble the first year, almost to the point of being dismissed from LAS. But Dad fought to keep him on. The next year, under Dad's guidance, he used his qualities constructively and became Mom's finest biology student.

For every student who took to Dad's methods or was repelled by them, there was another who reacted just as strongly to my mother. She had an infectious enthusiasm for the natural world, and her field trips to the Alpine ponds above Leysin or the intertidal realms of the Mediterranean coast were inspiring to the right sort—and incomprehensible to those who weren't interested. Bruce Bordett recalled her advice: "There will be enormous pressures on you to conform, to change your path to the more acceptable, to follow the path more comfortable. Don't do it. Stick with your dreams." If not for her, he said, "I'd probably have wound up in the shoe business with my father instead of being a filmmaker. Your mom taught me to believe in myself, and that being happy is often better than being first."

In the summer of 1964, after nearly a year in Leysin, my mother, sister, and I visited the States for the first time since we'd left five years before. Mom had received a predoctoral grant from the National Science Foundation to the University of Washington, where she was to attend a graduate course in marine algae. While she studied at the nearby Friday Harbor Laboratories, Andréa and I were to stay with our grandparents in the house that Mom had been raised in. After crossing the Atlantic, we landed in New York. On Sixth Avenue I looked up at skyscrapers for the first time; rather than being as impressed as I'd been told I would be, I remember feeling that they seemed small compared to the Eiger or Mont Blanc. But it was there, in the New York Public Library, that I saw a photo of a national park ranger on horseback. I determined that that's what I wanted to be—just as long as I could also be a scientist, like my mom.

We then took a long bus across the country to Washington State. The big events of the summer for me were learning new skills with my grandfather: shooting his .22 rifle, driving his tractor, fishing from his rowboat, and chopping wood with his axe. I was eight years old and Grandpa George fifty-seven, but he felt like an older brother who knew everything interesting and wanted to share it all with me. That summer we laid the foundations for a relationship that would become precious in my future fatherless world.

EIGHT

FRUSTRATIONS WITH THE EIGER DIRECT

THE AUTUMN we moved to Leysin, Dad wrote to a friend:

> I have never before had the opportunity of watching a seasonal change in the mountains. Every moment is a treasure of experience. With the lowering snowline there is a floral sleep, and the storms that bring the snow seem out of place in their violence. The greens are replaced by ambers and ochers, while an occasional late flower is a smile on the sober mountainside. Sometimes silence can scream of potential energy, but the quiet of our autumn is the restfulness of peace.

Living full-time in the mountains had a calming effect on Dad. It certainly brought out the best in him at home. The four of us would sit in the rain on the balcony, gather mushrooms in the woods next to the chalet, hike in the hills after school, swim in the freezing-cold local pool, and ski. When it was dark Dad loved to have us kids walk on his back while he lay on the living room rug listening to Beethoven, Mahler, Dylan, Baez.

In a different letter and another mood, Dad wrote, "I am becoming an animal of strength by climbing and training every day. I have never had an opportunity such as this, and it seems to be turning me into some sort of mountain ape. Oh well, it is better than being in a zoo!" For Dad mental tranquility and physical hyperactivity were mutually reinforcing, and the effect at home was happiness—the happiest we had ever known him.

Something else pleased him as well: people were paying attention. With a few exceptions, the routes Dad had climbed before the summer of 1963 had already been climbed by others, and you don't make much news in other people's footsteps. His list of climbs had earned him enough respect in Europe to have been invited into some tight circles, including as a guest of the Trento Film Festival, one of the inner sanctums of Alpine climbing, and a membership in the Group de Haute Montagne, an elite association of France's best alpinists (with an occasional invited foreigner). In Trento in 1961 he had met Walter Bonatti and Pierre Mazeaud, a few months after their Frêney Pillar disaster, and he struck up a future climbing partnership with the young French politician as well as friendships with alpinists across Europe.

In October of 1963 he returned to Trento for the third consecutive year. Though Dad despised nationalism, he was happy to admit that this had been a good year for American climbing. In May Americans had climbed Everest for the first time, which at the time was significant. Vastly more important was that Willi Unsoeld and Tom Hornbein had also completed the first-ever traverse of Everest—via a new route up a virgin face. It was one of the great climbs of history. A few months later Dad and friends established two of the hardest routes in the Alps. The Hidden Pillar of Frêney was perhaps the most challenging route on Mont Blanc, while the south face of the Fou ushered in a whole new era of technical difficulty in the heart of world alpinism. While Dad's deeds went unheralded in the States, in Europe—where the press made front-page news out of climbing successes and tragedies—Dad's star was bright. One colleague and climbing partner recalls, "It was fun to walk into restaurants or public places with him and watch the eyeballs click in his direction. And it seemed to happen everywhere, not just in Leysin."

Leysin was unknown to climbers at the time, but Dad intended to turn it into an international center for mountaineers. Immediately after arriving he started writing letters, inviting mountaineers worldwide to come, even work if necessary, and he brought climbers onto the staff at the American schools. He had plans, and the first big item on the agenda, no surprise, was the Eiger Direct. He wrote to Henry Kendall, an old friend from Stanford with whom he had climbed in the States: "Would you consider joining me and two others next on an Eiger direttissima? I can't hide the danger from you. There will be more risk than one is usually forced to accept in the mountains. But I'm game; how about you?" Kendall had made the first American ascent of the Walker Spur in 1962, with Gary, and thus had Alpine experience; but he was on his way toward winning a Nobel Prize in physics and founding the Union of Concerned Scientists, among other things, and an extended session of dangerous climbing didn't fit his schedule. Dad also wrote to Konrad and Gary, Mazeaud and René Desmaison, and various others. But most of all, he corresponded with Sorgato and Piussi, with whom he was firming up plans for the winter.

The Eiger Direct's time had come—not just for Dad, but for the entire Continental climbing world. Until the 1960s the prevalent attitude could be summed up in the words of legendary German climber Kurt Diemberger: "I never want to climb the North Face again. It is one of those climbs which one does in a lifetime, and finds it enough of a good thing." But by the early 1960s some who had climbed the Heckmair Route and others new to the Eiger were desperate to put a *direttissima*—or the "aesthetic line of attack," as Dad called it—on the greatest wall in the Alps.

The notion of a "direct" climb being the most elegant arose far earlier. In 1931 Italian alpinist Emilio Comici wrote, "I wish some day to make a route and from the summit let fall a drop of water and this is where my route will have gone." He was talking about the vertiginous terrain of his home turf in Italy's Dolomites, and he put his words into action, establishing in 1933 what some would call the first *direttissima,* on the north face of the 1,500-foot continuously overhanging wall of the Cima Grande. Others credit the German route on the same face in 1958 as being the first of the great *direttissimas;* the German Jörg Lehne, a young Saxon, would go on to lead the German team on the Eiger's own *direttissima* in 1966.

When Dad wrote to Sorgato from our new home in Leysin, he explained his belief that a winter climb would face considerably less rockfall. This extra safety would be worth the cost in logistics and difficulty. Sorgato agreed, and was already in touch with Piussi and two other Italians, Marcello Bonafede and Natalino Menegus, about a winter ascent. He thought that a five-man team would have the security and carrying capacity necessary for a winter climb. There would be one team of two and one of three. The team of two would establish the advance route by placing fixed ropes, while the second team would carry loads and prepare an early bivouac. Dad accepted this strategy—after all, Sorgato had recently directed the winter ascent of the north face of the Civetta with Piussi, perhaps the greatest feat of winter rock climbing yet done.

They decided that Dad should monitor the weather conditions on the Eiger, sending a telegram when they were favorable. In January 1964 he went to Kleine Scheidegg and spent a night on the Eiger with a friend of Konrad's to check out conditions. The snow and ice seemed perfect, but during the night it became clear that their clothing was not. Coming down, Dad met the Swiss climber Martin Epp, who suggested that they climb the north face of the Eiger's neighbor, the Mönch. Epp thought it could be climbed in a day or two despite the previous (and only) winter ascent having taken four days. As it turned out, Epp and my father reached the summit merely ten hours after leaving the hut, a phenomenal time. In celebration they sent off fireworks from the summit after Dad called my mother on the walkie-talkie; she was skiing nearby with students from LAS. On reaching Kleine Scheidegg, Dad telegraphed the Italians, reporting that Eiger conditions were perfect and they should come up as fast as possible. Unfortunately, they couldn't break free from their commitments, so Dad went to Chamonix instead to do the first winter ascent of a route on the Aiguille de Blaitière. Meanwhile at LAS, they marketed his fame in lieu of his teaching; his assistants could take care of those pesky students.

Four Munich climbers also had eyes on the Eiger's *direttissima,* and they started up shortly after Dad's Mönch climb. But after three days on the wall, including one spent in a snow cave hiding from a storm, continued bad weather forced them to retreat through one of the train-tunnel windows.

In February Sorgato and Piussi knocked on our door in Leysin, ready to make final preparations before launching on the Eiger. There was a lot to do, for as Dad put it, "The Eiger Direct presents a logistical problem comparable to Himalayan expeditions." Their gear list included a complete set of rock pitons, a large selection of ice equipment and screws, crampons, long ice axes for deep snow, short axes for climbing steep ice, expansion bolts, wooden wedges, ice daggers, Jumars, enough sling to fix more than 5,000 feet of rappels if they had to retreat, helmets, down jackets, gaiters, elephant's feet (short sleeping bags that are paired with a down jacket), bivouac tents, stove with fuel for twelve days, double boots, medical supplies including heart and circulation stimulants, two-way radio, piton hammers, daily change of socks, overpants, parkas, four sets of gloves, and food. Carrying twelve days' rations would be too much weight and volume on a climb this difficult, they concluded. Instead, Dad wrote, "we chose a progressive diet ending in the last few days with nothing more than carbohydrates and mineral-supplemented liquids."

The team spent two weeks in our basement preparing while the Eiger raged in continual storm. While skiing behind our house one day, Dad impaled his leg with a ski pole—the tip plunged four inches into his thigh, right up to the basket. Dad simply pulled it out and kept skiing to keep the leg from stiffening up. The next day, despite the unrelenting weather, they decamped to Kleine Scheidegg, leaving us in a sudden state of peace. Four days later a good weather report gave them enough hope to establish base camp in an alcove at the bottom of the face. By noon the following day they passed the first bivouac site of the Munich team that had abandoned their attempt three weeks prior. Dad's party climbed on, and in midafternoon encountered their first difficult rock pitches. The Italians' cold hands slowed progress, which frustrated Dad. He trained for such situations by almost never wearing gloves and by carrying snow in hands at every opportunity so that "the body adapts by not causing capillary shunts in the fingers."

As the Italians were waving their arms and smacking their hands together to stimulate circulation, Dad glanced into a nearby couloir, where he spotted a blackened arm sticking out of the snow with its hand "in supplication." It had belonged to Ernesto Navarro, one of the Spaniards who had died in the Spider on the Classic Route the summer before—the climbers Dad and the Italians had hoped to rescue. Somewhat demoralized, they climbed on.

The steep rock in intense cold with extremely heavy packs proved even more difficult than they'd expected. Ice clogged every crack, and they had to scrape off the rock with their fingers before they could find a place to drive a piton. As dusk descended they realized they wouldn't reach their planned bivouac site. They searched long and hard for an alternative, and in desperation Dad made a long traverse toward some slightly overhanging rock. Once there, he thrust his axe into the snow and it plunged into empty space. By luck they'd found a cave made comfortable by the Germans during their attempt, the one they'd holed up in during the storm.

Sorgato and Dad felt exhilarated as they teamed up for the pitches above camp the next day. That changed when they came across another piece of Navarro, this time his leg. The sight knocked the wind out of them just as they were reaching the most serious difficulties. But onward they climbed.

Sorgato and Dad spent the rest of the day forcing their way up the steep rock above, finding few cracks for pitons but refusing to place bolts on blank sections. By dark they had gained a few hundred feet and rappeled back to the foot of the cliff, where the others had dug a large, comfortable snow cave in the deep snow. But, Dad said, "the feeling of camping left as one crawled out the entrance hole to stare 2,500 vertical feet into the valley below." Despite the scattered body parts, the climbers were in excellent spirits, at least until they called Kleine Scheidegg on the walkie-talkie and discovered that a storm was forecast. After a quick powwow, they decided to continue climbing and hauling loads, but to enjoy the comforts of their cave each night until the weather forecast turned in their favor.

The next day Piussi and Bonafede took the lead, reaching the First Icefield early in the afternoon. They couldn't see any cracks in the wall above the Icefield, and they thought it would be necessary to traverse over to the normal route and use the Ice Hose to reach the Second Icefield. The lack of cracks above, the weight of their packs, the bad weather predicted on the radio, all turned their mood to depression. They spent the next day above the First Icefield, watching storm clouds bringing snow and hard wind. A radio report from the Geneva airport guaranteed adverse weather; they decided to escape through the refuse shaft leading to the railway tunnel, just as the Munich climbers had.

And then came the final demoralizing blow. "Somehow the frustrations of so much preparation and work, and so little accomplishment in the face of the storm," Dad wrote, "were not lessened when the Grindelwald police informed us that they required Navarro's leg to get legal certification of his death. I made a long rappel to retrieve the leg, and then jumared back up to the station window."

There was only one way to deal with such a depressing situation, as my father saw it. "The deep feeling of emptiness in me," he wrote, "could only be removed by another attempt at the Eiger Direct."

Life in Leysin went on as usual when Dad returned, and his feelings about the Eiger became just part of the standard family background, a kid's sense of normalcy. Our days overflowed with school, skiing, and the onset of spring in the mountains. In May the cows returned from the valley below, their exquisite bells heralding an approaching Alpine summer just as assuredly as the greening grass. And then Mom, Andréa, and I flew off to the States, leaving Dad to return to the Eiger in July with the French guides René Desmaison and André Bertrand. The weather began promisingly, and they found Piussi and Sorgato on the face as well. In thirty-six hours Dad and the Frenchmen reached the top of the Second Icefield by following approximately the Sedlmayer-Mehringer line, an easier though somewhat less direct version of what they'd tried in February. They might have joined forces with the Italians there, except that on the third day a storm forced everyone down. Already they'd endured bruising rockfall, just as Dad had feared on a summer ascent.

The previous April a Polish team had tried the *direttissima* and suffered a long fall low on the face, but no permanent injuries. That summer the Britons Chris Bonington and Dougal Haston, both of whom had climbed the Heckmair Route, were talking about climbing the Direct, but did not have a go. There were rumors of other interested parties. It seemed that climbers all over Europe were dreaming of this prize.

At the end of August, after being stormed off attempted new routes on the Shroud of the Walker Spur with Dougal Haston and the *direttissima* of the Dru with Lito Tejada-Flores, Mazeaud, and Sorgato, Dad drove to Luxembourg to meet my mother and us kids at the airport on our return from three months in the States. The symbolism was huge. Mom remembered years later, "The time was right for the Eiger Direct. John coming to the airport instead of heading back to the Eiger was about the biggest honor I could have." Andréa and I had bought plastic cameras in California, and I took a picture of Andréa clinging to Dad on the Luxembourg tarmac. I pause on this photo when I look through Andréa's album, and I can't help but wonder, what would life have been like if Dad hadn't come to meet us, but had completed his route instead?

A few months later Dad would give the keynote speech at the American Alpine Club's annual dinner, in Boston. It was his own first return to the States since we had moved to Europe, and the topic was dear to his heart: "The Problem of the Eiger Direct and the Mood of Alpine Climbing." Just as the 1938 Route by Heckmair and company had been the "last great problem" of Alpine climbing in the prewar era and took many attempts and six deaths before it was finally ascended, so climbing a direct or *direttissima* on the Eiger was the "last great problem" of the postwar era. The good news was that no one had died on the Direct.

NINE

ADVENTURES WITH DAD

THE AUTUMN of 1964 settled gently over the Harlin household. Dad's climbing season had been frustrating, with no great successes to show for it, but we all felt more comfortable entering the second year at our various schools than we had just a year before. Language was no longer an issue, and Andréa and I were learning the lay of the woods around our house. Along with Derrick and Ashley Eder, almost-our-age children who had moved in to the chalet next door, we found a clearing where we could play house using giant mushrooms for chairs, logs for tables, and a hollow stump as our precious toilet.

Dad sometimes took me to an abandoned quarry behind the house, where I belayed him in on what felt to me like a serious cliff—basically vertical and too high to fall off of. He would lead, and I actually thought I was safeguarding him, that I could hold him in a fall with my waist-belay. In those days belays consisted of simply sliding the rope around your back and holding it with your hands, and I now realize how unlikely it would have been for me to catch his 180 pounds during a fall. Later I'd return with Andréa or Derrick and we'd swing from pipes sticking out of the quarry's walls and climb up short cliffs, sometimes protecting ourselves with climbing hardware from Dad's stash and a rope that he'd given me. I had learned how to rappel out of our window in Bernkastel even before climbing in the Calanques and Chamonix, and I routinely went up and down the rope hanging from our balcony in Leysin, so the equipment felt completely natural. Dad would have me tie knots with my eyes closed while hiking up hills, just to make sure that I had them down pat.

In the short months before the high country went into hibernation, Mom led her students on hiking trips around Leysin, and I'd often tag along. She'd point out microcosms within forests and Alpine ponds, and we'd learn how each organism was adapting to the coming deep freeze. I remember the amazement of students almost twice my age when I'd tell them that lichen was in fact fungi and algae living together symbiotically. One student later remembered that Mrs. Harlin "opened my eyes to things I had previously walked past, stepped on, or otherwise ignored." My mother taught both chemistry and biology, and she used books like Rachel Carson's *Silent Spring,* which had come out just two years before, to impress on students the connections between human activity and nature, even at the chemical level. Many if not most of her students first learned from Mom about the importance of biodiversity and environmental preservation. I suppose I did, too, because the concepts already seemed obvious.

My sister's kindergarten and my second grade were in neighboring buildings, allowing us to walk to and from school together. In the fall we'd climb haystacks en route, being careful to stay out of the farmer's sight. Soon enough the snow season dropped on us like a blanket. Andréa and I would sit on our backpacks and slide down the last steep slope to school, wetting our papers in the process. We developed what we called our secret language at school: English spoken rapidly.

Andréa and Dad had a special rapport; she called herself "Daddy's little girl." Despite his great size and strength, he could brush her hair without making her cry, whereas Mom's efforts brought tears and resentment. Andréa knew instantly when Dad had returned from climbing, as she'd smell the dirty wet wool hanging up to dry and she'd exclaim, "Daddy's home!" He would leap out from behind a doorway, roaring like a lion, and we'd jump on him and wrestle him to the ground.

Often as not, there would be another climber in the house as well, for Dad's plan to put Leysin on the map was working. We loved the blur of strange accents, mostly Scottish or English, sometimes American, often various German dialects, French, or Italian. Andréa would don her tutu and put on ballet shows for them, while I'd do pull-ups off Dad's biceps. Particularly welcome was the smell of sausage frying in the kitchen, which meant Bev Clark, an English climber Dad had met in Wales in 1960, had arrived from London. One time the customs agents caught him, and they pulled the sausages out from his sleeves. We children were crushed that he arrived empty-handed. As winter progressed, I started giving ski lessons to various Brits who could haul themselves up overhanging walls, but who stumbled like clumsy puppies when they had skis on their feet.

Dad wasn't climbing with Gary anymore. They had finally decided that their friendship worked but their partnership didn't. There wasn't a hint of strife in Dad's account of the Fou climb, and maybe that's how he remembered it. Gary's diary, however, revealed that "we came as close as two people can come to killing one another from sheer hate and frustration with the other." Tom said that my father had an ability to forgive and forget, which likely made his conflicts with Gary less disagreeable to him than they had been to Stewart and Tom. "John and I got along famously on the Frêney," Tom said about the climb on Mont Blanc he made with Dad shortly after the Fou. "We were as one, in thought and action." Dad and Gary together, however, was another matter. "I believe Stewart and I were onlookers to a drama of basic incompatibility of two men under conditions of stress," said Tom. One of their ongoing disagreements concerned methods. Dad was willing to use fixed ropes to get up something if necessary, whereas Gary believed fixed ropes were impure under any circumstances. Another was that Dad was only too willing to accommodate and even encourage reporters, while Gary thought that talking about your deeds was selling out. Later Gary went so far as to refuse to speak about his climbs at all, even his new routes. He would simply disappear into the mountains, sometimes solo and sometimes with a partner, do hard climbs that were occasionally new, and respond to questions by saying he'd been for a stroll.

Gary roamed two continents trying to feel at home, though not to find a home. He was simultaneously attempting to write a novel, an autobiography, and a book about climbing in California, and he wrote incessantly in his diaries. Much of the time Gary's face was deep under a shaggy beard, which Andréa and I enjoyed filling with wildflowers while he dozed in mountain meadows. He was tall, blond, lanky, with an enigmatic countercultural poet-climber personality. Dad enjoyed him for his worldly, philosophical perspectives and good conversation, as well as their long history together, though in more formal company Dad felt embarrassed by Gary's long hair and shaggy clothes. Later, after Gary led the French rescue on the Dru in the summer of 1966 and became a media darling, much of the attention focused on his "beatnik" image, though he disavowed being a beatnik. He told a French magazine that the term had become pejorative toward a class who were parasites with long hair. The true origin of the movement, he said, was a blend of Zen Buddhism and spiritual discipline that contrasted with the external discipline required by the West. He didn't think it was possible to be a true beatnik because everyone has to mix with society. At the time of the interview, Gary was living under bridges in Paris.

Once they stopped climbing together, "all feelings of rivalry had disappeared, leaving behind the strength of a friendship built up over many years," wrote Mirella Tenderini in *The Beatnik of the Alps*. "John was the only old friend Gary had in Europe, and the only person with whom Gary had a past in common." Perhaps for this reason, Gary thought it a reasonable request for his child to be born in our house the first year we'd moved to Leysin. Gary also wanted Swiss citizenship for the child. Gary's Grenoble girlfriend, Claude, had decided to have his baby despite the fact that Gary would never marry. My mother and Claude were quite close and so Mom had agreed at first, assuming Dad would go along because of his friendship with Gary. But Dad exploded. He wouldn't have the baby born anywhere near our place, let alone living with us. It was Gary's responsibility to house and birth that child, he fumed. And so Claude had the baby alone in Grenoble while Gary kept moving. During our second year in Leysin we were almost as likely to smell Laurent's diapers as Gary's drying woolens.

Konrad, too, remained one of Dad's closest friends, but he rarely came to Leysin. When he wasn't engaged to his law studies, he was on multimonth expeditions to Afghanistan. The people I connected with among Dad's friends were those who worked at LAS, especially Ted Wilson, who came to teach in the sports program. Much later Ted served nine years as the mayor of Salt Lake City, but in Leysin he was my ski buddy; we roamed the mountain together, often with the high school ski team in tow. Ted remembered first meeting Dad, "with his large and strong body, his flowing wisp of blond hair, his huge handshake, and his embracing manner. It scared the hell out of me frankly." Ted was still jet-lagged after traveling to Leysin with his wife and baby when Dad ran him up the mountain and made him climb an icy chimney without a rope. Ted later realized it had been a test, and he said his high adrenaline level allowed him to pull it off well and earn Dad's respect. The future politician was already comfortable with forceful charismas, and he could relax around Dad as few could; they grew very close. He said my father "was full of ego and even bluster. But there was heart and soul there that would put a net over the world and absorb it all." Dad wanted Ted to climb the Eiger *direttissima* with him, but Ted refused, citing his new child. At first Dad scorned the logic, but later he apologized and admitted that family came first.

Instead Dad focused on Dougal Haston, the young Scottish

ice-climbing phenomenon with whom Dad had attempted the Shroud that summer. Dougal set up a semipermanent camp in our basement for the winter, though he complained about it later in his autobiography, *In High Places:* "Have you ever tried living with concrete all around at minus temperatures? My first move was to 'borrow' a stove from one of the disused summer chalets—it smoked badly but I preferred watery eyes to a frozen body." The food, he said, was "leftovers from the family meals at the American schools where John was sports director—'sports' being climbing and skiing."

Dougal was the silent type, given to hard drinking at Leysin's pub for expats, the Club Vagabond, when he wasn't shivering in our basement. Back in Scotland he had been a philosophy student, and Dad was able to engage him more than most. They spent much of the winter of 1965 hoping for the Eiger to come into shape, but the best they could do was an exploration of the 300-foot cliff below the First Icefield, which by now was known as the "First Band." To date, all *direttissima* attempts had either been blocked by this overhanging wall, or had bypassed it along the original line taken by Sedlmayer and Mehringer in 1935, when they climbed to the top of the Flatiron before freezing to death. Dad had grown increasingly keen on climbing all-new ground along a much more direct line, which meant somehow piercing the middle of the First Band. After three days of searching in intense cold, with the rock covered in powder snow and the ice so hard that they needed to chop steps everywhere, Dougal and Dad descended having learned little more than that getting through the First Band would require very difficult artificial climbing. Half jokingly, they guessed that the entire route would take three weeks.

Life at home was generally good, as Dad had mellowed considerably now that he was out of the military and was so much closer to the freedom he craved. But there were still plenty of arguments, often involving family responsibilities, like life insurance. He had started no policies, nor to the best of Mom's knowledge did he ever make a payment on the policy his father had started for him. He didn't go so far as to destroy the bills when they came, but he would give Mom a hard time when he caught her in the process of making out a check. "Profiteering by my death," he called it, even though she knew he expected his children to grow up with skis, ballet, musical instruments, and the other necessities of life. Mom's own feeling was that "mourning and starving is worse than simply mourning."

That winter she learned that his mountain judgment, which she'd had complete faith in, was also suspect. During a ski descent from La Berneuse, the high point served by lifts from Leysin, Dad wanted to take the Black Trail even though it was closed because of avalanche danger. Mom thought skiing it under these conditions was stupid, especially since it was still snowing and she'd noticed a crack in the snow that made the slope look especially risky to her. But she trusted Dad, and when he scoffed at her fears and swooped down the run, she followed a distance behind. Soon enough the slope between them avalanched, and then another set of avalanches cut loose behind her. Dad warned her to watch him closely so she'd know where to dig if he went under (a good chance of this, she thought). The situation was bad enough, and then he made it worse by yelling repeatedly, "Don't fall; it's your life." At the bottom of the hill he let out a great yodel. He was having fun. Meanwhile, all Mom could think of was the children.

They returned to news that a nearby avalanche had killed two people. Someone later told Mom that Andréa and I were so self-sufficient that it would have been days before anyone realized we were orphaned. After that she kept a silent resolve always to trust in her own judgment when it came to safety, even in the mountains.

I had my own character-revealing run-ins with Dad that winter. The first was on my return from the eighth annual Trofeo Topolino, a huge international ski race in Italy that Dad's parents took me to. While the parades and the crowds had been exciting, I returned deeply disappointed, as I'd not done well. My parents took the cog rail down to Aigle to meet us when we got off the overnight train from Italy. On the ride up the hill I felt the need to admit that I'd fallen twice in the race, not just the once that Dad's parents had reported. Dad's contempt was palpable. I don't recall any words, just a sense of being shamed.

The second took place in my school's playground. The class bully—an ignorant farmer's son in overalls—and I had a long-running conflict. He was on top of me flailing away with his fists when Andréa called from the steps to say that Mom was here to pick us up. I yelled back to get her so she could pull this kid off of me. Dad showed up instead, and the furious lecture he gave me in the car offered no sympathy for my being a victim, nor condemnation of me for being in a fight. What I still picture is his outline against the front window of the van glowering back at me in a rage of disappointment that I had been on the bottom of the pile receiving the blows instead of on top giving them.

Fortunately, in the mountains I was generally able to live up to Dad's expectations, though our outings weren't without incident. By now most of the ski slopes above Leysin felt familiar, and I was always looking for a chance to explore new ground. Les Diablerets, being the closest major ski area to Leysin, offered something even better than just another cut through the trees or a big open bowl: a real glacier that we could ski when all the other runs had long melted out. I jumped with delight when Dad invited me to pull the skis out of the basement to celebrate my ninth birthday, in May of 1965.

The gondola lifted us in three cliff-jumping stages to roughly 10,000 feet at the top of the glacier. Shortly after stepping out of the lift we stood on the flattest, smoothest glacier I'd ever seen. Normally glacial ice bulges into seracs and splits into crevasses as it reacts to the changing landscape a few hundred feet underneath the surface—rock shapes we can only guess at from above. Whatever lies below the upper Diablerets Glacier must be smooth and flat, since the surface we skied was like a gently tilted skating rink perfectly frosted with spring corn snow. We cruised along making huge turns that soon became boring in their monotony.

Then an idea came to us, and I don't recall if I thought of it first or watched one of the grown-ups do it first. I just remember swiveling my skis quickly so that the tails pointed downhill, and then carving the same arching turns as before, only backward. Soon we were all doing it, racing one another backward down the mountain, checking only occasionally to make sure nothing surprising lay below. Spring sunshine glittered brightly on the snow, melting it into a perfect buttery consistency. Rock bands hemmed in the glacier, and we swooped past and around one another in a ski game I've never been able to duplicate. This was close to heaven, and Dad cut loose a yodel that bounced off the rocky rim.

The grown-ups kept glancing over their shoulders downhill, checking for crevasses and also for the cutoff point. Eventually even the Diablerets Glacier has to reach the valley, and it makes up with a vengeance for all its youthful flatness. To escape from the icy maelstrom to come, skiers take a narrow path to a steep sidehill traverse. Finally we spotted our exit and reluctantly scrambled out of the Diablerets Glacier's great basin.

Suddenly the energy changed. The sidehill faces north and lay in shade, which crusted the snow into an icy, skidding track at roughly a forty-five-degree angle. This was Point A to Point B skiing, with Point B being many hundred yards straight across the slope on the right—meanwhile the top edge of a cliff threatened us below and left. To hold an edge on a steep slope in those old soft ski boots, you had to use the classic angular pose so familiar in ancient ski photos, with the ankles and knees aimed well uphill and hips twisted and aimed downhill. It is an insecure system on steep icy slopes, and soon enough it failed me.

My high-pitched yelp pierced through the chattering sounds of edges grinding down ice and then I was accelerating downward. I could see the cliff just below and it seemed inevitable that I would soon launch over it. Above I could see the receding ant line of skiers on the track. My gloved fingers clawed into the hard snow with no effect, and I tried to put my edges back in contact but they only bounced off the hard crust. I was in panic's full grip when a patch of rock bit into my clothes and held me fast. I lay on that rock like a pile of jelly as Dad stepped slowly and carefully down to help. My memories of the day end there.

Later that spring, after the snows had completely melted off of the Tour d'Aï above Leysin, Dad and Mick Burke brought me on their attempt to climb a several-hundred-foot-tall section of cliff that had no existing routes. Mick was one of my favorites among Dad's friends—a funny, outgoing, playful little British guy with glasses. Ten years later I was doing the dishes at my girlfriend's house in Connecticut when news came over the radio that Mick had disappeared on Everest on Chris Bonington's expedition (on that expedition Dougal made the first ascent of the southwest face and became the first British climber to summit Everest, along with Doug Scott). The news greatly saddened me, as Mick actually seemed a close friend of mine, too.

Mick led up the first pitch of the Tour d'Aï, smoothly climbing nearly 150 feet of chimney and wide crack. Following him on the crack was a real struggle for me, as it was about the width of my head, extremely smooth, and dead vertical. The sight of the ground so far below took the rest of the fun out of the experience. Then I shivered on the ledge for some time while Mick and Dad took turns struggling on something out of sight, maybe an overhang. They decided it wouldn't go, and we did a free-hanging rappel, the best part of which was at the bottom where we'd pendulum in huge sweeping arcs by running sideways along the wall until the rope swung us out into space. The outing had turned into a great lark by then, and I love looking at the pictures I took of Dad flying through the air.

What I didn't know at the time was that something went on up there that frightened Dad. He told Mom about it, and she was furious. Years later she told me that it was one thing for him to risk his own life, but he had no business doing anything that dangerous with me, though she didn't remember specifically what had gone wrong.

Dad was certainly more careful when Andréa was along. She usually wanted to come, though she had a lower tolerance for chilled digits on cold ski days, and was afraid of glaciers. Once when Mom, Andréa, and I crossed a glacier while checking on Dad's progress on a route above Chamonix, Andréa became unnerved at the snowbridge crossings, perhaps in part because I teased her that if we fell into the crevasse we'd end up in the river down in Chamonix. Instead of continuing with us, she sat down and waited for what to her seemed like hours. I don't remember the incident, myself, and if Dad had been there, Andréa probably would have crossed the glacier because she trusted him. She was game, and we nicknamed her "Me Too" for her desire to be included.

We all enjoyed a family outing that summer *inside* the Tour d'Aï. It was raining as we hiked up to the tunnel-like hole in the limestone cliff, but that didn't matter where it was always damp and cool and pitch black except for the beams of our headlamps and the flashes of our cameras. The cave pinched down so that sometimes we had to crawl sideways to slip through; in places we lowered down on ropes tied around boulders, and eventually Dad led up some steep bits and belayed us. When we finally saw daylight we were perhaps 100 feet above our starting point on the cliff and had to rappel back down to the entrance. A year later when our grandparents looked at the pictures, they asked Andréa, "Weren't you afraid?" She responded, "With Daddy we were always safe."

TEN

PREPARATIONS FOR EIGER DIRECT

WHETHER people loved Dad or loathed him, admired him or were simply confused, they noticed him. As Ted put it, "John would be a great general or even a gifted dictator of a nation. That's how deep his charisma ran. He could suck the oxygen out of any room." And one of the rooms he hung out in—or, some said, held court in—was the bar at the Club Vagabond, where the Gauloise cigarette smoke already displaced much of the oxygen. Dad's close friend Allan Rankin owned this multistory chalet at the top of the town, and he ran it as a refuge for English-speaking globetrotters who needed a welcoming, accepting, and comfortable place to unwind cheaply for a week or a month. You could dance until the middle of the night and crash on a bench if you weren't able to stagger to your bed, and the only danger would be from getting in the way of a drunk Scotsman. Allan himself was Canadian, with a quiet demeanor and a huge and generous heart, and it seemed the entire vagabonding world knew of his haven.

Allan had started the Vag before mountaineering came to Leysin. But when climbers arrived, the Vag became their unofficial headquarters. In the summer of 1965 the arrangement turned official when Dad established the International School of Modern

Mountaineering (ISMM) office at the Vag and made it the dormitory for students when they were in town. The Vag was off-limits to youth, and my mother didn't care for loud places or late nights, so neither of us saw much of the place. But Dad did, as it was where he went to converse and dream and plan with nearly everyone.

Planning for the school had occupied both of my parents for the last year, as well as Ted, Allan, Bev, and many others. Though a number of people helped to bring ISMM together, it was clearly Dad's baby, other than the "Alpine Mirror" component where Mom could teach about the mountain environment. Climbing, for Dad, was so much more than moving over stone, and his school was intended to build this awareness; it was also a low-investment way to introduce some of the concepts that Mom and Dad still planned to incorporate into their future International Institute, whether at Mont Blanc or in Leysin. You didn't simply climb a mountain, Dad wanted to stress: you lived the mountain. "By subjecting oneself to the pure and focused experience of survival, accompanied by careful introspection," he wrote, "one can approach an ultimate in self control." Or to put it in the words of ISMM's brochure, the school's goal was "To enable the individual to introspect into his character and then build upon it through analysis and adventure. . . . To strive, through the study of perfection in the sport of mountaineering, to understand and express our lives in the environment of our choice."

He still clung to his deep feeling that climbing could bring nations together. To the clinking of wineglasses at the American Alpine Club's banquet the previous December, he'd prefaced his words about the Eiger and the Alpine mood by saying:

> Whether it is justified or not, Americans are only associated with a certain exploitation or theater when it comes to real international exchanges. I believe it would surprise most Europeans if we took an active part in the internationalization of mountaineering, and I believe we would do a measurable amount of good for our country as a whole. It is hard for

Americans to realize how important mountaineering is in Europe; but it is a *fact*. And because of the connotations of fellowship, non-competition, mutual understanding and enjoyment, it becomes a vehicle for the sustenance of peace. I wonder how many people in this room have thought of mountaineering in these terms. I am saying that as climbers, Americans, and members of a world community, it is our obligation to start doing so.

ISMM was Dad's first big step toward turning his passion into something even more profound.

Dad was long on vision and short on time or patience for the squalid details of running a business, or even ensuring that the promised rostrum of instructors—nearly the entire glitterati of the Alpine world—knew that the school had been launched and their names were being marketed. And then there was Dad's teaching style, which Ullman summarized as, "What he wanted of the novices was for them to stop being novices as quickly as possible; and some, finding the climbs on which they were taken too rich for their blood, dropped out in short order."

To give himself more time to write his book, *Introspection Through Adventure,* to run ISMM, to climb big routes, and to make the Eiger Direct happen soon come hell or high water, Dad turned the directorship of the LAS sports program over to Royal Robbins, whom he had met at the American Alpine Club meeting. Robbins spent the summer in Leysin working part-time at ISMM and driving to Chamonix with Dad, where their goal was to complete the *direttissima* on the Dru. The previous summer Dad had been beaten back several times by storms and bad luck, and this year didn't start any more promisingly. Of the summer of '65, Dad wrote, "A new season comes—but what a season! It would have been better if it had stayed winter for one would at least have been able to ski." The Alps were so inaccessible that some ISMM classes were held in the Calanques instead.

Royal was the perfect partner for the Dru, for this route was technically even harder than the Fou, on which Royal's main big-wall partner, Tom Frost, had been the leading technician. Dad wasn't actually very interested in pure rock climbing, but he was American at a time when American climbers were developing new techniques and equipment that allowed them to push rock climbing to previously fantastic levels. Most of this innovation was taking place in Yosemite, where in 1958 arguably the world's greatest climbing wall—the 3,000-foot granite monolith known as El Capitan—had finally been ascended after forty-five days of climbing spread over eighteen months. That ascent broke psychological barriers, but it also revealed how much there was to learn. In 1960 the climb was repeated in seven days and without fixed ropes. While the first ascent of the Nose, as the route came to be called, established that such a wall could be climbed, the sheer labor that went into that first ascent made it an anomaly, an effort beyond the ken and interest of anyone but its visionary leader, Warren Harding. Even though Harding's effort had to come first, it was the second-ascent party who established the future of Yosemite big-wall climbing. That four-person team included Royal Robbins and Tom Frost (along with Chuck Pratt and Joe Fitschen), and the next year (1961) Royal and Tom teamed up with Pratt again to establish the second route on El Cap, this one accomplished in a mere ten days of climbing—a true revolution in difficulty and speed.

These routes, and shorter ones on other Valley walls, were well beyond the sheer technical difficulty of what was being climbed in the Alps at the time. Yosemite's famously good weather helped, in large part because it allowed climbers to accomplish their goals rather than spending all their time running for cover, weekend after weekend. Californians couldn't export their weather, but they could export the new techniques and equipment they were inventing. Yvon Chouinard, with an anvil in the back of his pickup, was taking pitons to new levels by changing the temper and alloy of the steel and aluminum being used, and by creating new shapes. Frost, a trained engineer, was helping to translate Chouinard's designs into practice. And Robbins, the most talented and dedicated all-around rock climber of his era, invented a system for hauling heavy loads of water and gear and for cleaning (de-pitoning) routes that radically improved efficiency on big walls.

Europeans long have credited Dad and Gary with raising the standards of climbing in the Alps by introducing American equipment and techniques. In fact, Dad had left California well before most of the new developments occurred. Gary wandered back and forth between the continents and was in closer touch with the Yosemite crew, but Gary also was much more of a European alpinist than an American rock climber. What Gary and Dad brought to the table—in addition to talents of their own—was an eye for unclimbed routes in the Alps and American friends who were establishing the trends back home. Among those friends were Frost and Robbins.

If the 1963 south face of the Fou with Tom marked the beginning of Dad's big new routes using Yosemite techniques, then the 1965 west face *direttissima* of the Dru with Royal marked the climax. Both became the hardest big-rock climbs of their day in the Western Alps (maybe in all the Alps), and the Dru *direttissima*'s reputation for danger and difficulty lasted for decades. The Fou, by contrast, eventually became a relatively popular route, especially after it was included in Gaston Rebuffat's book *Mont Blanc Massif: The 100 Finest Routes.* (Unfortunately, retreating glaciers have made the Fou's access couloir too dangerous to use and few people climb the route anymore.)

In July, Dad and Royal started their approach across the Mer de Glace hoping that the rain would stop. However, on the second day, the deluge only increased. On another occasion they reached somewhat higher when a bad weather report precipitated another retreat. Dad wrote of his frustration, then quickly added, "The dawn of a new day always brings more hope. It is amazing how this commodity is continually reborn."

In early August they tried again. Dad captured the mood of the approach in a new style of writing for him:

The long plod up the moraine—Those hours of back-bending weight—The same scenery—Tracks in the trail—Moving specks up the moraine—Others on the Rognon—"Good Lord, there's an army ahead"—Dusk—Bivouac among Germans, Czechs, Japs, French, Austrians, British, Poles—These numbers, a sign of accident or death to come in such a couloir—A resolve by everyone to be the first up—Morning preparation—Already ants mounting the avalanche cone by headlamp—I've put two socks on one foot and one on the other—Move out anyway—Time more important than symmetry—We don't rope up—The rocks whirl down the couloir barrel—Close calls already.

Soon the close calls turned into a real accident, as a German climber dropped a rock onto his partner, breaking his leg. And then a massive rockfall threatened to take out everyone at once; only luck prevented injuries. Eventually Royal and Dad entered virgin ground, where Dad led the most dangerous artificial pitch of his life, using skyhooks to avoid placing pitons that would have dislodged huge blocks of flaky granite (the entire wall to the right of their route fell off the mountain four decades later).

The route looked easier above, but Royal found it deceptively hard. And then Royal heard the whir of a falling rock and shouted a warning. Dad picked up the sound just before collapsing in white-hot pain—"Incredible pain that overwhelms, that seems to go to the core of one's being." He was certain that his leg was broken, yet when he could speak again, he told Royal to finish the lead. While jumaring those 135 feet to Royal's belay he broke down emotionally several times. He discovered that his leg wasn't actually broken, but doctors later told him that his sciatic nerve had been damaged and he was suffering from shock; his leg would bleed into the knee for three months.

On the belay ledge they discussed the pros and cons of going on. Dad couldn't fathom defeat after investing so much into this climb, and he trusted Royal implicitly in such terrain. They went up, though Royal would have to take over the leading, at least for the next day or two.

Dad wrote:

> When one has deliberately to torture oneself by continuous and regular movement of an injury, there develops a curious sensuousness to the pain. One tends to analyze its dimension in different terms, from color to form. About the only relief is the quality change of the pain varying from sharp spikes of accent to round deep rendering. White to red—Bach to Wagner—cry to groan. Forty meters become a never-ending journey into infinite variations on a single theme punctuated by the concentration of taking out pitons. Even the blows of the hammer and the feel of the rock take on sensual qualities, unpleasant except in academic reflection.

Two days later they reached the summit, by which time Dad's leg had improved enough that he had resumed his share of the leading. During the descent they met Bev and Lito, who had come to help Dad get down. Dad apologized for the wild-goose chase since his leg had improved so much, but everyone was happy that he wouldn't be a burden on the descent. They bivouacked together in an electrical storm, while rain turned to snow. The next day it was still snowing furiously and their mountain had a cold, white, sliding skin. The descent proved slow and treacherous. Still, Dad enjoyed himself, and by the time they reached the glacier, he said, "I feel like a dog tugging at a leash. I think to myself that it is wrong to feel so energetic."

Finally they did seat-glissades down the last slope to the hut, where, "much to the consternation of loved ones, friends, television crews and journalists, we hole up in our new shelter for half that day, the night, and half the next day. Finally, a helicopter routs us out to the unfortunate world of rebukes, congratulations, and misunderstandings."

Despite the final success, this was the end of Dad's good relationship with Royal. In Chris Bonington's words from the second volume of his autobiography, *The Next Horizon,* Royal and Dad were "both prima donnas in their own right, [who] could not have offered a greater contrast. John, flamboyant, assertive and impulsive—Robbins, very cool, analytical, carefully avoiding any ostentatious show, yet every bit as aware as John of his own position in the climbing firmament."

Ullman put it this way:

From Royal's point of view, John was disorganized, careless of the truth, bemused by his image of himself as a grand-design hero. In his own word, [Royal] became "disenchanted." For John's part, Royal struck him as plodding, unimaginative, and a bit of a cold fish. Of the two, John was the temper loser, and when annoyed he would flash out angrily. But he was also a quick forgiver of others' transgressions and a forgetter of his own. Royal was not. Whereas for John, to the end, their trouble was "some sort of misunderstanding," he, on the contrary, took the fixed, uncompromising position that here was a man he did not like.

Pat Ament, in his biography of Royal *(Spirit of the Age: The Biography of America's Most Distinguished Rock Climber, Royal Robbins)*, adds that "Royal found the records at the American School to be in shambles or nonexistent. It caused a few bad feelings between him and Harlin."

And Royal himself, forty years later, summed it up like this:

The first thing that struck me about your dad was his noble vision (or so it seemed). I was captivated by his vision of an International School of Modern Mountaineering. He thought big, much bigger than I did. We drifted apart when I began perceiving him as another flawed human being. He was also much stronger than I was and when I saw we were different I took refuge in principle, a rather chilly outpost. Your dad once told me the truth about myself, and I have never forgiven him for that though I am well aware of the curative properties of forgiveness.

The enigma of the last line will likely remain forever.

That autumn Dad wrote an essay he titled "On Stage." He is alone in the moonlight in the Calanques, seeing his moonshadow on the white limestone walls, and feeling on display: "As I looked on from the wings, my body walked out on that stage. And I felt a surge of revulsion for the melodrama of this overpowering symbolism. I wanted to leave this fool, this clown. And yet, for Christ's sake how could I? The moonlight had become the dramatic vehicle of realization, while the darkness was the security of lost identification. So I watched this buffoon on the white stage of life, and I was sick. Deep sadness of futility. At last the darkness of the trees on the other side again fused my two selves, but for a long moment I had seen myself. I was alone, and no one would help me. The experience brought home to me the need, the difficulty, and the horror of standing alone. I saw the spectators watching, disapproving, whispering, but not helping."

THE MOST important person in the rest of Dad's life, at least outside the immediate family, was Chris Bonington. Tom Patey, the English doctor and well-loved climbing satirist, brought Bonington to our house in Leysin, in August 1965. I don't recall the visit specifically; so many British climbers passed through our chalet that my brain has amalgamated most of them. None of us knew that Chris would go on to become the most famous and most financially successful climber in Britain, and most likely in the rest of the world until Reinhold Messner took over the stage. In 1962 Chris had been the first Briton to climb the north face of the Eiger, and starting in 1970 he would lead multiple expeditions to the Himalaya to make the hardest climbs of their day, including the 9,000-foot southwest face of Mount Everest, an idea he got from Dad. Chris's first Himalayan success was the 12,000-foot wall on the south face of 8,078-meter Annapurna, in which Tom Frost played a key role and Dougal made the summit. Dougal would be held in reserve for summit duty on several of Chris's big climbs, including Everest. In 1986 Chris was awarded a CBE (Commander of the Order of the British Empire), a knighthood in 1996, and numerous honorary degrees, all for the exploratory climbs he made or led, the books he wrote and photographed, the management-consultant work he did based on his Himalayan successes, and the adventure-oriented charitable organizations he headed.

When Patey brought Chris and his wife, Wendy, by our house, however, Chris was trying to get published as a photojournalist and had his eye on the Eiger *direttissima*. He regarded Dad as "a potential competitor for the Direct Route," he recalled. But as they talked, Chris's "suspicions quickly subsided—[John] appeared outgoing, frank, and immensely enthusiastic." They decided to climb the *direttissima* together, along with Rusty Baillie, a Scot to whom Chris was already committed; Dad had had a falling-out with Dougal, who was back in Scotland. Chris and Dad decided to wait until the end of the summer, when the wall freezes over, locking the stones in place. Meanwhile, the Brits set up their tents in the quarry behind our house.

For the Eiger, Chris would have to jumar, because that was the efficient way to follow a steep aid pitch. But most alpinists at that time didn't use Jumars, even the good climbers like Chris. In the rare instances when they climbed something so hard that the leader had to hang from pitons, the second would hang from the same pitons as well, and more often than not those pitons remained fixed for the next party, too. So Dad took Chris to the Dents du Midi across the Rhône Valley from our house to teach him how to jumar.

Chris recounts that they'd had a fondue party in their tent in the quarry, and then they hiked up to the Vag for a long night of drinking. As they "staggered" back downhill at 2 a.m. (Vag closing time), they noticed that the night was clear—a precious occurrence that summer.

"We could do a route tomorrow," said Chris.

Dad didn't miss a beat. "I know a new line on the Dents du Midi—how about trying that?"

They piled their stuff into our Volkswagen bus and reached the trailhead sometime near dawn, and the bottom of the cliff a couple of hours later. The goal, wrote Chris, was to "try out the American Big Wall climbing technique" because it "was the technique we proposed to use on the Eiger." The only trouble was, Dad picked a harsh place and method to teach him. The place was a huge overhang, from which Chris would swing out into space. The method was to tell him nothing.

"I hated the thought of committing myself to that slender strand of rope . . . ," wrote Bonington about having to jumar the rope that Dad had fixed. "Was even more determined not to show I was frightened, especially to the Blond God. . . ." Eventually he made it up the rope and things went better, but he learned that "Climbing with Harlin was a hard school—a constant game of Chicken, with no one prepared to call off first."

While waiting for conditions to improve in the Bernese Oberland, where the Eiger collected snow all this terrible summer, Dad, Chris, and Rusty went off to finish Chris and Rusty's near-success on the Right-Hand Pillar of Brouillard, just left of the Frêney Face on Mont Blanc. To make up two ropes of two, they invited Brian Robertson, a Scotsman. Chris and Dad would take the first rope. "Age and experience sometimes have their compensations," Dad explained. Dad had just turned thirty, and Chris was thirty-one. "This was the first big climb I had been on with John," wrote Chris, "and I liked the steady rhythm of his movement, the confidence of his decisions and his speed of climbing. We were on the same wavelength, climbing with the minimum of verbal communication." The weather turned on them, but they decided to climb into the storm anyway. Three days later they were back in Leysin, having completed their new route, though they hadn't been to the summit.

August dragged into October, but the weather remained so unstable when it wasn't downright bad that the Eiger never came into condition. They decided to delay their attempt until winter.

"In some ways," Bonington wrote, Wendy and he "were relieved to escape from the close confines of Leysin and from the demanding, all-embracing presence of John Harlin. For eight weeks I had been caught up in his dreams and plans, like so many others before me, having arranged to climb the Eiger Direct, help with the International School of Modern Mountaineering and with plans for a mammoth flight down through the Americas.

"As we drove from Leysin, the spell lifted and the ideas seemed distant, far-fetched and improbable. . . . Our return to the Lake District was like an escape from enchantment. Becoming too involved in John's fantastic schemes, I had felt my own individuality and freedom of action curtailed."

Immediately they began a correspondence. Dad reminded Chris how he felt about the Direct. "This will be the culmination of our climbing experience," wrote Dad. "We're never likely to get onto anything harder. I feel that everything I've done in the mountains leads to this, and we'll be calling on all the experience we have gained in our climbing careers."

But Chris's feet were already getting cold. And then he pulled out. He listed his reasons in *The Next Horizon,* including that he had never climbed in the Alps in the winter and didn't know how he would adapt; that Dad's plan for a ten-day ascent relied on an impossibly hard-to-predict weather window and "What would happen if you got three-quarters of the way up the face after seven or eight days, and then the weather broke? Would you have the strength left to fight your way out or retreat—especially in a winter blizzard? I doubted it"; that "although I had complete confidence in John Harlin as a mountaineer, and had struck a rare accord with him on the Right-Hand Pillar of Brouillard, I was less certain about his practical planning ability"; and finally he worried about "becoming a gladiator, at the mercy of the watching public." He concluded that if he went on the climb he might become "trapped in the cleft stick of the professional mountaineer, faced with the pressure to climb for the sake of a position in the climbing firmament, and it was a position which I abhorred. After an agonizing day of indecision . . . I wrote to John telling him how I had let him down. It was now early November and he was not going to have long to find a replacement."

Chris was still willing to help with Eiger planning. Earlier that summer Dad had worked with *Life* magazine on sponsorship of an attempt. *Life* was going to send photographers and publish a cover story if the climb was successful. But the chance never came. Now Chris acted as a liaison with the *Weekend Telegraph,* sometimes interpreting the editor's views and Dad's to each other. Dad wanted the *Telegraph* to pay for the climb in exchange for primary coverage, and the fees were arranged according to whether enough altitude was reached to "draw international publicity, thereby creating a marketable story," according to Dad's correspondence. The *Telegraph* would send a reporter to Kleine Scheidegg, and in an ironic twist, they would hire Chris to take the pictures.

Dad was stuck for a replacement. He broke down and called Dougal at Christmas to patch up their quarrel and suggest the attempt. In a follow-up letter, Dougal wrote, "I'm willing to accept the conditions you state. You obviously have the plan. I offer my climbing ability which I have every confidence in." Dougal would be the ice specialist. He finished his letter by asking for a job at ISMM.

The rock specialist would be Layton Kor, a phenomenal climber who happened to be in Europe at the time. Layton and Dad had met at the American Alpine Club banquet, where Royal had also been. There Layton learned about the Eiger Direct attempts, and Dad learned more about Layton's legendary status as perhaps the most energetic, enthusiastic, and peripatetic climber in America—and one of the most talented as well. A Colorado bricklayer by trade, the loose-limbed, six-foot-four-inch prodigy ranged across North America in search of big new routes, which he would dispatch with a restless hunger before moving on to his next meal of virgin rock. His energy was always positive—people compared him to a puppy—if sometimes overwhelming. Royal later wrote of him (as quoted in the book *Climb! The History of Rock Climbing in Colorado*), "Kor was one of the very few highly competitive climbers who never criticized the efforts and achievements of others. He was interested in action, life, joking conversation, and plans for the next climb. . . . He was the first climber to break the hegemony which Californians had long enjoyed in Yosemite [that] would inevitably take the piss out of the arrogant visitor. . . . He astonished us all by his ability to immediately do the harder routes in the Valley, and in record time as well." He was also a "genius at route finding," in the words of another famous climbing partner, Bob Culp. And he always kept a level head. In classic Kor language, Layton told journalist Peter Gillman, "It's no good when [partners] go white and start shaking and lose a grip of themselves."

Mom later wrote Ullman, "John liked Layton very much and was furious with the treatment those pseudo-intellectuals of Yosemite circles had given him. Layton had a heart, which they were too cruel to recognize in their love of castigating him. It had nearly made a wreck of that man."

And finally the time came to climb. Dougal came down from three days with Bev on Ben Nevis in Scotland to find a note tucked under the windshield wiper of Bev's car. Apparently, Dad had "rung Bev's wife in London; she had rung Dougal's girlfriend in Edinburgh; she had rung Graham Tiso, the owner of an Edinburgh climbing equipment shop and a climbing friend of Dougal's; he had rung Hamish MacInnes, a climber who lived in Glencoe; and he had rung a friend in Fort William who had fixed the message onto the car. It said: 'Please ring at once. John.' " The Eiger's weather forecast was good, and Dougal was to arrive in Leysin immediately.

By his own estimate, Dad had already been to the Eiger a dozen times, and he desperately wanted to get the job done. For this attempt he planned to leave as little as possible to chance. On February 2, 1966, immediately after Dougal arrived, the three-man Anglo-American team rented a helicopter (with *Weekend Telegraph* funds) to fly them from our home in Leysin to the Eiger for a detailed study of the face. They wanted to climb up the very center of the face, the plumb line, the way a drop of water (or in the case of the Eiger, a rock) would fall from the summit. The most valuable piece of information they learned from the flight was that from the Spider up there was a system of ice gullies that would let them climb more directly than they thought possible. They figured Layton would somehow get them up the First Band.

The helicopter flight had also revealed perfect conditions on the face. The climbers returned in the afternoon of February 2 in a panic for last-minute food and gear. Despite Dad's best efforts at preparation—he had meticulously planned the food for maximum calories, chosen drinks to rebalance ions missing in melted snow-water, designed a new style of double boots and gaiters—there is always more to be done for a ten-day gear-intensive winter route involving every style of climbing. Rucksacks would weigh fifty pounds each, in addition to twenty pounds of climbing gear draped on the body, and every ounce had to be carefully considered.

There was real pressure for Dad to finish this project, not just because it had already consumed so much of his time, but because there were rumors of a team in secret training in the Black Forest with German climber Peter Haag as leader. Apparently they had invited Dad to join them at some point. Piussi and Sorgato were still very interested, and so was Desmaison. In November of 1965, the Swiss guide Hilti von Allmen had observed, "People are thinking about it all over Europe." It was very definitely the latest "Last Great Problem" of the Alps, and everyone was waiting, even the nonclimbing public. Earlier that year Dad had actually received a postcard addressed simply, "Eiger John, Switzerland."

ELEVEN

THE JOHN HARLIN ROUTE

O N the 4th of February, Layton, Dougal, and Dad decamped from our chalet to Kleine Scheidegg, establishing themselves in the top floor of the Villa Maria. After a complicated search Bonington was found on the evening of the 5th in a hotel in England. He arrived at Kleine Scheidegg on the afternoon of the 6th, just in time to watch a storm bury the face in a fresh blanket of unconsolidated snow. Day after day went by with snow building ever thicker. The climbers skied gloveless to condition their hands against the cold as their frustration mounted.

Given the conditions and the weight of their packs—which contained all the food for the expected ten-day push to the summit—they decided to use an unconventional aspect of the mountain to give them unconventional aid: Dougal and Chris brought the heavy sacks up the railway tunnel inside the mountain and delivered them through the Gallery Window to the foot of the First Band, where most of the heavy rock-climbing gear and nine-tenths of the food could await a speedy unencumbered ascent of the lowest, easiest part of the face. This approach was not entirely unprecedented, as the first and only winter ascent of the face (1961) had taken place in two stages because of weather: stage one took them to the tunnel window, where they dumped their gear and climbed back down in a storm. Stage two, six days later, took them out the window and to the summit. The tactic had raised hackles among purists, but the controversy was blamed in part on the fact that at first the climbers had tried to conceal their actions.

Dad phoned home occasionally, and replied to a letter from Andréa. He had missed her eighth birthday on February 6, and she was thanking him for the matchstick chalet he had given her (ironically it had been crafted by the former director of LAS while in prison for embezzling school funds). She was now in first grade at our village school, and writing in French was as natural as in English:

> Dear Daddy
>
> Comment est l'eiger? Merci pour la jolie chalet fait en allumettes. A ma fête j'ai reçu une bougie rouge avec quelque chose qui la tien. I saw a puppet show. There were witches and ducks. There was a show called Mexico at night. Please come back home soon. I love you very much Daddy. Gary is here. I love you. Much much love, Andréa

> Dear Andréa,
>
> It was wonderful reading a letter from you and it warmed my heart very much. I love you. Mother tells me that you will be able to go to Topolino too [where I would be racing again]. That's terrific—I'm very happy. Please tell Johnny good luck for me and that I love him very much. Both of you be careful for me.
>
> Tomorrow I will start on the climb but don't worry for we will take no chances. Everything will be all right. Well, I must go to sleep now so goodbye and please give Rongo [our German shepherd] a hug for me.
>
> Love all of you very very much. Dad

In fact it wasn't until the 15th of February that the weather report was decent enough to raise their hopes at beginning the ascent. But that very day Dad tried a fancy ski trick where he'd wrap one leg over his shoulder. He crashed and felt his shoulder pop out of its socket. When Peter Gillman arrived in Kleine Scheidegg to cover the story, he found that the demoralized team had gone back to Leysin. Dad's doctor ordered bed rest for five days and no climbing for three weeks. Dad would have none of that. When Mom grumbled about whether he really wanted it to heal, Dad told her it was *his* shoulder and she could mind her own business.

On the 18th the *Weekend Telegraph* recalled Peter to London until the weather improved. Chris stayed, and hours later he was startled to see a team of eight Germans start up the Eiger to climb the *direttissima*. That a team of Germans was attempting the wall wasn't a complete surprise; they had, after all, invited Dad to join them. But the size of the team was shocking, something never before seen in Alpine climbing.

In fact, the only thing Alpine about their climb was the fact that it was taking place in the Alps. Their methods were entirely Himalayan, where the standard style was still to "siege" the mountain by fixing ropes and using them to haul supplies to camps and to alternate lead climbers. When one lead team wears down from hard work and cold, another moves up to take its place, which keeps fresh climbers in point position while other climbers rest or bring supplies all the way from the bottom. Dad and the Italians had tried the Direct with five people just two years earlier, but the difference was that everyone was always working, either hauling or climbing, and they moved up the face together; there weren't enough people for anyone to take real rest days. On the Eiger the Germans intended to succeed no matter how long it took. This also meant that they didn't need to wait for a forecast of extended good weather in order to climb—they could take advantage of momentary breaks in the weather, moving hour by hour, day by day, without concern for the weight of their packs or whether they'd be trapped on the mountain. These were highly controversial tactics, but they were designed to accomplish the mission: this winter the *direttissima would* be climbed.

The next day, the 19th of February, the Anglo-American team rushed back to Kleine Scheidegg to find the Germans 1,500 feet up the lower, easier section of the face and ferrying their sacks up. On February 20, despite the unsettled weather, Dougal and Layton made a 3 a.m. start up the mountain to try to gain new ground above where the Germans were. At first they took advantage of the Germans' fixed ropes, but then they climbed the ice instead, finding it surprisingly challenging and even vertical in places. At the First Band, they encountered climbing every bit as difficult as had been expected. More difficult, in fact, because the Germans had established themselves on the logical line (off to the right), and Layton had to make do with a relatively blank wall instead, though at least it was the shortest distance to the steep ice runnels above the First Band. It took him four hours of artificial climbing to gain 90 feet, where he placed a bolt—one of only two or three bolts he would place on the entire climb—from which he and Dougal rappeled to a bivouac at the bottom of the cliff. (The Germans used many more bolts on their line, highlighting Layton's genius at artificial climbing.)

That night a storm blew in, with winds measured at 75 miles per hour in Kleine Scheidegg, and 110 miles per hour at the Jungfraujoch above. Dad said it was the worst storm he'd ever seen, and it knocked out power and water at Kleine Scheidegg, and train service down to Grindelwald. Avalanches poured over Dougal and Layton as they shared a bivouac sack much too short for Layton's six-foot-four-inch frame. The sack kept filling with snow, and as soon as one person began to doze, he would slide off the little seat they'd carved, dragging the other down with him. They left at first light. Dad wrote Mom, "We had anxiously hired a special train next day to go up to the window to let them in but found the bivy spot abandoned and a rappel rope going down."

During the next two days storm raged outside, and diplomacy brewed inside. The rival teams hashed out their plans and talked about joining forces. But the intended styles of ascent were fundamentally incompatible. The Anglos wanted a fast Alpine-style ascent. They still figured on ten days just as soon as they could actually climb. The Germans intended to get their whole team up. They figured on eighteen days—or whatever it took. The complete team consisted of Peter Haag and Jörg Lehne, leaders, with fellow climbers Günther Strobel, Roland Votteler, Sigi Hupfauer, Karl Golikow, Günther Schnaidt, and Rolf Rosenzopf. Even though press sponsorship of a climb in the Alps was a novelty at the time, a publishing firm had also underwritten the Germans, and they had Harri Frey as their full-time press coordinator.

While Dad was negotiating and worrying about the weather, he received a letter from Mom. She wrote, "Johnny did a good [ski] jump yesterday—13 meters. Says one loses points on style if legs bend to gain greater distance. One instructor banged his head on this jump. Kids say it was bloody and awful. Johnny fell in this morning's giant slalom but thinks his time still alright. This afternoon is special slalom. Then—when all is over, he wants to play with Rongo in the snow."

She also mentioned Gary, who was staying with us:

Gary is reading *Either/Or* and is <u>now</u> violently upset because it turns out that a portion of the book had been lifted and published out of context in France. As a result people have misinterpreted Kierkegaard. Many expressive statements have gurgled forth this morning. "Kierkegaard would turn over in his grave." He has certainly been doing a lot of thinking on philosophy and has shown some original synthesis.

Surely hoping for the best with shoulder . . .
Much, much, much love . . . Mara

And Dad wrote her back,

Dear Mara,

It really warmed my heart to hear from you during a particularly difficult time for me. The journalistic end of it is really messy. I wish now that I had launched the project on my own despite the risk financially. Oh well, we will weather this storm along with others.

My shoulder still pops, grinds and hurts so I don't know what to think. Improvement though is considerable.

I loved your line 'and when it's all over, he wants to play with Rongo in the snow.' That's how I too feel about this only I'd substitute you for Rongo.

Love you immeasurably, John

As the weather improved, both teams started out, but the avalanche danger was too great to make progress. Still, given the developments, Peter flew back from England and Don Whillans showed up to belay Chris as he got into position to take photos. As expected, Dad's shoulder was healing faster than the doctor predicted.

At 2 a.m. on the 28th, Dougal, Layton, and Chris started up. Don and Dad were to follow with loads a few hours later. At the First Band, the original three-man team would carry on to the summit in a nine-day push, while Chris and Don fell back to take pictures, later coming up the west flank to shoot the climbers as they approached the summit.

It was a glorious plan. Reality struck while Layton was engaged with the next aid pitch on the First Band. The sky started spitting snow, and soon avalanches swept over Layton while he was pounding delicate pitons. He'd had enough. Layton jumped onto the fixed lines and zipped all the way down to Kleine Scheidegg, leaving Dougal and Chris to dig a snow cave at the base of the First Band. (The Germans had already dug themselves an "Ice Palace" at the foot of the First Band, a snow-cave advance base camp capable of holding all eight climbers and gear in comfort.) Don and Dad had only made it to the start of the fixed ropes when they decided the avalanches made climbing impossible—they'd already seen three huge powder snowslides engulf Layton and Dougal on the First Band.

By now Dad's team was forced to admit that the weather

wasn't working for them. Since they couldn't change the weather, and weren't willing to give up the first ascent of the *direttissima,* the only thing left was to fix ropes until the weather looked like it might finally give them a break for a dash to the summit.

While they were changing plans, Mom drove over to Scheidegg with our friends Sam and Sara Jane Elliot, who also taught at LAS. Mom was wildly excited to see Dad again. They had celebrated their tenth wedding anniversary the previous October by eating out at a nice restaurant. Neither of them were anniversary celebrators, but Dad had told her that they would celebrate their tenth—if they survived it. Now he told her that he wanted to grow old with her. He felt that they had gone through enough in their ten years of marriage and one of courting to have worked out the basis for a lifetime companionship. Mom wrote, "Never before had he considered the future with me in it to the end." As Mom remembered it, his last words on leaving Leysin had been, "I love you so much. Don't let Gary bother you." The Elliots kidded her about dressing up for her husband and being sure that her hair was combed just before he'd enter. "You'd think it was your first date with him," they teased.

In the next few days the Anglo-American team carved out their own much smaller snow cave, Layton finished the First Band, and Dad and Dougal led up mixed ice and rock above, heading toward the Second Band. The Germans were paralleling on the right, and then moved left to join the Anglo line. The forecast looked to be improving, and the team again consolidated for a summit push. Another snowstorm dashed their hopes. Not until March 9 did they reach the Death Bivouac at the top of the Second Icefield after multiple up-and-down trips hauling gear between snow holes and sometimes recuperating in Kleine Scheidegg. Earlier in the same day the Germans had found a good place to dig a snow cave and had stopped 300 feet from the top of the Flatiron, but Dad's crew was determined to reach Death Bivouac itself, where they figured there would be another good cave opportunity.

It was "a howling blizzard," Layton recalled, when Dougal,

Layton, Chris, and Dad all reached the intended bivouac site with heavy loads. Only one headlamp worked properly, and holding wires to batteries with bare hands kept another one alight. Though a bulge in the snow promised the possibility of a cave, it would be a hard-earned bivouac. Over the next four hours they alternated chopping at the snow and ice until it finally opened into a room big enough for all four to stuff themselves into. Finally they could brew up hot drinks and dinner—except the stove was in one of two packs fixed to a belay station 300 feet away at the end of a dangerous traverse (dangerous because the fixed rope initially was poorly positioned to protect a climber). Dougal went to fetch the pack with the stove, and then Dad followed to get the other. Back in the cave an hour or two later, Dougal thought the stove had run out of gas. He examined it by the light of a candle, and then started unscrewing the canister from the stove. Fuel sprayed forth, bursting into flame as it hit the candle; the cave seemed to fill with fire. Dougal threw the fire-jetting canister at the door, but missed. Chris dived for the door to escape and caught himself right at the edge, staring at almost 4,000 feet of space below. Dad grabbed the flaming canister and threw it into the storm.

They screwed in another canister and supplemented their brewing with a legless paraffin stove, which Dougal had to pinch between his knees while holding the pot of slowly melting snow in his hands. Gradually they rehydrated with their first liquids in twenty hours of climbing, and in the small hours of the morning sleep finally came to the dog pile of weary climbers.

They awoke late and discovered daylight filtering through the snow cave's thin walls. Despite the cramped interior, it was obvious they couldn't expand outward. Dad stabbed an ice axe into the floor's outer rim. When he pulled it out, they could see Grindelwald through the hole, nearly 8,000 feet below. They had carved their cave into a cornice, and the floor actually overhung the Third Icefield. Karl Mehringer's body had emerged from the snow right here only four years prior.

Because that day offered a break in the weather, Chris decided to take advantage of it to bring his film down for processing and to let the actual climbing team carry on without him. He bid the team good-bye and good luck, believing that the final summit dash was just around the corner. Chris would meet the victorious team soon enough; for now, he clipped into the fixed lines for some 3,500 feet of rappeling. Meanwhile the Germans had started up a chimney system that Dougal thought would dead-end, and Layton and Dougal scouted leftward to pick their own line. After the previous night's tribulations, this would be a day of rest and organization for tomorrow's big final push; Dad sorted gear and food for the next week of climbing. It was now March 11, the helicopter flight had been February 2, and they had been actively climbing since February 20 or 28, depending on how you look at it—two to three weeks on the wall already, another couple of weeks in the hotel below. With any luck at all, the summit would be just a few days away.

Chris also brought down a hastily scrawled letter from Dad, with "Death Bivouac, March?" in the upper right corner:

> Dear Mom & Kids,
>
> I'm certainly hoping that Trento [Topolino] was enjoyable—also that the exams were not too miserable [I had just taken intensive exams to enter the Swiss secondary school system].
>
> We are hoping to make the top in a few days but we are being very safe so don't worry.
>
> Love you all very, very much. Dad

The storm pounced that night, blowing spindrift through every crack and seam in their flimsy cave. Moving up was out of the question. The summit push was off again. To conserve food, fuel, and snow-cave space, Layton dropped back to Kleine Scheidegg despite the weather, attaching a tent sack across the outside of the door to seal out the blowing snow. Dad and Dougal decided to wait it out on the mountain, expecting Layton to return in a couple of days. They had food and fuel for five days, and Layton would bring more back up when conditions allowed. Two people needed to stay on the mountain since the Germans also had climbers pushing higher, and likely whoever first reached the Spider would stay in the lead to the top. At the earliest sign of a break in the weather, both teams would be moving upward.

Meanwhile, down in Kleine Scheidegg, another kind of storm was raging: the need for hard copy by the media. Much earlier in the climb, Don Whillans had been interviewed at the foot of the face for British television. He'd been asked if the climb were a race, and he replied characteristically with a one-liner: "If it's a race, it's the slowest race in the world." It was left for Chris to explain how each team had planned their climb independently, that naturally each team would like the satisfaction of the first ascent, but that "there's a definite feeling of friendship and cooperation between the two parties." Peter wrote in the *Daily Telegraph,* quite tongue in cheek, "British American team takes 15-foot lead in Eiger climb." With less irony, a German newspaper reported on how badly equipped the Anglo team was: they'd even had to borrow a shovel to dig their first snow cave. Various newspapers took the angle of asking whether the climbers were doing it for the money. Chris explained that the climbers weren't paid, but that a protracted climb like this cost a lot of money, hence the underwriting.

With the climbers high on the face, and the long-promised final push seeming imminent, more and more journalists showed up in Kleine Scheidegg. As the storm dragged on, some of them began speculating about the climbers being trapped on the mountain, and that a rescue effort would soon be mounted.

Up in their snow hole, Dougal and Dad fought the spindrift, which would blast around the fixed door several times during the night, forcing them to get up to clean it off themselves. As Layton remembered it to me, "Your dad was very organized as far as how you get in the cave: you take your boots off, brush them off, take your parka off, and brush it off. Everything had a spot it had to go, because otherwise you're getting stuff everywhere and you're getting wet sleeping bags in a place like that, and that's not so good. He had all these things thought out very carefully since he'd done a lot of winter climbing." In order to keep their down and wool clothing from getting wet, Dad kept waking Dougal up during the night for brush-down sessions. They would hear the hissing of snow running down the Third Icefield, and occasionally loud cracks as their cornice shifted. Each time the cornice cracked a huge plume of spindrift would fly into the cave and they'd worry that the entire snow-mass would fall down the mountain. Dougal had strange dreams, imagining a third man in the cave who was squeezing him against the rock wall. By radio Peter asked, "What are the survival problems involved up there?" To which Dad answered, "Staying alive."

On the fourth day (March 13) the cave dwellers were running low on food. Much worse, Dad announced that he had a high fever and a racing pulse—an illness that would soon turn into bronchitis. On the 14th five doctors who were skiing in Kleine Scheidegg showed up for the radio call. Dad was temporarily feeling better, and they announced that he could remain in the cave for now. News of Dad's illness was kept under wraps so the other media and the German team wouldn't know.

London's *Daily Sketch* ran a piece that read:

It began as a light-hearted race, almost in the mood of a boyish escapade. But there was no laughter on the Eiger today and no dancing in the valley below, where the wives and sweethearts of the climbers wait. For sheltered in a tiny snow-hole, 11,200 feet up the wall, Dougal Haston (24) from Edinburgh, and John Harlin, a 30-year-old American, have sent a walkie-talkie message to their three comrades: "It is terribly grim up here. Can't you help us?" They have been marooned on the mountain since digging in last Thursday. . . .

The happy hours seem so far away, when Marilyn Harlin, pig-tailed Wendy Bonington, and Audrey Whillans would take turns at the big telescope on their hotel roof and tell each other what grand chaps their husbands were.

Today the adventure has gone sour. . . .

As a result of stories like this, a mountain rescue team from Munich prepared to offer assistance, and my mother called from Leysin to find out what was going on. Wendy was still back in England, where she'd always been, and Audrey in Leysin.

Another newspaperman recounted, "The attitude of the Swiss establishment has not helped the climbers. They have complained that the climbers were not dressing for dinner during their rest periods in the hotel. Whenever Harlin walked into a local restaurant the band played an adaptation of a German pop song they called 'Don't Fall off the Eiger, Johnny.' "

The antics of this overpublicized climb didn't escape the community of real climbers, either, most of whom didn't approve of either the sieging of the route by Himalayan tactics, nor the constant media attention it was getting.

My mother wrote to her parents:

I am taking the children to Kleine Scheidegg this weekend to watch John on his last siege of the climb. It has gone on much longer than he expected: pitches were more difficult, weather has been bad, he dislocated his shoulder in training. I spent last Sunday at the telescope. I *really* hope this goes thru, for it would be a culmination of his climbing career. Weather looks good but hints of cirrus clouds antagonize and agonize.

The Elliots drove us, and when we arrived Dad was in Death Bivouac. We all spoke with him on the wall. For us kids, or at least for me, it didn't feel that strange. Dad was up there behind the clouds, and I'd talked with him through the walkie-talkie on climbs before. He said he was fine, and I took him at his word. What I mostly remember from the trip was doing somersaults off the second-story balcony into the deepest powder I'd ever seen. Eventually I talked Andréa off the balcony, too. She sunk in to her neck. For Mom it was different. "When I talked with Dad that time my throat was tight and my eyes were moist," she told me much later. "It was terrible to poke the antenna from a warm room into a terrible storm, to know that he was freezing, hungry, sick, but that he talked optimistically of little things, such as hoping I enjoyed the skiing, that he was comfortable, how were his parents, etc. It was as if I was talking with a trapped miner when there did not seem to be much chance. That was one of my worst experiences. Hearing his voice made it so much worse."

On the 15th of March the weather reports were still bad. The long-expected high-pressure system had stalled over Wales, blocked by another air mass from Scandinavia. Weather patterns had broken from their usual scripts; forecasts were proving completely unreliable, and yet that's all the climbers had to go on. Chris, Don, Layton, Jörg Lehne, and Karl Golikow beat a ski-trail to the base of the face to deliver supplies, finding conditions desperately difficult and dangerous. Whenever the face briefly revealed itself, it was plastered with a new layer of white. The Anglos returned in the daylight after depositing their loads, but the Germans carried on up the fixed ropes a ways to deposit theirs higher. They returned late that night, and shortly afterward the hotel owner, Fritz von Almen, told Peter how lucky the men had been. An avalanche had killed the local guide Hilti von Allmen the day before. Hilti had been a close friend of my father's.

On the 16th Dad revealed that his illness had turned into mild bronchitis. They were also out of food. It was time to come down. With the shovel they pushed six days' worth of excrement out the door—for it had been too stormy to open the covering Layton had affixed—and clipped themselves to the rope. They moved clumsily for some distance, their bodies unused to motion, and their heads felt light from lack of food, but they managed to get down safely after repositioning ropes that had been blown around horns of rock. By the time Dougal and Dad reached Chris and Peter at the Alpiglen train station they were bathed in sunshine and the wall above stood crisp in every detail, though trapped in shade. Peter recalls that Dad had a long black streak on his face. " 'The stove blew up,' he said, and laughed again and then coughed badly, spitting into the snow. 'It's great to be back. It was really cold up there this morning.' "

The sun stayed brilliant the rest of that day and the next while Dad went to the hospital in Interlaken and Hilti von Allmen's funeral. On the 18th Chris and Layton went back up the face with three Germans. Chris figured that he would remain up there for at most three or four days until Dougal and Dad returned, depending on what Dad learned about his lungs. Chris remembers being frightened by the idea of ascending those fixed ropes. They were a mere seven millimeters in thickness (about ¼ inch), not at all intended for the kind of vertical abuse on rock that they were being subjected to. He noted some signs of wear as well, but he put these observations to the back of his mind. It took them a mere eight hours on the fixed ropes to reach Death Bivouac, which had taken almost three weeks to reach by climbing, and had been occupied during another week of storm.

After the funeral Peter asked Dad if he had lost many climbing partners. "I've already lost three in the last year," he replied, "including the one who would have been with me on this climb now—Erich Friedli." (The others were Lionel Terray—author of *Conquistadors of the Useless*—and Marc Martinetti; Dad went to all four funerals.) The next morning the Swiss tabloid newspaper *Blick* reported that Dad had been admitted to the hospital with pneumonia and wouldn't be able to finish the climb. In fact it was bronchitis and he left the hospital with medication, fully intent on climbing immediately.

That day Mom wrote a letter to Dad, in which she warned:

Don't play with the gods up there. It appears they are jealous
of you and thus manifest their wrath in peculiar ways. To
convince you, mortal man, that you ought not to defy them,
they have inflicted the worst winter, journalists, competitors
(for security I am happy they are there), Layton's toes, Don's
vertigo, Dougal's odor, your shoulder, your lung problems,
and then *Hilti!* Now the "blond god" returns. Perhaps by
now the others submit, and when they do, you will finish in
fine spirits, fine weather, and rapidly return to the hearth of
Pollux. Yet the battle may not be over. We all give our support thru this last stretch.

  Much more love, Mara

And Andréa wrote:

Dear Daddy
  I hope you come back home pretty soon. I love you very
much. Love Andréa and Kuzma

While I added:

I passed the examens for the collège secondaire. I wish you
good luck! Try to make it to the top! Love Rongo & John

Meanwhile in Death Bivouac, Chris and Layton looked out
the door on the 18th and saw a gray sheet of clouds. They thought
they could squeeze in a day of climbing before the storm hit, but it
blasted in by the time they reached the high point of the fixed
ropes not far above the cave. They rappeled back down to the snow
cave, which Chris declared "bloody fabulous—really comfortable"
in a radio call, and they settled in for another siege. The main problem was a shortage of fuel. Dad had given some to the Germans,

but after Chris went over to ask about it he told Dad by radio, "Trouble is, they don't seem very keen to give any of ours back."

Dad called Mom that night from Kleine Scheidegg, giving her butterflies of excitement. He told her how eager he was to have it all over so that he could get back to us. Mom suggested giving up the climb, but Dad felt the family could not afford another winter on it. Besides, he was sure things would go smoothly from here on up. He said he was looking forward to taking care of the kids when she led the school field trip to Greece in April.

Dad's knowledge of meteorology from air force training told him that the winter weather from Scandinavia was finally breaking through and would likely deliver a more normal winter pattern, with an extended good spell coming shortly. The next day the forecast remained bad for the short term, but the sun was out (never reaching the face, of course) and Chris and Layton headed up to prepare new ground. The predictions for a long stretch of good weather were still two days out; the climbers would simply take the ropes a little higher and return to Death Bivouac to sleep and wait. As it turned out, on this day they solved a key section of the entire route.

Layton led a delicate three-hour aid traverse across the base of the Central Pillar, and then Chris took over to lead an equally delicate pitch of nearly unprotected thin ice that kept threatening to break out from under his feet. He was eighty feet above a bad piton by the time he reached firm snow, risking a fall of 160 feet assuming the piton held, and much worse if it didn't. While Layton was seconding the pitch, Chris beamed with satisfaction. "I gaze[d] down, across the face, with a rich feeling of contentment," he reflected in *The Next Horizon*. "It had been the hardest, and certainly the most spectacular ice pitch I had ever climbed. The complete lack of protection made it, in effect, a solo ascent, for had I fallen, I don't think Layton could have held me." It would be the only pitch on the entire route that Chris led (he was, after all, only supposed to take pictures), but in combination with Layton's traverse it proved the key to unlocking the upper face. Hearing about the progress via the walkie-talkie, Dad thought that they had reached the turning point of the climb. The Germans came over and reported having failed on their line to the right; they asked Chris and Layton to drop them a rope from the top of the Central Pillar.

The next day, the 20th of March, Jörg Lehne came over to Layton and Chris in their snow hole and suggested joining teams. He didn't think it sensible to continue the competition, nor to climb on separate routes a few meters apart, nor even for them to simply follow the Anglos up this section of the climb. Jörg suggested that Layton and Karl Golikow climb together that day, allowing Chris to take pictures. Chris agreed, thinking, "If we could all end up climbing together, it would be the perfect climax to the successful conclusion of the route." Layton and Karl started up together immediately, but longer-term cooperation depended on Dad's ratification of the plan.

At the 11:45 a.m. radio call, Chris presented the situation, and Dad replied, "Well, it's a lot to swallow at the moment, Chris. I'll have to think about it. Offhand it sounds good except I think it should have come a hair later, after we had already reached the top of the Pillar. How did this decision come about?" Chris explained. Dad was sympathetic, and indeed had dreamed of an international ascent of this route from the very beginning. But he was worried that the large size of the German party would seem to swallow the smaller Anglo group, never mind his continued determination to blast for the top, Alpine style, whereas the Germans still intended to bring everyone up by fixing ropes to the summit. He told Chris, "I don't want it to come out in the press that we were taken up the mountain." And later he told Layton, "I don't want us to be committed to climb with the complete German team. This is just too big and it isn't in our scheme of things. Now if they want to join up with us, say just Lehne and Charlie [Karl], to go with us to the summit, then that's fine."

Meanwhile Layton and Karl, undoubtedly the two most

cheerful climbers in the whole group, climbed together to the top of the Central Pillar. The Anglos loved Karl's perpetual smile, and his constant refrain of "It's a hard life," given at every opportunity, and always accompanied by an ear-to-ear grin. Karl had a happy-go-lucky nature, and by this ascent had already racked up over 250 meters of falls during his career. In Germany his nickname was "Catastrophe Karl" for all his wrecks. His lead to the top of the Pillar played havoc on Layton's nerves, as during a short slip with no protection beneath him, Layton thought "he was going to kill both of us."

Dad told a reporter that day, "This is not and never has been a race. We are sharing ropes, routes, and, when times are hard, even rations. For example, the Germans radioed today that they needed another 600 feet of perlon for the fixed ropes, and I shall take that up to them tomorrow. You can't have lads like Karl Golikow dancing about on crampons totally unroped, and that's what he is doing. What they lack in equipment they make up in nerve." (Karl would die in 1972 in a climbing accident on the Piz Badille.)

That evening, the 20th, Dad radioed up to the face from Kleine Scheidegg, "The weather report is a go, is a go. I want to organize things to the point of a complete departure for the summit. . . . Our plan is to either bivouac at the Death Bivouac tomorrow night and then leave very early, or else take our bivouac gear up to the top of the Pillar and make a platform there." Layton didn't think there was enough snow on top of the Pillar to make a ledge, and suggested a departure from Death Bivouac. Nor did he think the Germans would split their team to include two of their climbers with the Anglos. No matter. Layton, Dougal, and Dad were blasting for the summit, with or without Germans in the team. Dad told Layton to continue climbing with Karl the next day, expecting to reach the Spider, but to have his personal gear packed and ready for him and Dougal to bring up from Death Bivouac. At 1 a.m. Dougal and Dad in their full winter-Eiger regalia walked past the late-night drinkers in the bar on their way out into the star-filled night, headed at last to the endlessly awaited summit push.

Dad had heavy coughing sessions the whole way up the fixed lines, which slowed him, but shortly after noon they arrived at Death Bivouac with their loads. The weather report was for three good days and they couldn't be wasted, bronchitis be damned. The day was spectacular, so still that Layton and Dougal had conversed from a thousand feet apart, with Layton swinging from slings beneath an overhang while Dougal was down in the Second Icefield. From Death Bivouac they could see the progress that Jörg, Karl, and Layton had made, all the way into the lower leg of the Spider. Things were finally looking good, very, very good. With weather like this, nothing would stop them.

When the 3:45 p.m. scheduled radio call came in, Dad was busy organizing gear. Peter called in, "Scheidegg to Eiger, Scheidegg to Eiger, how do you read, how do you read. Over." Dad replied, "Roger, Pete," and continued with the news about Layton and Jörg before saying, "We're getting ready for the final push. We've sorted out our three days of food and we're planning on prusiking up the ropes in the morning and blasting for the summit. I hope you've got a good weather forecast for us. Over."

Peter delayed a while before responding. He didn't want to deliver the news, but finally he had to: "Regret to state that preliminary weather reports from Zurich and Geneva say that there is a cold front approaching. This should arrive sometime tomorrow night. Regret, a cold front arriving sometime tomorrow night. We are checking this. But it does not look good. Over."

Off the radio, Dougal and Dad swore violently. "Christ, when are we going to get a break?" said Dougal, while Peter told his mates, "God, we're fed up." Back on the radio, Dad replied in a deadpan voice, "We'll just have to sit it out until we get a good forecast."

Early on the next day, the 22nd of March, Dad called down for fresh weather forecasts. Chris replied, "There now seem to be two cold fronts," and explained how a smaller one would deliver some snow that night and a larger one would deliver more snow the next night. Layton offered to descend to Kleine Scheidegg and bring up additional food when the weather improved. Reluctantly, everyone agreed that would be for the best, and Layton beelined to the hotel.

Later that morning, Mick Burke, who had come to replace Don Whillans as Bonington's belayer, looked through the telescope and saw a German entering the Fly, the next icefield after the Spider. Everyone had thought it would be very difficult to get from the Spider to the Fly, and this surprising progress electrified Dougal and Dad. I have heard these taped radio conversations so many times that I've almost memorized them. The emotions on the crackling end of the conversation are hard to interpret. Dad's voice is measured, controlled, almost fatalistic. The emotions on the Scheidegg end, where the recordings were made, become exuberant. Peter spoke: "We have four weather forecasts for you. The cold front is just as strong, but it has slowed. The forecasts mostly agree that it will not now arrive until tomorrow night."

Chris asked, "John, what exactly are your plans now?" After a few exchanges, Dad concluded, "I'm thinking we might modify our plans and go just as high as we possibly can with the idea that we might be able to climb all the way out to the summit tomorrow." After a bit more discussion, he concluded, "Apologize to Layton that we've pushed off like this, but I think he'll understand." They had in fact discussed such a situation, and Layton had agreed to summit with the second team of Germans if it came to that. Guido Tonella, a Swiss journalist friend of Dad's, spoke into the radio, "I'll come tomorrow with a bottle of champagne." Peter fixed the next radio call for 3:45 p.m., but Dad told him, "We're going to be working awfully hard and I don't know if we're going to be able to make that broadcast." To Peter's question about Dad's health, he replied, "Real great. Okay, Pete, I gotta get going. Anything else? If not, Eiger out." On the tape one can hear a jumble of voices wishing them good luck, and Peter saying, "Just go, go, go, and we'll see you on the summit."

Dougal and Dad exchanged huge grins. They were going for it. Dougal later wrote, "I felt I was on the way to the completion of my greatest dream." Dad paused for the final Death Bivouac cleanup while Dougal started up the ropes. Sigi Hupfauer jumared just ahead of Dougal, carrying his own heavy pack full of supplies. Each time he reached the top of a fixed rope, he yelled down to Dougal to start up. These were terrifying trips up the ropes, spinning in space under overhangs, with a 4,000-foot drop to the foot of the wall, and another 4,000 vertical feet of steep valley-side to the village of Grindelwald. The ropes they were jumaring may have been a mere seven millimeters in thickness, but at least these ropes had only been here a few days. Dougal was fighting his way up the overhanging prusik on the side of the Central Pillar when he saw Dad come around on the Third Icefield, about to start up the steeper ropes. On the final overhanging prusik to the Spider, Dougal noticed the rope "going over a particularly bad spot," as Chris remembers Dougal telling him. My mother recalls Dougal telling her that he noticed a fray there, but he thought the rope would hold.

A few minutes later Dad clipped his Jumars to the free-hanging rope leading to the Spider and started up. For all the time he'd spent on the Eiger, this would be his first time on the Spider since the summer of 1962, and what a difference four years makes. Last time he had been in the twenty-eighth team to climb the classic, and still the only, route on this wall. Now he was poised to be in the first team to complete the greatest route of his generation, the most sought-after climb in the Alps, the route he had been trying to climb for three years now, the one that meant more to him than all the rest put together. This rope was taking him to the Spider, and after that a single day of fast climbing would transform his all-consuming dream into the greatest satisfaction he'd ever known. He slid his Jumars up the rope, left, right, left, right, left, right, gaining about a vertical foot with each step, and fighting to keep from spinning, when suddenly the rope above went slack and he felt himself hurtling downward, the Third Icefield rushing toward him at breakneck speed.

AT 3:15, Peter put his eye to the telescope and was following the ropes from the Death Bivouac upward when a red figure fell through his field of vision. It was "stretched out and turning over slowly, gently, and with awful finality."

Peter yelled up to Chris's window, three stories above.

"Chris! Chris Bonington! Chris, come down here!"

When Chris arrived, Peter brought him to the telescope, and as Chris bent over to view, Peter spoke quietly into his ear, "I think someone's fallen, Chris. I'm pretty sure it was someone. I don't know who it was."

Chris asked if it could have been a rucksack. Peter said he didn't think so.

Fritz von Almen was at the telescope now and trained it to the bottom of the face. Soon he spotted what he was looking for, a dark mass on the snow about 500 feet below the start of the fixed ropes. Chris took over the telescope and among the scattered debris he saw a blue rucksack, the color of Dad's. Chris was pretty sure the red mass was a body, and thought it was Dad. He went to get Layton so they could ski over to it immediately. Layton looked through the telescope and thought it was just a bivouac sack. They trained the telescope on the Spider and it seemed clear that everyone there was acting normally, like nothing had happened. But a few minutes before, Guido Tonella of the *Tribune de Genève* had seen a figure on the ropes below the Spider. Now that figure was gone.

Still the radio call was scheduled for 3:45. Dad, who was carrying the radio, had said they would be working awfully hard and might not be able to make it. At 3:45 Peter pushed the transmit button:

"Scheidegg to Eiger, Scheidegg to Eiger, how do you read, how do you read. Over."

There was only a static crackling of radio silence.

Five minutes later Chris and Layton were skiing in silence to-ward the face, dreading what they expected to find. At 4:30 they reached some scattered gear.

"It's only a sack!" Chris shouted in a wave of relief. And then they saw something else above them.

It was Dad. Or what used to be Dad. Chris described his body as "grotesque, distorted by the appalling impact of his 4,000-foot fall, but still horribly recognizable."

"There was a strange, terrible beauty in the juxtaposition of the bent limbs of this man, who had devoted everything to climb-ing, and finally to this project and to the face towering above," Chris wrote in *The Next Horizon*. He thought it would make a "per-fect photograph—a picture that said everything that could possi-bly be said about the North Wall of the Eiger." But the next instant he was "horrified with myself that I could even think in this way; I knew that I could never take such a picture." Instead he forced himself to put his hand on Dad's heart, just to formally con-firm the obvious. And then he came on the radio, sobbing.

"It's John. He's dead."

Chris asked for a team of Swiss guides to bring the body down. Von Almen insisted that Chris and Layton do it, but they were too emotionally devastated; they simply couldn't bring themselves to do it, despite Von Almen's directive. "We can't, Pete, we can't," Chris radioed back, in a voice he couldn't control.

Wendy Bonington had already been sent by car to Leysin to deliver the news, in case it proved to be Dad. She would call en route to get the facts. But at five o'clock Don Whillans called from Leysin, where he was working at the American School. On learn-ing the news he offered for his wife, Audrey, and him to go over to tell my mother. They arrived ten minutes before the news hit the radio.

I was playing on a bed with my sister and friends in the chalet next door. One look at Mom, coming through the door, told us something was terribly wrong. I don't remember what she said exactly, just that in the next moment people were crying and I was stupefied. Mom remembered my first words as, "I thought he'd make it this time." I just remember confusion. How could Dad have fallen off the mountain? It didn't make sense. Falling and hitting a ledge I could understand, but all the way off the mountain? I needed information, to learn that he hadn't made a mistake; I couldn't imagine him not tying in, or not clipping himself to a fixed rope. Dad didn't make dumb mistakes like that. So how could he have fallen off the mountain? Somehow the information about a broken rope must not have reached me. On the back of a photograph I found recently, someone—I have no idea who—had written, "Son Johnnie very good skier. Commented on hearing of father's death: 'It wasn't his fault.'"

Andréa's first words, again as Mom remembered them months later, were "Why did he go up that damn mountain?" Decades later she told Maria Coffey, in *Where the Mountain Casts Its Shadow,* "I was furious because he was supposed to come home and be my daddy. I was so mad, I wasn't even sad. I had to fake crying. I kept that anger for so long."

While Andréa was struggling with her anger, and Mom was struggling with her grief, I struggled with my need to know, to understand causation. I'm sure this helped to transfer my emotions to the rational, rather than dwelling only on the intangible: the fact that Dad was now gone forever. But then my thoughts started turning from what went wrong to what remains. I understood permanence, the complete finality of death. And what remained was that Dad was gone. I wasn't thinking about the impact on me, because I didn't know what, if anything, in my life would change, other than that Dad was not coming home. But I did know that for him it was over, and for that I was terribly sad. I could also feel Mom's overwhelming grief, and I always felt wired to her emotions. I turned to the wall and gently cried.

Two weeks earlier, after delivering me from the Trofeo Topolino ski race, Dad's father had flown to Africa and his mother to California. Mom tracked them down and they arrived in Leysin the next day. Mom had Dad's body transported to Leysin, where he would be buried, and she set the funeral for March 25. She refused to see his body. She did not want to remember him mutilated. But she was told that he was wearing the sweater that she had hand-knitted for him as a Christmas present, and this meant something to her.

On the mountain Dougal waited an hour for Dad to arrive in the Spider, growing increasingly apprehensive. When Dad never appeared, Dougal jumared another pitch toward the Fly, while Roland rappeled down to fetch supplies. A few minutes later Roland raced back up the rope. At first Dougal was elated, thinking it was Dad, but then felt "shattering depression" when he identified Roland. Roland yelled up that the rope had cut over the edge. Shortly after, Sigi appeared from above after speaking to Kleine Scheidegg by radio.

"John's dead," he yelled down to Dougal.

Dougal sat down, stunned. "We didn't speak," he wrote. "There was nothing more to say. A broken rope, and gone was one of my greatest friends and one of Europe's best mountaineers."

When they did speak again, the automatic action was to call off the climb. But as the immediate shock settled and reason returned during the night, they realized that they were poised to fulfill Dad's greatest wish and that the ultimate tribute to him would be to finish the route as his memorial. They would call it the John Harlin Route. There would be considerable public criticism of this action, but everyone who knew Dad realized this was right. There can be no doubt that Dad would have wanted it that way.

Early on the 23rd Layton raced up the ropes to join the climbers. He had been devastated by Dad's death, but desperately wanted to finish the climb, both in Dad's honor and because it wasn't in his nature to quit a climb. He later told me that if there were too many climbers on the Direct finish, he "was ready to grab one of the Germans and use the Exit Cracks. I didn't care how I got to the top, I thought, 'Layton, climb the thing and get it over with!' " But by the time he reached Death Bivouac, where the lower set of Germans were, Karl Golikow had decided on his own that all the ropes below the Spider were too damaged to use. He had stripped them on his descent, effectively cutting off the five climbers above the Spider from retreat, and the climbers below from completing the route. "I don't know why he did that, it was strange," reflected Layton. So instead of climbing up, Layton helped to bag up gear and toss it off. They stripped all the rest of the ropes on the way down, and cleaned up the jettisoned gear when they reached the bottom of the wall.

Dougal spent a miserable night in the Spider, which proved to be typical of the three days that it took to reach the top. A vicious storm set in, the worst of the entire winter, through which they simply had to climb, as there were no more places to carve a reasonable bivouac ledge, let alone a cave. They were low on food, and sleeping bags were frozen solid from lack of proper coverings. They got almost no sleep. Toes and fingers were starting to freeze, and many amputations were to come.

The German team sent a telegraph to my mother:

THE UNTIMELY PASSING OF YOUR HUSBAND HAS DEEPLY MOVED US STOP WE ARE UNABLE TO EX-PRESS DEEPLY ENOUGH OUR SENSE OF SHOCK AT HIS LOSS STOP THE FOUR OF US CAME DOWN FROM THE BUEGELEISIN TO BE PRESENT AT THE FUNERAL STOP MOST UNFORTUNATELY OUR FOUR COMRADES AND DOUGAL HASTON ARE IN EXTREME DIFFICULTIES JUST UNDER THE PEAK STOP WE THEREFORE HAVE TO CLIMB TO THE TOP AND BE PREPARED TO LAUNCH AN IMMEDIATE RESCUE OPERATION SHOULD IT BE NECES-SARY STOP WE ARE SURE YOU WILL UNDERSTAND OUR SITUATION STOP WE SINCERELY REGRET NOT

BEING ABLE TO BE PRESENT   STOP   WE WILL ALWAYS
BE THINKING OF YOU   STOP   HAAG SCHNEIDT GOL-
LIKOW ROSENZOPP

Meanwhile, Chris and Mick went to the summit via the west
flank to be ready for the climbers. They dug caves in the snow 400
feet below the top and occasionally ventured to the summit to try
to spot the climbers. But conditions were so miserable that they
could not see down the face and so cold that a half hour at a time
was all that they could spend on top. Chris radioed, "It's really
grim, it's desperate."

On the 25th Sigi Hupfauer, Jörg Lehne, Günther Strobel,
Roland Votteler, and Dougal Haston finally scratched their way to
the summit after the fight of their lives. Chris stayed on the summit taking pictures with five cameras that froze up one by one,
leaving only one in the end that worked. Mick and Karl Golikow
shuttled climbers down to the snow cave they had prepared on the
west flank. Eleven climbers were crowded into a snow cave built
for four. Many hands didn't work, but everyone was joyous. Dougal later wrote, "We were united by the spirit of extreme climbing."

The next day when they descended to Kleine Scheidegg,
a telegram awaited them, signed by my mother and by Dad's
parents:

WE EXTEND TO EACH OF YOU OUR HEARTFELT GRATI-
TUDE FOR YOUR CONTINUING THE CLIMB IN JOHN'S
SPIRIT   STOP   WE REALIZE YOU CONTINUED UNDER
THE MOST DIFFICULT AND HAZARDOUS CONDITIONS
STOP   WE CONGRATULATE YOU UPON YOUR SUCCESS
AND PRAY FOR YOUR SPEEDY RECOVERY

On their day of triumph, as the climbers were staggering over
the summit and down to the crowded snow cave, we in Leysin were

filing into the church for Dad's service. It was a small church, and people spilled out into the street, where snow dropped from the sky by the handful. Konrad drove from Munich through the storm to be with my mother and to give the dedication at the funeral. I don't have the words he spoke there, but they must have been something like those he wrote for Dad's obituary. In addition to an overview of Dad's background, it read:

> Achievements and tangible successes in the mountains are ultimately only a matter of appearance. To base a judgment on these criteria alone would not do justice to John. The publicity of the last weeks may have given the public another picture of John. But I know that John was not a climbing machine, but a real mountaineer. And being there for others had been for John one of the most significant features of a mountaineer. John was what the French call "un alpinist complet" and for him, mountain climbing was a way of life in the noble sense.
>
> In this context, two things were remarkable with John: First his awareness of what mountain climbing is able to give to men, especially to their soul and character. To perceive this was certainly due to his artistic side. But his strength exceeded perceiving and describing. He wanted to pass along; he taught, was an example. His work at the Leysin American School and the founding of the International School of Modern Mountaineering were only the beginning. Ventures like the one he did not return from were, in the last resort, only a form of expression, were only the means, not the purpose.
>
> John belonged to those who saw mountain climbing as something uniting, as a way of life independent of language, origin, and nationality. The term "international understanding" was for him not a cheap phrase but an incredibly important and extremely difficult task.
>
> It is not a symbol we have lost, but a force incarnate.

Allan Rankin, the Club Vagabond's owner, was also at the funeral. I don't believe he spoke to the assembly, but a letter he wrote two weeks later to a friend also stands as a eulogy:

> Death is not unknown to we, John's friends, but one cannot yet fully understand that this profusion of thought and energy will not return. His effect was far beyond his years, the culmination, the synthesis, of what he hoped to do was only beginning to emerge.
>
> This, of course, is an irreplaceable loss for us. His mountain school that had begun reflected ideas that were only his, his other school might have emerged [the International Institute at Mont Blanc]. The ideas that were about to help us to do so much are still here, but their continuation, their expansion, are so reduced with the loss of the dynamo. In my own person the things undone, unsaid, undiscussed, and the responsibility of recall, are of dominating importance.
>
> He will not be replaced—he was John Harlin.

Mom did not speak at the funeral, but if she had she likely would have said what she wrote down later: "John offered me a world of feeling, observation, and participation that I could never have experienced on my own. One cannot measure him by the yardstick used for ordinary men. It would be like measuring an elephant in microns."

I only remember the sight of people spilling out the door, the processions of mountain guides from France and Switzerland, all in their guide's clothes; later walking up the steps to the grave site, where wreaths of evergreen boughs and huge bouquets of flowers were piled into small mountains under the falling snow, and a crowd of people looked down as Dad's casket was lowered into the freshly dug earth. The president of Dad's chapter of the Swiss Alpine Club gave the final words at the grave, calling Dad their brother. But most of all I remember driving from the chapel to the cemetery down a long winding lane in the snowy forest. We followed a car with a gigantic wreath attached to the back that had been sent by the German team still on the Eiger. A wide ribbon stretched across the wreath with the words,

"Goodbye John."

TWELVE

PICKING UP THE PIECES

MY MOTHER had been warned that she would have dreams about Dad if she didn't see his body, and this came to fruition. In her dreams Dad's death was a hoax: he had gone to Algeria to escape his family commitment. Then she'd meet him on ski lifts or trains, and always she'd ask, "How could you do that to the children?"

In my own dreams Dad would simply show up at the dinner table—or also on trains. He was silent, and I silently observed him and wondered where he had been. My dreams faded much sooner than Mom's did. Eight-year-old Andréa had the hardest time, and her confession to Maria Coffey in *Where the Mountain Casts Its Shadow* shocked both Mom and me nearly four decades later. Andréa told Maria she never cared that Dad "succeeded" on a climb, so long as he came back to her. Furious at him in his death, Andréa turned her anger onto Mom. Her tantrums grew worse than ever, and when Gary tried to spank her in Leysin to bring her under control, her reaction was, "You're not my father." She started building her fantasy, which she would cling to for seven years: Dad was not dead. The coffin was empty. He would come back and take Andréa with him to wherever he had gone. She was a junior in high school, she told Maria, when suddenly she stood still and realized, "No, he's not ever going to come back. He's dead."

Wendy Bonington was a great comfort to Mom while Chris was still on the mountain, but then Wendy left to spend three days in a hospital with Chris, where they treated toes that had been blackened by frostbite. After that, they returned to England, where their two-year-old son was waiting.

In a letter to Chris a week after the funeral, Mom wrote:

> I, too, miss him very, very much. Yet I dare not have regrets, for my life has been enriched for the last 11½ years. The children are proud of their dad and know of the foundations he built for them—foundations of solid qualities which some children never get, although they have a father all their life. Beyond ourselves, the effect upon the community and a good portion of the globe has not just been *shock*, but *stimulation*. Regrets, when one lets them seep in, lie in what he might have done, or inspired to be done, in his full evolution.

Even before Dad died, we had loved the town, and it in turn loved us. We knew the shop owners, the restaurant owners, the guides, the ski instructors. One coach, Albino Viecelli, treated me like a son, and we alternated our business between his ski shop and Hefti's, a friend who had been an Olympic ski trainer. Andréa's and my schoolteachers came over for dinner, and Dad had offered to take them climbing. Dad spoke often with the mayor, who was also the printer. And he spent time at the police department discussing how Leysin was going to keep out the climbing ruffians while welcoming the more civilized legion.

The community council had given Mom unprecedented permission to build a mountain hut for Alpine research—I remember scouting for caves at the base of cliffs to convert into Mom's shelter. We were going to buy a large chalet in Leysin with apartments to rent out—the final bank and paperwork processing was to be made when Dad returned from the Eiger. After Dad's death the villagers generously extended themselves to us.

Both the Protestant minister and the Catholic priest had spoken at the funeral; there were the town officials and leaders, and the policemen keeping journalists and television cameras in check; but just as important, there were also janitors and shopkeepers and teachers and students. We were told that no funeral in Leysin had cut so deeply across all the social and religious divisions in the town. The American High School and College had their own memorial service in order to avoid crowding the church for those who had come far through the terrible storm. One of the college students, a young Sylvester Stallone, made a painting about Dad called *The Day Superman Died* (the words used on local newspaper headlines), which I didn't see until it was printed in *Rock & Ice* magazine in 1992.

Dad would have been thrilled to know how much the community cared. Before my parents were married, he had told Mom that he wanted his permanent home to be in the mountains above Montreux. Now Dad has his wish; this country is forever his home.

Within the family we referred to Dad being "away on an expedition," and we tried to live as best we could by pretending this was a normal absence. Life for me was so full and difficult that I barely had time to notice that Dad's "expedition" extended ever longer. I had done reasonably well at the Topolino race. There had been 689 contestants overall, and I'd finished second in my particular ski club, which made me something of a star to them. I'd been in good spirits on my return, which helped in my exams for secondary school. Those tests were very hard on me—two full days from eight in the morning until four in the afternoon, with a short lunch break. Mom had told me that one part would be an intelligence test, and to relax me she'd said it would be like playing games. So I was crushed when nearly the entire testing was French vocabulary, reading, dictation, grammar, writing samples, definitions, implications. I did at least enjoy the math, but I came out of the exams thinking I'd failed. Not only did I hate failure, I badly wanted to go on to the "big school" in the valley that year. I had hoped the children there would be wider in outlook than my village schoolmates, and I wanted to get away from the bully.

It turned out that I'd passed the exams, and as a result I rode the train to the valley each morning, struggled all day with very difficult classes, and then worked all evening to complete my homework. There was no time to discover how broad-minded the "big school" kids might have been; it was hard enough to catch up to them.

One weekend in early June, about three weeks after my tenth birthday, Mom and I went to Zermatt, where we hiked under the north face of the Matterhorn and slept in an abandoned grain house. We had hoped to reach the Hörnli Hut, but Mom was out of shape after all the trauma of the winter and spring. Then we wandered down to the town, through exquisite little villages. We hiked through a group of whistling marmots, and with Dad's 35mm camera I took close-up photos of flowers, lichens, old chalets, and rock formations. Mom wrote Sandy Bill afterward, "Johnny has not given up his intention of being the youngest climber of the Matterhorn, despite the fact that the original guide is no longer around. He showed me where his route went on the mountain and where the others were. He has never felt about the Eiger the way he has for YEARS about the Matterhorn. Told me yesterday that if no one takes him up before he is 17, he will solo it. I do not know if that was meant as a threat or a fact."

I don't remember or understand how Mom managed her time. She was chair of the science departments for the high school and college, and taught at both institutions. The end of the year included field trips to the coasts of France and Greece, lab preparations, reports, exams, grading, ordering supplies. She was working with the Super 8 movie film Dad had shot on the Eiger, from which he'd intended to make a commercial film. Mom sorted the radio conversations from the climb, and pulled his writings together in hopes of publishing his book, *Introspection Through Adventure.* She had legal and business affairs to deal with, illnesses, and general household management. She was in touch with the Oceanographic Institute in Monaco and the University of Washington about jobs and graduate studies. And by the end of April she had agreed to work with James Ramsey Ullman on Dad's biography. She accepted his offer, she wrote him, "based on your expressed desire to extend beyond the individual. I believe that you could capture the ideals and inspirations of John. A mere statement of his activities and the culminating drama would be far from my interests—or John's." It was the start of almost two years of massive correspondence, none of which I saw until I discovered her letters in the Ullman Papers archives at Princeton University nearly forty years later.

An LAS student, Carol Florell, recently remembered Mom's depression during the Greek field trip. To cheer her up, Carol and her friends gave Mom a "makeover," complete with styled hair and a manicure. "The idea," Carol said, "was to let her know as best we could that we cared about her." During that trip Mom decided she must return to her field of study immediately. On her return to Leysin she arranged with the Oceanographic Institute in Monaco that if the French government sufficiently funded the next Cousteau project, she would work as a research assistant studying radioactive isotopes in algae. She'd been visiting the institute for four years, and Professor Vaissiere, the research director, suggested that she coordinate her work with advanced graduate studies toward a thesis. We kids would spend the summer with our grandparents in the woods outside Olympia, Washington. If Mom got the job in Monaco we'd return to Europe; otherwise, Mom would study marine algae at the University of Washington.

My sister flew to Olympia in May, and I was scheduled to fly there at the end of July—each of us being delivered on TWA by Dad's parents. On the day of the accident Mom's father, George Miler, had begun building a small guesthouse for us so that we could have privacy and independence; he didn't know if we would come and hadn't asked, but he was an impulsive man. Mom thought that Andréa would get more attention with them than she'd be able to get with us during these complicated times. From her parents Mom learned that Andréa seemed to be happy, but after Andréa had been there about a month, Sandy went by to visit and take her hiking. She had adored Sandy, who had packed her up the hill behind our home in Leysin just after he'd been released from the hospital from his long climbing fall. (The doctor had told him only to walk on horizontal planes, but he was no better at following doctors' orders than Dad had been.) It turned out that Andréa wasn't happy at all, that she felt she had been abandoned to live with people she barely knew.

Mom wrote back to Sandy, "Andréa is very much the female counterpart of John—the imagination, the idealization, the affection, the sensitivity, the generosity, along with a certain deceptiveness and impracticality which can upset others. She is so advanced in some ways that one forgets she is a child and expects too much from her. I am guilty of this. She outmaneuvers me and befuddles me." Whether Andréa would have been better off in Leysin is an open question. She certainly would have been better off with her father.

Gary Hemming had been in Paris when Dad died. He became so emotional that his young girlfriend's father called the police to throw him out of the house. He arrived at our place not long after the funeral, intending in part to protect my mother from the crush of events. Gary helped Mom look back at Dad's life and death as no one else could. But Gary talked a lot, assuming that Mom wanted to hear all he was saying. If she was at all distracted, he became wounded or enraged.

Not long after Gary spanked Andréa, Mom remembers him storming out of the house. He had been complaining to her about her materialism, and telling her how generous Dad had been in comparison, until finally she explained how he was living under her materialistic roof and eating her materialistic food and consuming her precious time. Gary left a conciliatory note behind that included:

I've learned many many things of the greatest importance during this stay here and I want to thank you sincerely for the "trip," for the long talks, for everything in this respect—not to mention such material aspects as replenishing my body fibers and fluids with food and drink! So long as I'm not a truly free spirit I'm obliged to rely on people being kind enough to do this for me now and again! I hope as well that you are better able to see the unreality of death and likewise the unreality of our own lives. Je t'embrace encore, Gary

Many believe that Gary never recovered from Dad's death, that he saw it as "a premonition of his own." According to Mirella Tenderini, Gary "had always maintained that if someone died in an accident, it was because they wanted to die. . . . He became convinced that John's subconscious fall towards death was caused by a desire to punish himself, for his guilt in wanting to own, to possess the Eiger, by means of brute force."

After thinking about it, Gary wrote in his diary:

And John? His so called death. Is it real? What has really happened to his becoming? How does one become anything after he loses all physical contact with the world? . . . John is one of my dearest friends. His death I refuse to accept and so far as I am concerned he is still very much alive; you can interpret that as you please but his fall from the Eiger last week means that I cannot climb alone next summer. I have spoken with him about this and because of our long past together, because of our friendship, I must do these climbs with him. . . . You John are my best mate. It is to you I give the reign. . . . That's the best way for us to climb the summer, John—each in solo and you come along whenever you please and you leave whenever you please.

The other major event of Gary's year came that summer, after a season of soloing, when he led a rescue on the Dru that earned him superstar fame in France. At first the fame amused him, and then he couldn't escape from it, and eventually it led him to question even more deeply the strange injustice of the world. He wrote, "I am still the same person I was before. Before I was already me, just as I am now. Why then did no-one notice me? Why was I shunned, pitied?" It wore him down, as did other circumstances of life.

Ted Wilson saw Gary again in 1969. He wrote me:

> Gary came to Jackson Hole where I was working as a Jenny Lake ranger. He stayed with us, and one afternoon we drove to a guide's meeting at Leigh Ortenburger's house together. I asked him about John's death and how it had settled with him. Gary missed him deeply. He told me a story of going to Leysin soon after John died. He said he got drunk one night in the presence of your Mom and finding a lot of lust in grief, tried to take liberties with her. Marilyn rebuffed him and told him she was not into that stuff. He told me he felt really badly about what he had done. I said to him that Marilyn is a wonderful woman and would probably forgive if he were to tell her how badly he felt. He said that it was too late for that. The next night he got drunk around a Teton campfire at Guide's Hill, got into a fight, and was beaten up pretty badly. Gary went to the trees away from the campfire and used a gun on his head.
>
> Now I don't think for a moment that Marilyn's rebuke had anything to do with that. I think the circumstances of the evening and his embarrassment of not winning a fight when he had such a tough reputation was more in play. But I have often thought of the certain Hemingway type fatalism that persisted in the mountaineering world of the time. And how that affected your dad and Gary and many others. Like Hemingway, they lived large, took life by storm, and were willing to die young if necessary. They were truly a committed generation.

Relations with Dougal Haston had never been good, and they only got worse. He told Mom that after spending weeks in snow caves with Dad, he—Dougal—knew John much better than she did, and that he therefore was entitled to remove most of Dad's climbing and ski gear from our chalet, since that's what Dad would have wanted him to do. And then after many battles he took over ISMM, to which he also felt entitled. Dougal virulently rejected any input on Dad's visions and dreams for the school, which my parents had worked out together. "Dougal ended up with your dad's life, his summit, his book [*Eiger Direct,* which Dougal coauthored with Peter Gillman], and his climbing school," my mother would tell me later. "That would be almost bearable," she continued, "except that he squashed any attempt to include John Harlin's genes or my input into its structure. Instead, he responded with obscenities." Dougal more than anyone kept Mom from wanting to return to Leysin, and she never has. He went on to a legendary Himalayan climbing career, but in 1977 an avalanche killed him above Leysin.

THE ARRIVAL of our dog, Rongo, and cat, Kuzma, in mid-July, 1966, cheered Andréa two weeks before I showed up. When I landed in Washington, Andréa told me how she'd called out Rongo's name at the airport and had identified his cage as the one shaking from side to side from his excitement at hearing her voice. Kuzma immediately took to purring on her lap, and suddenly her world was less forlorn. With me in the picture again, her family was coming back together.

The grandparents who for Andréa had been caretakers of a lonely exile, for me opened a fresh and magical new world. Grandpa's passion was the self-sufficient life. He worked for money as little as possible (not at all when I knew him) and instead spent his days spading the garden, cutting firewood on his eighty-acre forest, and reading books—stacks and stacks of books. His home had electricity, but the wood he cut on his property provided all the heat, hot water, and even the cooking fuel. It was a huge disappointment to me many years later when he replaced the stove with an electric version, though Grandmommy had been asking for one for decades. Grandpa reminded me how to shoot (he'd taught me two years earlier during our visit), and I would take long hikes in the forest with a .22 pistol on my hip and sometimes a .25–.35 rifle in my arms, both of which he gave me. He taught me to accurately swing a double-bitted axe (the lumberjack kind with a blade on two sides). He taught me to drive the tractor and haul logs out of the woods with it. He taught me to fish, to love a garden's soil, to notch logs for a fort, to split wood with a wedge, to look for old gouges in the hillside where oxen and steam donkeys had dragged logs when Grandpa was young, and to think about the Big Bang and everything that came after.

We would lie in bed in the dormer as rain tapped on the tin roof and the creek roared in winter flood, and I would listen. A cool wet breeze usually flowed into our room as I learned of his own Puritan roots on the *Mayflower,* and how and why he'd come to renounce that lineage. Grandpa's father had been born near San Francisco, as had he (and my mother and me), and the extended family had largely prospered as scientists, doctors, professors, and similar "professional" sorts. But Grandpa rejected them all—he did not like what he considered to be their pretensions. He dropped out of college, and after his father's farm in Walnut Creek was foreclosed on early in the Great Depression, Grandpa decided to bicycle to the wilderness of British Columbia. Passing through Olympia he took shelter from the rain on the porch of what turned out to be a real estate office. On the wall was a notice for forty acres with a cabin, creek, and spring for $400. He took $4 of the $5 hidden in his bicycle handle and used it as the down payment. He then hopped freight trains back to California, where he worked to come up with the missing $396. But he didn't return to Olympia for eight years; in the meantime he met Gertrude Turula, they married, and had children. When the family finally moved north they discovered the cabin had burned down, so they lived in a tent for nearly a year—but he was able to add another forty acres to his land, also for about $400.

Since Grandpa dominated the talking—as well as the household—it was he who told me most of Grandmommy's stories as well. Her Finnish immigrant parents had first worked deep in a Montana mine before concluding something to the effect of, "We didn't come to America to live like this." Grandmommy was born just north of San Francisco in a Finnish commune where they raised grapes. She'd left home at fourteen and when Grandpa met her she was in college in Berkeley earning room and board working for Grandpa's favorite aunt, Susan, a retired missionary doctor who used to rescue female babies floating down Chinese rivers.

I lapped up these stories, every one of them news to me, and felt a new concept of family—all the way from roots buried in history to branches unknown. But most of all Grandpa and I talked about the moon and the stars and nature and self-sufficiency and books. Grandpa read every issue of *Scientific American* from cover to cover. He would think about what he'd learned while handspading his garden, and then he'd share his insights with me.

Though Grandpa had built the small guesthouse—we called it "the cabin"—on an impetuous whim to help his daughter in a time of crisis, we did in fact move in to it. The Monaco funding didn't work out, and Mom was accepted into the botany department at the University of Washington in Seattle. In those days before the modern freeway, Seattle was a good two to three hours from Olympia, and a few months after Mom arrived, she began commuting to school. Because of its distance, she made four-day round-trips to Seattle, leaving us with her parents. When Mom wasn't there, Andréa slept downstairs with Grandmommy, while I slept under the rafters in the attic with Grandpa. School was hideous, as I did not fit in with the provincial country kids in sixth grade, in part because I had been put ahead by a couple of grades.

It seemed that every boy wanted to beat me up, and I lived in terror from when I stepped onto the yellow school bus until it dropped me home again at my grandparents'. But life with Grandpa was a boy's dream.

On weekends Mom came home and Andréa and I moved to the cabin with her. She did her best to raise us with maximum freedom, hoping this would eliminate our need to rebel later on. At the same time we were expected to contribute our share to the family, and Andréa and I were responsible for the cooking, dish washing, bed making, and the wood fire that provided all of our heat. Andréa and I carved trails on the hillside above the cabin, and once we picked up Dad's oil paints, which he hadn't used in nearly a decade. We made large paintings of a butterfly and a fish, respectively—both subjects that we'd grown up with in Dad's paintings on our wall in Switzerland.

In addition to her schoolwork, Mom would write endless letters to Ullman. In February, she wrote:

> Last week we had Andréa's ninth birthday party. This was the first time we had a party in English! Some of the girl talk was what I remember from high school. When a nine-year-old is in the minority without a bra—I am prodded to ship the kids back to Europe where they are children a little longer! . . . Andréa let me know that in three years she could have a baby—and, as Johnny said, "like Claude she doesn't have to get married."

Most of Mom's letters to Ullman were about Dad and the life that had come before. But often she'd digress into her immediate surroundings, the life that was happening now, and she'd proudly tell him how we kids helped her to "maintain perspective" and how much fun it was to observe the combination of "genetic shuffling and environmental molding" that shaped us. "We are enjoying these moments while we have them," she wrote, "and we are all three growing up."

In the spring of 1967, a year after the accident, she wrote:

The children have been talking a lot about John recently—
Andréa in particular. I neither bring up nor avoid the subject. It is their very high regard for him that always
permeates the conversation, and their intense love—here
again Andréa far more than Johnny. A couple weeks ago her
teacher wrote that Andréa had nearly made herself ill crying
so hard about missing her father. She is just now beginning
to use the past tense. An outsider commented to me on her
shift from "Daddy picks out Mommy's clothes" to "Daddy
used to. . . ." This was on the botany field trip last weekend.
Yesterday she was telling me about what a good father he
was, how much they used to hug one another, what a tease he
was. "Daddy was so funny." She referred to the monster faces.
John would contort his expressions, his hands, and stalk in to
the children as a Frankenstein. They would scream delight-
edly. Then they would pounce all over him, and he'd roar.
Within the family he showed unreserved tenderness and support. To me in the last year or so when confessing his deep
love for the children, he told me how he would give his life
unhesitatingly for them and questioned whether I loved
them enough to do the same. I suggested he save his life for
them. That, as you might guess, was not taken favorably—
my comment that is. I tried to explain that my saving my life
for the children might be weighed in the category of his giving his. I was only hoping to seed ideas which might later become his "own."

I remember little about my own emotions during this period,
at least as they concerned Dad. I remember my fear of my schoolmates, the wild joy of yelling "Timber!" when a big tree fell, the
stress of being lost in the forest, the sting of nettles as I slashed
through them with Grandpa's machete. I just don't remember what
I felt about Dad during this time, and I've long wondered whether

that means I forgot what I felt or whether I didn't feel, and what that might mean about me. Discovering Mom's letters to Ullman was a revelation. It seems that I'd moved on, for better or worse.

The mountains came back into my life not long after we moved to Seattle that autumn. The Harlin grandparents, whom we rarely saw, paid for me to join the Mighty Mite ski racing program at Crystal Mountain, a ski resort with bus service from Seattle that allowed me to ski on Saturdays. Graduate student friends of my mother's started taking me mountaineering, simple Cascades volcanoes and Olympics hike-ups with a few tricky moves. But I didn't need high-standard climbing to enjoy myself. When Ted Wilson came for graduate school at UW he took me to a real cliff, and I had fun until I crawled under what felt like a difficult overhang perhaps 100 feet up the vertical face. I have never been afraid of heights, but then and now I'm very afraid of falling, and I simply didn't trust the rope above me.

The weekend wilderness outings that Mom's graduate student friends Steve and Ginny Burger and later Ken Davis took me on were exactly what this eleven-year-old boy needed, along with frequent doses of the manly country life with Grandpa, working wood, throwing knives, and shooting bottles. I attended one meeting of the Boy Scouts in Seattle, hoping this would take me even more frequently into the hills, but it was immediately clear that the citified Boy Scouts would not be my ticket to adventure.

In Seattle, school was once again a living nightmare. The Olympia hicks were replaced by junior-high black kids with giant chips on their shoulders—they told me menacingly how when they grew up whites would be their slaves. America seemed in a revolution thanks to the Vietnam War and race riots, and the day after Martin Luther King, Jr., was assassinated I stayed home from fear. It was an ugly time to be a small white boy in a mostly black inner-city school, but the attacks on me amounted to little more than being pushed around, and the one time I was hit with a chain didn't hurt physically, just mentally.

I found my daily sanctuary in books, and started devouring boy-and-his-dog and wilderness-survival stories until the school's library ran dry. I was looking for more at the Seattle Public Library when I spotted the book that would change my life. Displayed on top of a cabinet was Farley Mowat's *Never Cry Wolf,* a novelized version of the author's year with a Canadian wolf pack. Suddenly the Arctic was everything to me, and wolves its living symbol. I would become an Arctic wolf biologist. I started calling Ken Davis "Uncle Albert," the nickname Mowat gave to the male wolf who selflessly helped the breeding couple to raise their pups, and I passed the book on to the Burgers. I like to think this book helped to change the fate of wolves in North America. Mowat also wrote wilderness survival stories and other Arctic tales, cementing my passion for polar realms.

In the spring of 1969, just before my thirteenth birthday, came one of the happiest days of my life: Ken asked if I'd like to go to the North Slope of Alaska that summer. A large group from the Seattle Mountaineers would take floatplanes to a lake in what was then the Arctic National Wildlife Range (later upgraded to Refuge) with the primary goal of climbing the highest peak in the Brooks Range, 9,020-foot Mount Chamberlin. I was delirious with joy.

That summer we climbed the peak despite a pitch of steep ice, and on the summit Ken and I tossed a Frisbee across the Arctic Divide, where the waters split between the Beaufort Sea (Arctic Ocean) and the Yukon River (which ran to the Pacific). As big a thrill as the climb itself was rediscovering my leather glove in the tundra near camp and finding two fang marks in it, perfectly spaced for a wolf jaw. While we saw no wolves during that trip, the Arctic hook had been thoroughly set, and a splinter group of a half dozen Mountaineers, myself included, would return to ANWR the following two summers for increasingly long hiking and kayaking adventures.

When I came home to Washington, I found Andréa and

Mom already ensconced at the Friday Harbor Marine Labs on San Juan Island, where we would live for the next year. A static-filled black-and-white television crackled with the image of Neil Armstrong landing on the Moon, and soon after we drove out to our new house in the country. Rippled-glass picture windows overlooked the Strait of Juan de Fuca, where orcas swam in the foreground and the Olympic mountains rose behind. The open landscape swarmed with rabbits just begging to be killed by my single-shot .22 rifle, and I fed them to my new dog, Ranger, and to the hawks and eagles flying overhead. My ninth-grade class was small, smart, and without a single bully.

The 6,000-foot north face of the Eiger being viewed from the telescope at Kleine Scheidegg in the early 1960s. The 1938 Route is the Classic, or Heckmair, Route, which Dad climbed in 1962 and I climbed in 2005. The 1966 Route is the John Harlin Route, also known as the Winter Direct. Dad's rope broke at (x). From this vantage it appears that the Direct angles up the face from the left. A more straight-on view would show that the route is, in fact, direct. Dad's body landed very close to the start of the route. These were the first two routes on the north face. Now there are more than twenty.

Dad, Mom, and me outside our home in Los Altos, California, in 1956.

Dad standing beside his F-100 at Hahn Air Base, circa 1961.

The castle above Bernkastel, as viewed from the trail from our house to my kindergarten.

Andréa and me in Germany, circa 1961 (ages roughly 3 and 5).

6

Dad meeting Konrad Kirch for the first time as he and Henri Briquet approach the Gamba Hut below Mont Blanc in 1961. Gary Hemming is on the left.

7

Dad and Konrad immediately after their ascent of the Classic Route on the Eiger in 1962.

With Mom at the borders of Austria, Italy, and Switzerland on my first big ski tour, in February 1963, age 6.

8

Andréa and me planting Alpine flowers in Gary's beard.

The Refuge de l'Envers des Aiguilles, where I waited for Mom to return during the storm.

The Fou team at the Refuge de l'Envers des Aiguilles: Dad, Tom Frost, Gary Hemming, Stewart Fulton.

11

10

On the way down from my first climb in the Alps, age 7.

Mom carrying gear from Chamonix to the base of the Fou, 1963.

12

13

Chalet Pollux, our home. The Dents de Morcles are on the left, while the peaks at the right rise above Chamonix, France.

Dad and Andréa in Luxembourg on our return from the States in 1964.

Grandpa John and Grandma Sue visiting Leysin in 1965.

With Dad's paintings in our living room, 1965.

The Tour d'Aï rises behind me (age 9) at the top of the Berneuse gondola, above Leysin, 1966.

Layton Kor, Dougal Haston, and Dad with their gear for the planned nine-day ascent of the Direct.

Chris Bonington in storm on the Brouillard Pillar (Mont Blanc) the previous August.

Dad filming Layton early in the climb.

Dougal, Layton, and Dad at the start of the fixed ropes.

Peter Gillman radioing to Dad on the face.

Dad with Layton and Dougal on the first morning inside the Death Bivouac cave. Note the daylight coming through the walls.

24

25

At the funeral in Leysin. From left to right: Grandpa John, me, Grandma Sue, Konrad, Mom, and Andréa. Directly above Andréa, facing the camera, is Bev Clark.

26

The funeral procession in Leysin's graveyard.

Grandpa George (Miler), my mother's father, working wood on his property in 1967.

27

Approaching the summit of Mount Chamberlin, the highest peak in the Brooks Range, during my first trip to the Arctic National Wildlife Range, in 1969.

28

29

Ranger about to enjoy his daily rabbit on San Juan Island, 1970.

On my third trip to ANWR, in 1971, we paddled the Sheenjek River to Fort Yukon. This northern pike came from the junction of the Sheenjek and the Porcupine Rivers.

30

Mom gathering specimens in Rhode Island on her way to class, early 1970s.

31

Chris Metcalf nearing the summit of Mount Ritter in January 1977.

Wayne Sawka bouldering at Dead Man's Summit on the east side of the Sierra Nevada, 1977.

32

33

35

The south face of Mount Robson, showing: (1) Wishbone Arête (2) the Schwarz Ledges route of my solo ascent; (b) Wishbone bivouac site; (h) Ralph Forster Hut; (x) where Chuck fell.

34

Buildering with my cast on the UCSB campus in 1978.

Chuck Hospidales on the spectacular last move of the Photo Finish Route on Mount Andromeda, Columbia Icefield.

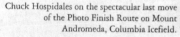

36

37

My first pilgrimage to Dad's grave in Leysin, Christmas 1980.

Reinhard Karl in the Pfalz, Germany, in 1980.

38

Nico Mailänder in the Verdon, France, in 1980.

Charlie Fowler on the third pitch of our new route, Seven Arrows, in Rocky Mountain National Park.

39

40

41

42

At the cabin with our puppy, Lupine, shortly after the wedding ceremony.

The Hammond family at our wedding: Stanley, Cherry, Adele, Cheryl, and Rose.

The east face of Longs Peak, showing the route of Jimmy Katz's and my ski descent in 1984. The previous year I skied the peak via the north face (around the right skyline).

With Jimmy Katz after making the first ski descent of the left Y-Couloir on Mount Ypsilon, Rocky Mountain National Park, in 1984. The route starts on the summit snow slope directly above us.

43

44 Jimmy Katz in the Notch Couloir on the east face of Longs Peak.

45

The town of Huaráz, Peru, and the summit of 22,205-foot Huascarán Sur, which we skied on 3-pins (Nordic equipment) in 1985.

46

47

With Craig Sabina, *Summit*'s publisher, in front of our home/office barn in Pennsylvania, 1990.

Me on a climbing route to the 28-foot-high ceiling inside Adele's studio portion of the barn in Pennsylvania.

48

Our initial foray into Heinrich Harrer's multi-thousand-photo collection from his years in Lhasa, from which we crafted *Lost Lhasa: Heinrich Harrer's Tibet*. Here we are in his Austrian home in 1991.

49

50

Looking for our line on the true south face of Mount Waddington, British Columbia, in 1995.

51

The surprise airdrop at about 13,000 feet on Mount Waddington's shoulder glacier, just below the summit pinnacle

52

Our Matterhorn traverse in 1999 started in Zermatt, in the valley below right, hiked over to and climbed the left skyline, and descended the right skyline.

5

Mark Jenkins on the Italian summit of the Matterhorn.

Konrad Kirch in his beloved Calanques, early 1990s.

54

Mark pointing to our chosen peak in Tibet, a 21,000-foot virgin with various names, including Namla Karpo. We made it partway up the left skyline in 2002 before retreating from fear of avalanches.

Siena, age 7, on the summit of Germany's Zugspitze.

56

55

58

ulie-Ann Clyma at the lower Eccles bivouac hut in 004.

The south side of Mont Blanc, showing, left to right: the Brouillard Pillar route Dad climbed in 1965; From Dawn to Decadence on the Innominata Ridge, which I climbed in 2004; and the Hidden Pillar of Frêney, which Dad climbed in 1963. The beautiful dihedral with icicles is at (d). The dotted line marks my approach in 2003.

59

Me on the roof on From Dawn to Decadence after knocking out the icicles in 2004.

60

Robert Jasper on the Ice Hose in perfect conditions.

61

62

63

Daniela Jasper finishing the Second Icefield, with a helicopter hovering near the Death Bivouac on top of the Flatiron.

Robert on the Traverse of the Gods.

Me at the end of the Traverse of the Gods.

Robert and Daniela with the MacGillivray Freeman camera crew on the Summit Icefield.

Final steps to the Eiger's summit.

65

Konrad and I are holding an old Eiger piton and Eiger rope, along with a rose, that Daniela and Robert Jasper gave to me after our ascent in 2005.

66

Michael Brown with the big IMAX-film camera and Jochen Schmoll with the video camera on the summit of the Eiger in April 2006.

67

The Hammond-Harlin family nervously awaiting good conditions on the Eiger in September 2005.

Siena, age 9, and me enjoying each other's company at Kleine Scheidegg prior to my ascent in 2005.

68

Many more photos can be viewed at www.JohnHarlin.net.

69

THIRTEEN

YES, HE WAS MY FATHER

LIVING on the island, I gave up ski racing. I had been showing some promise, and even had my eye on racing in the Olympics
one day, but I never loved the formal competition and training of
racing, where gates dictate turns and lift lines replace adventure.
The best part of each ski year had been when the coach—who was
from Austria and had mountains in his blood—took us to ski a volcano after the racing season was over. The first year it was Mount
Saint Helens (before it exploded), and the second it was Mount
Hood (we climbed to the summit, but skied from lower down).
During our year on the island I spent more time than ever in nature, and I missed the snow surprisingly little.

When we moved back to Seattle I attended a suburban school
where Ken Davis taught; this kept me out of the riots at the inner-
city high school. Ken and other adult friends took me back to the
Arctic National Wildlife Range the next two summers for month-
long hiking and paddling journeys in the Brooks Range, in addition to the easy mountaineering climbs we were doing in the
Cascades and Olympics. Fishing had become my new love of loves,
and between my quest for Arctic char, Washington steelhead, and
Canadian kokanee, there was hardly enough time left to read my
books on fly tying.

Mom finally earned her long-awaited Ph.D. in the spring of 1971. She must have been tremendously proud and pleased. Likely I took her joy somewhat for granted, as what I remember more is her early stress at the dearth of openings for professors of marine botany. She was thirty-six years old, had been through a lot, and wanted to finally do research science and to mentor graduate students, not teach at a state college, which she had been offered on both the West and the East coasts. She was also offered a National Science Foundation fellowship to Scripps Institution of Oceanography in California, but that was only guaranteed for a year, and she was worried about putting her family through yet another move. In her last letter to Ullman, three years after *Straight Up* was published, she explained why she chose Scripps: "My son decided for me: 'Do what you want to do most, NOW, because we won't be around for long and it is your career.'"

In the end a promising professorship opened up at the University of Rhode Island, and our sights shifted east. She would be the first woman faculty member in science at the College of Arts and Sciences. A long ordeal with chauvinist colleagues was about to begin, but in the next three decades she would help to transform the ossified institution until it reached a stage where her young female colleagues could take the whole painful process for granted, eventually seeing Mom as part of the old guard instead of the revolutionary she had been.

In the late summer of 1971, when I was fifteen, we packed up the station wagon and drove three thousand miles to what for me seemed like the last place on earth. Rhode Island was not only the most densely populated state in America, but its maximum elevation was 812 feet. What kind of place was this? Fortunately, I'd been around enough to know that living situations are only temporary, with each offering its own kind of adventure.

In the "Ocean State" I finally fell in with a group of friends my own age. It started in math class where a half dozen of us motivated kids split off into our own fun-loving working group, and it extended into after-school activities where I finally learned to socialize. My hair grew to my shoulders (where it stayed for the next nine years), and Mom says it was my year as a teenager, when I went from adult to teenager to adult again in about that span of time. Soon I had a car to drive three hours north to ski in New Hampshire, where an old friend from Bernkastel-Kues lived.

Thanks to the grades I skipped coming back from Switzerland and an early admissions option at the University of Rhode Island, I started college in the winter of 1973, when I was sixteen years old. I chose zoology as my major because studying Arctic wolves remained my life's goal. College suited me, though I found myself enjoying calculus and physics more than biology. In order to get my grades I found that I had to resort to the same trick my mother had used at Stanford: studying. Mom called it her form of cheating, since Stanford was full of gifted students who were used to coasting on their intelligence. By studying harder than they did, Mom found she could compete quite effectively with less natural talent.

URI hardly compares with Stanford, except that I had inherited Mom's need to excel academically, and this tended to keep me glued to the books. The trouble was that I was too restless to keep it up indefinitely. Much though I loved learning, I couldn't stop my mind from wandering to the outside world—not outside the ivory tower, but *outside* outside: adventure. First I dreamed and then planned in some detail a drive to Patagonia in my little Fiat 128. Not to climb, because I didn't know any climbers and was only playing around on rocks with Rhode Island friends who'd never known a rope that wasn't attached to a boat, but simply to explore. Unfortunately the South American Drive Fantasy was built largely on the notion of doing it with my girlfriend in Connecticut, and as it turned out her mother wasn't convinced it was the best thing for her sixteen-year-old daughter (who, ironically, was about to enroll at Stanford).

But I needed to *do* something. Sitting around Rhode Island

wasn't holding my attention. After a year of college I took a semester off to go back to Washington State. Sandy now worked for Weyerhaeuser, the giant timber company, and he had offered to find me work logging and to let me stay at his house. I had to lie about my age because eighteen was the minimum for work as dangerous as a choker setter. I worked long, hard hours with massively powerful machinery and huge logs that sometimes rolled over men on the steep hillsides. Mom and Grandpa weren't thrilled about the risk, but Mom was especially keen that I didn't go climbing with Sandy. By now he had put up, among other things, the first ascent of a brilliant route on the Lotus Flower Tower in the remote Cirque of the Unclimbables in Canada. But he had also taken a huge fall while rock climbing in Germany and broken nearly every bone in his body. Before that he had been a downhill-ski racer, and had twice skidded into the trees and been dragged out on stretchers. And he had rolled two Porsches. Perhaps out of respect for Mom, he didn't offer to take me climbing.

After a wet spring of dragging logs out of western Washington's clear-cuts, I had enough money to join my old North Slope friends for another trip to ANWR. Our plan was to land a ski plane on overflow ice at the head of the Kongakut, the northeasternmost river in Alaska, and then make its first descent. We found fiberglass kayaks that we could cut into three pieces to fit them inside of a little bush plane. Ward Irwin, a Boeing engineer, designed a fiberglass sleeve and a bolting system that allowed the boats to be reassembled in the field and be strong enough for Class III waters with heavy loads inside. The two months we spent paddling in ANWR followed by hiking in the Arrigetch reaffirmed my love for the Arctic. We saw numerous wolves and grizzlies, and about ten thousand caribou. It also bought me enough *Sitzfleisch* credits to allow another two semesters in academia.

Then I needed another semester off, and I spent it delivering boats, including 100-foot ferries that we brought from Rhode Island to Puerto Rico, and Rhode Island to the Yucatan Peninsula.

On the Yucatan we dropped off the boat with a developer who was building some of the first hotels in Cancun. The rest of the crew flew home, but I wanted to save money and experience more by taking the bus back to Rhode Island (that year I rode buses for eighteen thousand miles). The day after we landed, the captain, who was amused by my history of wandering, asked me if I would change rooms every night in the hotel; I responded with the only thing that made sense to me: "Depends on whether the view is different." Later the captain was contracted by the army to do civilian testing on a new ship, and so we brought an army LCU (a beach-storming landing boat capable of carrying three tanks) from the Great Lakes through the Erie Canal and then put it through its paces by landing it eighty times on various New England beaches, much to the confusion of the sunbathers we displaced.

Back at URI that fall I once again lived at home studying my butt off. I had no social life at all. I didn't miss it, but I knew it would be good for me. Mom and I decided that I needed to live on campus to meet my peers. My heart and soul were completely Western, and the University of Washington would have been ideal except that I already knew Washington and figured I'd end up living there eventually. I applied to Stanford because my parents had gone there, but the school didn't want me (Mom insisted it was because they take few transfer students). So I decided on the University of California, Santa Barbara. They had a great ecology department, which was a prerequisite. But the main reason for that choice was that I had never lived in Southern California. The last two years of college seemed like the perfect chance to try out something with a different view. In the fall of 1976, at twenty years old, I got off the bus at dawn at a campus that looked like a beachside tropical paradise. The dorm I'd selected was called Tropicana Gardens. It felt as exotic as anywhere I'd ever been.

A week or so later the UCSB Mountaineering Association had its first meeting. We filled out forms, and during a break in the presentations I perused copies of magazines I'd never seen: *Moun-*

tain, Climbing, Summit. It brought back memories of my childhood, kindling a sense that here was the forgotten door to My World—and that I should enter it. I was lost in the magazines when a half-laughing voice boomed out from the middle of the lecture hall: "John Harlin? Who's this John Harlin?"

Startled, I looked up. There was a tight knot of jocular friends going over the application forms. I said, "That's me."

Now it was their turn to look startled—they assumed my name had been put in as a practical joke. "But John Harlin died doing a new route on the Eiger," said a long-haired fellow. The others were all staring at me. My face flushed under the sudden curious glare of a whole corner of the auditorium, and I blurted out, "Yes, he was my father." I could feel my body almost go tipsy with nervous pride that these people knew of Dad. It felt like I was meeting my kin, my kind. Where would this lead?

At that meeting I added a pair of rock-climbing shoes and a rope to the club's mail-order list. I only owned Dad's old shoes, which were too big for me and besides, the leather was rotting. Dad's old climbing rope wasn't much better.

A few weeks later the club's van was waiting for Chris Metcalf and me to descend from Tahquitz Rock, a superb granite climbing area just southeast of Los Angeles. Chris, with hair to his shoulders like mine, thin and highly intellectual, loved the sport but was no expert. We made a great team and became best friends. The day before, we'd climbed a five-pitch route called Sahara Terror, graded 5.6, which put us onto thin face climbing with what felt like tiny handholds and footholds sometimes a long ways past the protection. With my pulse racing, I felt like I'd rediscovered an old friend. The next day we climbed a longer, harder route, the Long Climb, graded 5.7 (now raised to 5.8). It felt just as natural. The sun was setting into Los Angeles's smog as we descended, and darkness settled upon the impatient crew as they waited for us in the van.

Chris and I flopped onto the floor of the van, lying on our

backs on the pile of gear. The drive back was quite possibly the most magical feeling I've ever had, before or since. My head floated on the weekend's memories: delicate moves on steep slabs, empty space beneath my feet, carefully controlled fear, the sweet, heady rush of triumph. I felt myself a lost child suddenly returned to home's warm embrace—a home filled with wonders beyond any I remembered. Each delicate passage replayed itself over and over in my head; there was no stopping the mental imagery. Chris seemed equally entranced, and we talked and dreamed and remembered in an enchanted cloud. Over the following decades of climbing I've tried to rekindle the magic of that first romantic blush, but somehow familiarity or loss of innocence blocks its perfect bliss. I hope I never forget how it was.

Chris and I decided to climb the Direct Route on Washington's Column in Yosemite that Thanksgiving. It was an all-day route with relatively easy climbing (5.7) and I'd heard that Dad had climbed it. But we weren't a fast team, and we carried too much stuff, including big pac-boots (Arctic hiking boots—all I had) lashed to the outside of my rucksack because we intended to hike ten miles past Yosemite Falls to return to the valley floor. We were several ropelengths shy of the summit when the sun went down and the campfires started twinkling 1,000 feet below. Food was scant, water bottles were empty, and we could almost smell the Thanksgiving turkey feasts taking place below. Still, we were comfortable enough on separate sloping ledges wedged into the shallow chimney. It was far too early in my climbing career for me to feel bad about climbing slowly. The experience we were having seemed infinitely better than a full stomach in the woods below.

Thanks to an exceptionally dry year, that winter Chris and I climbed Mount Ritter deep in the Sierra. We chose a rock route and again nightfall surprised us, this time during the descent, where we had to sleep without bags on a windy ledge at about 12,000 feet in January's cold. By then my closest friends were all in the Mountaineering Association's leadership, and later that winter our little clique searched out frozen waterfalls to learn how to climb ice. During that trip the club's vice president, Wayne Sawka, and I noticed the Northeast Buttress of Mount Morrison, a pyramidal face that dominates Highway 395 just south of Mammoth Lakes. Mount Morrison looks positively Himalayan in scale from that vantage, especially in winter with snow. It surges upward in an intimidating monolith one can't ignore—and consequently, we had to climb it. It proved long, cold, loose, and wonderful, and that night on the long drive back to Santa Barbara I shared kisses with Paula Brooks, the woman who had platonically shared my tent the night before the climb. Romancing Paula, a beautiful graduate student several years older than I, completed my transformation. I was giddy with happiness during this year of discovery, the only problem being that my grades were now slipping. It seemed a small price to pay for an otherwise perfect world.

That summer I decided that life was too short to get a job. I was lucky in that as long as I was in school I could collect enough Social Security to live on, which besides my name and some memories is what I'd inherited from Dad. Money rarely influenced my directions, and so I'd happily given up the Social Security payments each time I'd taken semesters off from college. That summer I took an apartment for a month in Ventura so that Paula could join me several days a week from her summer job in Santa Monica. In Ventura I could do a little work for my friend Del Johns who was setting up a second store for the Great Pacific Iron Works and its nascent brand "Patagonia." We were given an empty warehouse and we filled it with boxes of Foamback rain gear with defective stitching, climbing nuts with oddly spaced holes, and ice axes with tiny cracks in the handle stamped with the number "2." Yvon Chouinard himself seemed to approve of what we did, and he didn't mind that we kept the best for ourselves in lieu of some wages. Then Del and I and a few of his friends headed to the Wind River Range in Wyoming for wilderness mountaineering to round out the summer.

On the twenty-five-mile approach hike to Gannett Peak, the highest in the Winds, I lashed Dad's climbing rucksack to the top of my Arctic frame pack. This was for practical reasons—I needed the room for climbing gear in addition to two weeks' worth of food and camping gear—but it also felt metaphorical, since by now I was starting to think that my future career in science should perhaps include the Alpine zone as well as the Arctic. The two have a lot in common, other than wolves. And tundra that leads to a big granite wall felt more practical than tundra that just leads toward more tundra. We took a basic route up Gannett, and I reveled in my first steps on a real glacier since the volcanoes I'd climbed and skied in Washington. A few days later we started up an ice face on neighboring Fremont Peak. I don't know exactly how high or steep it was: steep enough to be interesting, low enough angle to feel completely secure, long enough to feel very real. I'd never been on a proper ice face before, but once again, the climbing seemed just right. The front points of our crampons penetrated only when we'd kick them in firmly, and the slope was gentle enough that we could rest by putting one foot flat against the ice with a bent knee, thus relieving our straining calf muscles. We never pulled the rope out of the pack, and it became the first technical route I soloed—or in this case, simul-soloed, in that two of us climbed unroped side by side. It was another giddy moment for me, standing on Fremont's ragged summit deep in a very wild range, with not a sign of humanity anywhere. We looked down at great sweeps of granite in the next valley west and dreamed of going there someday.

I called Paula when I returned to California and found out she'd dumped me. It felt like a golden carpet had been yanked out from under me and I'd been sent spinning into a dark void. I just couldn't believe it. She wouldn't say why. She wouldn't let me see her. Finally, after a love letter arrived that I'd mailed to her just hours before our fateful phone call, she agreed to drive up from Santa Monica and talk. We sat in her car as tears streamed down my face, and she told me that her previous boyfriend had also been a climber and had left her often and caused her to worry, and she did not want that life again. That's the only reason I could get from her, or at least the only one I remember. There must have been more to it, but of one thing there could be no doubt: I had very definitely become a climber. My senior year at UCSB started in a week, and the first duty on my agenda was to prepare the opening meeting of the Mountaineering Association, of which I was now the president, just as Dad had been at Stanford exactly twenty years before.

F O R the Mountaineering Association's meeting I put together a slide show that merged my passions: Arctic travel, climbing, and classical music. Back in Rhode Island I had built a complex slide show synching my nature photography with Vivaldi's *Four Seasons*. That had been just for fun, and this time it had a larger purpose. In that fall of 1977 I still had no idea that my life would go anywhere but to a career in science. To pay for my room and board I'd taken a job as a "resident assistant" in my dorm (too much policing for my taste, as it turned out). The night of the Mountaineering Association meeting the dorm manager introduced the other RAs to the assembled Tropicana Gardens residents and announced that I wasn't there because of my commitment to the club.

One of the freshman girls was becoming curious who her RA was, since she'd still not seen me and my room was just a couple of doors away. So she came by the dorm's office where there were photos of all the RAs. My photo showed me in a kayak with a Norwegian elkhound on my lap. She figured she had to meet this guy, and a few days later she was in my room with questions about a field trip to one of the islands off the Santa Barbara coast. And then there were invitations to play ultimate Frisbee, and pretty soon we were discussing homework, and then walking on the beach, lightly bumping shoulders to see how the other would react. By the time we kissed two weeks after meeting we were already in love.

Adele Hammond was an eighteen-year-old Colorado girl. She'd grown up in the same house in Denver that she'd been born into, and she had never seen an ocean before arriving in Santa Barbara. On our beach walks I discovered that she believed the tide went out during the day and came in at night. The ocean at night intimidated her, a fact I exploited by promptly going for a night-time swim in the surf. But she had a deep appetite for the world; she was every bit as eager to see new places and experience new cultures as I was, the main difference being that for her these experiences would be much fresher. And her mind was wide open. She had enrolled on a scholarship to the College of Creative Studies, a small campus within UCSB's broad tent that had been set up after the famous burning of the Bank of America building during Vietnam War protests seven years earlier. CCS had been established in part to give especially talented minds a place to express their creativity, and while the protests belonged to an earlier generation, the school's grade-free and self-directed system of study appealed to some. The small school is hard to get in to, requiring applicants to show that they'd already performed in their field of study. In Adele's case, she had submitted twenty slides of her paintings to get in to the art program. She showed me her work, which I found brilliant, and the next quarter I signed up for art history classes so that I'd have some idea of what she was doing.

That Thanksgiving we drove to her roommate's house not far from Yosemite and I continued on to the Valley to meet Chris Metcalf for another go at Washington's Column, this time on a much steeper and harder route. The summer before I'd climbed the north face of Yosemite's Sentinel Rock, my first real "wall," which by the Yosemite definition is a climb big enough to require a deliberate bivouac en route rather than an accidental bivy due to slow climbing. On Sentinel Rock I'd found that my equally inexperienced partner moved far too slowly when he was leading, and I took over to lead the rest of the climb. The South Face Route on Washington's Column proved to be the same experience. I felt in my element on the climb and moved accordingly. For Chris it just wasn't gelling, and he found that dangling in slings from a vertical wall 1,000 feet above the deck didn't suit his more sensitive nature. In fact, he didn't seem to enjoy it much at all, and we crept only slowly up the wall. After a planned bivouac on a big ledge a few pitches up, we spent an unplanned second night at the top of cliff. Long out of water, we found a patch of snow and melted precious liquid in a used sardine tin over a smoky fire. The taste was as vile as it sounds, and there was no food. So once again we had to eat vicariously 2,000 feet above the Thanksgiving fireside feasts we could see twinkling in the Valley below. It would prove to be our last big climb together. While our friendship was strong, our goals in climbing were diverging. This confused me at the time, as it seemed to me that if one loved to climb then one would always want to climb harder, bigger, longer, more. Chris didn't seem to want that, or to be comfortable with it. He wasn't launching himself into the climbing world, but was happy enough fitting climbing into his world.

My own climbing also lost momentum during my senior year, replaced in part by romance. Instead of spending Christmas vacation in the mountains, I spent it taking the bus to Rhode Island with Adele so she could meet my mother. I'd spent so much time on buses that they were second nature to me, but Adele found it tedious. We flew home. Most of spring break went to studying, and much of what should have been climbing time went to the club and to the small demands of my job. But my mind always wandered to the mountains. It clearly wasn't time to continue straight on to graduate school. No, I needed a couple of years off to shake climbing from my system. I had to scratch the itch hard enough to make it go away for a while. That was the theory, anyway.

The first problem, however, was money. The Social Security stipends had run out with my graduation, and I was now in the real world. The quickest, most flexible way for me to make money was to go back to Willapa Logging, the small outfit I'd worked for before. It was run by nice people who said they'd take me back whenever I wanted to work. While the effect of logging on the Northwestern forests was troubling, the fact was that I tremendously enjoyed the work itself. Plus, my feelings then and now have not much changed: it's not logging per se that's bad, it's how it's done. And whether logging is dangerous or not is similarly dictated by how it's done. It is very much like Alpine climbing in that way. If you stay alert, if you don't reduce precautions just because you're tired, and if you work with safety-conscious people, then the risks are relatively minor. If you take shortcuts for whatever reason—usually exhaustion—logging and climbing can turn deadly in a heartbeat.

My primary job in logging was working as a choker setter. Chokers are thirty- to forty-foot-long, three-quarter-inch-thick cables that are ganged three or four to a group. One end of the cable is wrapped around a log, and the other end is connected to the fat "mainline" cable, which runs up the hill to the "tower" where a big motor pulls the log to waiting trucks. A small "backline" cable pulls the chokers and the mainline back down the hill after the logs have been unhooked.

I loved the smell of the cut trees, working in the clean open air, and especially the adventure of walking on branches and tree trunks suspended sometimes twenty feet in the air—relying on the spikes on my "corked" boots and my balance to keep from falling off. We raced one another to wrap our logs fastest, and we raced out of the way in order to get the logs to the tower quickly. We hauled eighty-pound steel pulleys up and down steep brushy hillsides. And we endured cold soaking rains that no rain gear can keep out.

It took periodic reminders to keep us on our toes. Sometimes a thirty-foot log two feet in diameter would somersault in the air after hitting a stump as the log was being pulled up the hill. Sometimes the logs would come unhooked and roll down the slope. Sometimes cables would break under impact, zinging back from the tension. Once we'd been too tired and lazy to get fully out of the way when the chokers were zipping toward us along the ground as the backline pulled them to us. We watched the three cables tangle briefly in some vine maples and the rigging slinger (the man in charge) instantly cried out, "Duck!!!" We all plunged flat to the ground as the cables whipped over us; they might have cut us in two if we'd not ducked fast enough. We should have been waiting farther out, where the chokers couldn't have touched us, but we had let our guard down. You just can't do that, in logging or in climbing.

Wayne and I had a plan to meet in July to fly to the Devil's Thumb, in southeastern Alaska. A magazine article had just come out describing an attempt on its unclimbed 6,000-foot north face (which is still virgin twenty-eight years, thirteen attempts, and two deaths later), and we thought we'd have a go. It was to be my first major quasi-expeditionary climb. Two days before we were to meet, my boss drove out to the logging site where I was sleeping in my truck and told me I needed to call Wayne. After two hours of driving to reach a phone, I called Wayne and learned he was canceling the climb. Devastated, I drank a six-pack of beer and ate a dozen donuts on the drive back. I figured I might as well keep making money while I was at it; I would find something else to climb later. I'd bought a truck and needed to pay it off. Still, I felt like my immediate purpose in life had been removed, leaving me hollow, and a little adrift. Adele was in Colorado working for the Youth Conservation Corps, and without a goal in sight, I suddenly felt lonely.

One afternoon we were all holding the "bells" of our chokers overhead and disentangling a braid of cables when a free-swinging choker bell slammed into my thumb. I bellowed in pain, but kept on setting chokers for two more weeks using my index finger as an opposable thumb and believing that I'd only sprained it badly. But the pain didn't stop, and finally I drove to a city to see a doctor. The X-ray revealed that the thumb had been smashed and that the bone was growing back together in a lump. Without an operation I'd lose motion in the topmost joint. I decided to have the operation not so much because I needed to wiggle the tip of my thumb, but because I hadn't been under the knife since my tonsils had been taken out as a kid, and it seemed like it would be an interesting experience to have. What's more, during six weeks of official recovery I could collect 80 percent of my salary while living with Adele, who by then had returned to Santa Barbara. I was paying half her apartment rent at school so that I could be her roommate during extended visits.

My first full school year without school didn't end up with much to show for it. At first I reveled in shocking people in California by climbing in my cast (the fingers showed through, allowing me to face-climb, but because the cast encased my wrist it looked like the damage was much worse than it really was). When the cast came off I went back to work in Washington for a few months before returning to Santa Barbara. I wrote to Pakistan for their expedition application forms because I wanted to climb a striking line on Paiju Peak; this expedition would come in 1980 after I returned from Europe, where Adele was going to spend her junior year in France. In Europe I planned to climb my heart out. First I would repeat all of Dad's big routes, then I'd finish his Direct line on the Eiger. After that I would do new routes of my own.

I also wrote a lot of fiction, just for the fun of it. Most of my stories put protagonists into mountain situations where they had to battle moral conflicts. In one story a climber and his partner disagreed over the safety of continuing their climb. The partner insisted on going up, while the "hero" insisted on going down. Eventually the "hero" was forced to take the rope and descend on his own, condemning his partner to death, a decision that drove him insane. In another story a guide was climbing with his client when a big storm rolled in. The client weakened and clearly wouldn't be able to make it. The guide could have abandoned his client and saved himself. Instead he stayed with his client, and by the time the client died the guide was too exhausted to save himself. In another a young man was trying to finish a route on which his father had disappeared many years before. Eventually the son froze to death next to his father's corpse, which he discovered crouched on a ledge while he was waiting out an electrical storm. I wanted to explore philosophical conundrums, and the morally difficult situations that mountains can throw participants into—much like the sea and the jungle in Joseph Conrad's stories, which I loved.

When looking back at the strange dichotomy between my climbing ambitions and my actual deeds during the 1978–79 academic year, I see the beginning of a lifelong pattern that would bind me to hearth and home (in other words, Adele) because I craved her company. She was not a climber and never would become one, which has always meant that climbing would take me away from her, something I rarely wanted to happen.

But the year wasn't spent entirely in dreaming of future mountain conquests while lounging with my girlfriend in tropical paradise. I spent a bit over a month in Yosemite in the spring, living the Camp 4 ideal of becoming one with the dirt. My skills had improved enough that I was dabbling with 5.11's, though my growth in climbing always has been limited by, among other things, an intense fear of falling. This fear isn't as rational as it sounds. Clearly there are circumstances where falling can do great damage. But in most rock climbing, a properly protected fall is safe. Usually the only result of a tumble is a bruised ego, or maybe a skinned knee. Breaking a bone by hitting a ledge is extremely rare. Actually killing yourself is almost unheard of in roped rock climbing. Mom never had much worry about my doing what she called "Royal Robbins style" climbing. She identified Royal with protected rock climbing without the extra risks of the Alpine world. She either didn't know or chose to ignore that Royal had done many routes that took those additional risks, but on the whole she was right about the relative dangers of rock climbing in a place like Yosemite versus mountain climbing in a place like the Alps. Still, in the final moment before falling off a rock my brain seizes up with terror no matter how safe the situation; I just don't dare to drop onto the rope. Sometimes such fear pushes a climber to the top of something he might otherwise give up on. But more often it switches his focus to the fear itself. You imagine failure, instead of imagining success, and then you fall. It's a classic paradigm for life, made immediate by a surge of adrenaline.

Between rainstorms in the Valley I hooked up with one of the heroes of 1970s American climbing: Tobin Sorenson, a man who did not suffer from the disease of fear. We only did one route together, a three-pitch crack called Moratorium, but I already knew many a Tobin legend. Tobin first made his mark at Tahquitz Rock and its neighbor Suicide Rock. At the latter was a notorious broad jump that only the bold would take, or those whose masculinity was being challenged. The problem was that it launched from one 150-foot clifftop and landed on another one considerably lower, compounded by the fact that the destination sloped at a challenging angle. It required great precision to stick the landing. Most jumpers were happy just to survive. Tobin added an aerial 360-degree pirouette to spice things up. He also climbed a vertical 5.11 crack back when 5.11 was near the top of the difficulty grade—only Tobin did it with the rope tied around his neck. Tobin's antics didn't stop when he discovered Jesus, but he switched his focus to Alpine climbing. During trips to Europe where he smuggled Bibles into Romania, he'd stop by the Alps and make fast and bold ascents wearing his trademark helmet with an arrow pointing upward. People said he had a top-rope from God.

Six months before I met him, Tobin had made the fourth ascent of Dad's route on the Eiger with an equally legendary Scot named Alex MacIntyre. When the Japanese made the route's second ascent (in 1969) they had spent three *months* on the climb and drilled many bolts into Layton Kor's hard aid pitches, which radically reduced the climb's intensity. A Czech team made history in

1976 by making the route's third ascent, but doing it Alpine style in seven days in summer—climbing ability, perfect conditions, and boldness made this possible, but the Japanese bolts and fixed pitons sure didn't hurt. Tobin and Alex climbed the Direct in a mere five days in October. Tobin told me it was the best route in the Alps when climbed as he had done it. He said the trick was to climb in the autumn when the face was sheathed in ice but before the deep snow and intense cold of winter. He had done the entire climb in crampons, and claimed he could climb nearly any 5.10 rock route in crampons. His approach presaged the M-climbing revolution that would begin a decade later and become relatively mainstream in the late 1990s. "M-climbing" means using ice tools (modern ice axes) and crampons to climb "mixed" ice-and-rock routes with little or no actual ice. The picks on the ice tools and the front points on the crampons hook on ledges and slip into cracks, allowing a strange form of hardware-assisted "free climbing."

Dad's route had already been much on my mind, and Tobin's description pretty much locked it in, especially with the revelation that October provided the ideal window to climb it. The coming autumn of 1979 would be the time, then. Not that Tobin's opinions were entirely comforting. Tobin was bold beyond anything that I ever aspired to be. It came as little surprise when two years later his top-rope from heaven reeled him in. He was found dead at the base of the north face of Mount Alberta, a particularly notorious climb, with a single piton clipped to the rope between him and his pack. Evidently he'd been climbing with a rope using his pack to counterweight a risky self-belay system. The piton must have pulled when he fell.

It rained a lot that spring in the Valley, and we spent most of our time dealing with the wet. When Peter von Gaza, a friend from UCSB who had taken over the Mountaineering Association, came up for his spring break, we decided that one way to deal with the rain was to climb something entirely overhanging. The Leaning Tower fit the bill: two of the ten pitches are vertical; the rest overhang, sometimes radically. And it worked. It rained both days we were on the face, and at the bivouac ledge we watched sheets of rain far outside our reach. Finally, on the last move of the last pitch, we pulled into the downpour and instantly were soaked. This was the first wall on which I didn't do almost all the leading: Peter and I alternated pitches in the standard fashion. And I discovered something quite unexpected: when you're 1,000 feet off the deck it's terrifying to jumar a single strand of rope that disappears over an overhang. Our ropes were 11mm, not 7mm like Dad's, but still I just couldn't get myself to trust that the rope wasn't sawing itself in two. I hadn't experienced this before, as I'd done the leading on my previous walls. We had planned to make this climb with three people, but the third had bailed. Once we were several pitches up the route I started wondering if psychologically I even could have done it with three people. When you're just two, the second person cleans the pitons and nuts that were placed by the first. This keeps you close to the rock, even when it overhangs. There is always protection to grab, and you have a greater feeling of safety. But with a team of three, somebody has to jumar a rope hanging free in space. On the Leaning Tower this rope was sometimes twenty or thirty feet away from the wall, as affirmed by the free-hanging haul sack. I'd see the haul sack swing, and I couldn't bear the thought of being out there in its place.

While the terror is real, the danger is mostly an illusion. Eleven-millimeter ropes never break and only rarely cut over edges. There is very little rockfall in Yosemite, and besides, on the Leaning Tower a rock would fall into space, not onto the rope. In steep rock climbing like this you can get scared but not seriously hurt unless you do something stupid. The Alpine climbing world, as Mom well knew, is pretty much the opposite: the illusion is safety. Instead of teaching yourself to believe in equipment and rock that is inherently trustworthy, you have to teach yourself to distrust everything—yet work with it anyway.

An old saying goes that the greatest attribute in a mountaineer is a short memory. By the time you see another mountain, you've forgotten the manifold pains of climbing the previous one. In Alpine climbing the goal is to reach a lovely summit, preferably via an aesthetic ridge, face, or other "natural" line. With luck there may also be good climbing on your route. Since the actual quality of the climbing ("doing the moves") ranks lower than the merits of the feature or the summit, one tends to put up with bad rock and ice that one would never tolerate on a lowland route. Bad rock might be defined as rock that isn't solid enough to dependably hold your weight, or rock that won't hold a nut or piton when you fall on it. Bad rock can also fall on you from above, particularly when sun hits the upper face and softens the bad ice that's holding bad rock together. Good ice will hold screws for protection and won't crumble under your ice axe or crampons. Bad ice breaks.

It's never okay to fall on bad rock or bad ice since you don't know when you'll stop. In the Alpine world it's very hard to get home with a damaged body, especially because some of the primary attractions of a climb are that it's big, high, and remote. In Alpine climbing you're generally trying to cover a great distance in a short time (to avoid a bivouac, to avoid a storm, to avoid the sun warming ice above you). To save time you tend to not place as much protection even when the rock and ice are good enough to hold it. In any case you probably don't have much equipment with you because you're trying to save weight so you can move faster. And therefore if you do fall the distance is greater. And because Alpine rock generally isn't as steep as pure rock-climbing rock, and mountains tend to have more ledges, the chance of hitting hard enough to break a bone is pretty good. As another old saying goes, it's not the fall that hurts, it's the landing. If you fall 100 feet from an overhang on the Leaning Tower and the elasticity in the rope catches you gently in midair, only your nerves will be shot. If you slide 10 feet down an easy slab and slam into a ledge with your crampons on, your ankle could break. In the mountains most of us climb at a lower technical standard than we do on our local crag. This tends to make us feel safe even with an ankle-breaking ledge just below. But there are many things that can make you fall besides pure difficulty: a falling rock can crack your helmet; you can be exhausted from the altitude and from climbing since 3 a.m.; maybe you had a hard time sleeping on the tiny sloping bivouac ledge and now you're doing the stupid things that sleepy people do: tripping on your shoelaces or catching a crampon in your pant leg or dropping your protection or not noticing a dimple in the snow that indicates a hidden crevasse.

But the danger from falling is just a small part of a mountain's web of illusions. There's the weather, which may be crisp and blue in the morning and sizzling with electricity or frozen with blowing snow in the afternoon. There's the snowfield that looks soft and beautiful from a distance and cuts loose into an avalanche when you step on it. There's the distance to the summit, which seems so close in the spell of the morning's foreshortening magic, and seems bitterly unattainable as exhaustion closes in and the sun stretches into the horizon. There's the glacier that seems all smooth and white and then collapses to reveal a monstrous crevasse underneath. There's the wall of ice above that hasn't dropped any chunks in days and suddenly crumbles in a flash flood of cubic bowling balls. In short, there's pretty much every danger you can imagine, and the trick is to imagine which apply to your climb and how to avoid them while still doing the climb.

To an alpinist, all these things are attractive. A true alpinist follows the Siren's call because he loves to dance with her and believes he can escape her clutches afterward. Depending on the level at which one likes to play, much of the thrill of our game is prancing through the vertical minefield in a jolly test of cunning, bravery, and physical prowess. An alpinist can't specialize exclusively in any one discipline—rock, ice, crack, face, steep, slab—because he'll face all of these and more. A little apprehension quickens his pulse and adds value to his sense of accomplishment. But excess angst makes him think too much of unpleasant alternatives, so he bottles his fears as best he can.

There is another road to becoming a mountaineer: a passion for raw natural beauty. A mountaineer doesn't necessarily love mountain splendor any more than does a balcony sitter in a Swiss chalet. But the mountaineer also loves being inside that beauty, being a part of its panoramic, vertiginous, elemental power. And we find that the challenges of getting there, both physical and mental, have sharpened our senses. On a good day, the air feels brilliant and crystalline and your eyes see crisply, even insightfully. On a bad day you feel Earth rage and you never forget her splendor.

Love of challenge, love of beauty, and tolerance for risk (or love thereof)—all rule the world of mountaineers and alpinists. Each of us mixes these ingredients to his personal taste, and we can all find similar satisfaction despite wildly diverging levels of skill and bravery.

Finally, we climb to be with our partners, who, if we're fortunate, are somehow more than simply friends. We're teammates, bonded by the "brotherhood of the rope." We help one another, need one another, and make one another laugh. We become close through sharing intense experiences, the way couples are said to feel closer after seeing a scary movie. Our sport isn't performed in a few of hours of individual effort, nor are we competing against one another. Instead we're working together over the long haul, eventually sharing a triumph—or at least a valiant effort—that we could only have achieved together.

These days climbers hate the term "conquest" when used with mountains, and in general we resist battle analogies. We never defeat a mountain; we only defeat the things inside ourselves that would keep us from climbing the mountain.

Of course it's not all a metaphysical morality tale. It can also be a heck of a lot of fun.

For all these reasons I considered myself a mountaineer more than just a climber. I had big plans for the coming summer to climb real mountains in the Canadian Rockies. These peaks would train me for Adele's and my year in Europe. At the close of the school year, I drove Adele home to Colorado, where she would spend her third summer building campgrounds and trails with the Youth Conservation Corps, this time as a crew leader. From there she'd fly across the Atlantic to Pau and then Paris to spend her junior year studying at French universities. I would use her pads as home bases while I climbed in the Alps. First priority on my post–Canadian Rockies Alps agenda: the Eiger in late September or October.

FOURTEEN

MOUNTAIN GUIDE

I **PULLED** the car to the side of the road and gaped. A few miles later I did it again, and then again every few miles thereafter. Thrusting out of the ground north of Banff, Alberta, were the most magnificent mountains I'd seen since the Alps. To a climber, driving from Banff to Jasper is like watching a great parade go by and knowing you can jump on any of the floats, each of which is an adventurous world of its own. Glaciers plunge over multithousand-foot cliffs, while huge ice faces reflect the morning sun. On the seat beside me lay an open copy of Chris Jones's masterpiece, *Climbing in North America*. Chris brings to life the pioneering climbers and the places they discovered and transformed; his book had become my bible during my tumble into climbing obsession. And of all the stories in this book, the ones that grabbed me hardest took place in the mountains right alongside this road. To a mountaineer, this drive is so much more than pretty scenery.

I arrived in Jasper expecting Peter von Gaza to be waiting for me, or to arrive shortly after. He wasn't there, and a telephone call to Adele revealed he wouldn't be coming, at least not for a while. But the famous Rockies clouds were parting and the peaks looked perfect. My heart was already set on the highest summit of them all: Mount Robson. At 12,972 feet, Robson sits just west of the north end of the Banff-Jasper picket line of peaks. I hadn't seen it yet, and in fact it has a reputation for not being seeable. I'd read that it could only be viewed from the highway for a total of two weeks per year. West of the crest of the Rockies, Robson forms a bowsprit against British Columbia's many wet storm fronts. And even when BC dries out, Robson is so big and isolated that it generates its own weather. On both counts—bowsprit and self-generating weather—Mount Robson is much like the Eiger. The other thing Robson shares with the Eiger is a reputation for being built out of the worst rock in a notoriously loose mountain range. Still, Robson has what a climber wants: it is the tallest in the land, which strokes our egos when we've climbed it; and all routes are technical, which means only real climbers can get up it, further stroking our egos. It also has a magnificent climbing history even from before its first ascent by the great Canadian Rockies pioneer, the Swiss guide Conrad Kain, in 1913. Each of its ridges is renowned and even infamous, from the Emperor Ridge's long line of ice pillars that have to be bypassed one after the other as a climber weaves his way along the knife-edged crest of two great faces, to the Wishbone Arête that steeply cleaves the massive south face via multiple bands of supremely loose rock.

Robson seemed like perfect Eiger training. Except that I had no partner.

While wondering what to do, I wandered into the Jasper weather station. As with the Alps, the first thing you need to know in the Canadian Rockies is the weather forecast—not that you can depend on it for long, but it helps for making short-term plans. I asked about conditions on Mount Robson. The person at the desk was a climber, or at least familiar with them.

"You should have been here a month ago," he said. "We had a great spell of weather then. But it's been snowing for most of the last three weeks, and it's not looking good for the next few days. No one has climbed Robson yet this year."

It was July 19. There was still plenty of time in the summer for the pattern to change. And I'd studied the guidebook, so I knew there was a hut at roughly 8,500 feet on the south side and that the route above the hut was the easiest on the mountain: a little bit of technical rock and a lot of moderate rock, ice, and snow. Being south-facing, the snow would melt off or solidify fast if the sun came out, as it seemed to be doing now. The solution was obvious: Hike to the hut with lots of food. Wait to see what happens while enjoying a good book in a cozy mountain shelter. Go up if the weather stays nice. That night I bivouacked in the bushes in the lower valley (not recommended on account of grizzlies), and the next day "hiked" up, up, up almost 6,000 vertical feet of the steepest quasi-trail this side of technical climbing. Trees could only cling to the lower elevations, though a few gnarly evergreens managed to take root all the way to perhaps 7,000 feet, providing the occasional something to grab hold of. If it weren't that the rock had crumbled to dirt, the official climb would begin somewhere near the valley floor.

By the afternoon, though, I'd reached the Forster Hut. The tiny wooden hut sits on a gravel terrace poised in what feels like the center of the mountain. The lower Wishbone Arête plunged two or three thousand feet below on the left. Above, the upper mountain quickly disappeared into cloud, but I could hear the booms and crashes of active glaciers. I unpacked my food staples—peanut butter and jelly—and prepared to see what the weather had in mind.

All the next day the clouds rose just high enough to tease, then dropped again to hide their queen. Up enough for me to see the first section of the rocky route above, then down again to say not yet. Up again to reveal where the rock turned to snow with rocky ridges, then down again to say maybe later. By afternoon I'd seen high hanging glaciers, and I knew where I'd have to traverse steep rock beneath one. I decided to set the alarm for 1 a.m. and see what the night revealed.

When I poked my head out the door, a thousand stars lighted

the night's black envelope, and the snow-plastered mountain glimmered lightly in their glow. The air felt crisp and inviting, the mountain silent, frozen into place. I suited up. To calm my nerves, I told myself that I could turn back wherever I chose to; the summit was entirely optional. The ruse worked pretty well, and mostly I felt tuned and ready, albeit careful to guard nerves that weren't quite sure if I was up to the test. There was almost 5,000 vertical feet of climbing coming up on a bigger and more legendary mountain than anything I'd yet experienced, and I was not (and never would become) a solo climber with a solo climber's deep inner faith in himself. But I could always turn tail—I mean, turn back.

Summer dawn breaks slowly at this latitude, and the first few thousand feet passed under my crampons in the starlit dark and then the pre-sun gray. Just before the hanging glacier I turned around to see my footprints along a knife-edged ridge—each foot sticking to its own side, my safety ensured because if a foot slipped I'd catch the ridge in my crotch. The sun finally found me scampering up hard windblown snow on the summit ridge. At the top I was beside myself with joy. I had defeated my nerves and climbed the biggest mountain in my life, the tallest in this realm. The panorama wrapped endless mountains and a vastness of wilderness. The only sign of man was a tiny thread 10,000 feet below: the two-lane road to Jasper. And I was the first person to stand here in a year. Self-portrait photos reveal a Pacific-sized grin under Dad's Peruvian hat.

The snow had softened by the time I started the descent, and I punched through the surface crust as I plunge-stepped downward, an ice axe in each hand. I was headed for the top of an ice cliff, which I'd skirt on the right during the descent. My eyes were searching for the route ahead when suddenly two snowballs came bouncing down to my right, and then I felt one hit me on the back of the head. Without looking or thinking, I plunged my axes full-shaft into the snow and lay flat on my stomach below them, holding on. An instant later I could feel the avalanche sweeping over me. It was a surface-snow slide that covered me like a wet blanket, and it dragged and plucked at me as it slid over my back. I had time to start worrying about air when finally it slid past, leaving me intact and in place. Below I could see it sliding toward and then over the cliff. I jumped up and started running down, before another had a chance to take me with it.

That afternoon I walked back into the Jasper weather station.

"Why aren't you on Robson?" the condescending voice rang out. "The weather is perfect!"

"Already climbed it," said I, trying to disguise my pride.

I asked about partners again, and this time the weatherman gave me the address of his friend Chuck Hospidales.

Chuck and I hit it off immediately. A first-generation Canadian of Venezuelan parentage, Chuck was dark, a bit shorter than I, and overflowing with enthusiasm. Talk flowed, plans made themselves, and he invited me to settle on his couch. Only there wasn't to be much settling, because the next two weeks presented an unrelenting series of punishingly clear days. Chuck and I developed a pattern of spending a presummit night with little if any sleep thanks to 1 a.m. starts, followed by postsummit fourteen-hour sleeping binges. We'd wake to find the sky still clear, forcing us to get up at 1 a.m. the next morning to climb yet another peak. It just wouldn't do to waste the most precious commodity in the Canadian Rockies: sunshine.

On the north face of Mount Athabasca, which we climbed after a day of crag climbing, we established that I would do all the leading. Though Chuck had been climbing for several years—at least as long as my return to the sport—I was more experienced, more driven, and stronger. I was twenty-three and he about a year my junior. On Athabasca we learned about 55-degree icefields. On the Photo Finish Route of Andromeda we learned about Rockies "rock" when the only piece of protection I could get was a hand-placed piton under a loose stone—this is what's called "psychological protection," meaning that it makes you feel better to see a piton in the rock even if you know that it won't hold; by feeling better you can continue the climb, whereas if reason ruled you'd turn back. Of course, there's sometimes a chance that psychological pro would actually hold a fall; you wouldn't bet money on it, but sometimes you bet your life.

We then turned to Mount Robson. I really wanted to climb the north face, but there was still a lot of snow on the mountain and I didn't want to turn what had been called the greatest ice face in the Rockies into a mere snow slog. Instead we settled on the Wishbone Arête because it is such a stunningly beautiful line, and because we figured it must be good since it was in the popular book *Fifty Classic Climbs of North America.* Chuck was nervous; living nearby, he had been doubly steeped in Robson's reputation. The route was also big, much bigger than our previous climbs together. As we hiked in we noticed some high thin clouds for the first time in a week, which quickly metamorphosed into a mackerel formation. The clouds were enough for Chuck to call the climb off for himself. I wasn't convinced the weather would turn serious, and besides, there was a big ledge system almost halfway up the arête that offers a traversing escape to the Forster Hut if necessary (in fact, using the ledge in the reverse direction is a common approach to the Wishbone, but it avoids lots of climbing on the logical direct line). I thought it worth climbing until the weather showed what it really had in mind. So I started up on my own while Chuck waited in the valley. I felt really keen to solo the Wishbone, as it would clearly be my proudest achievement yet. But without a partner it felt like my backbone had turned to jelly. Suddenly the mountain swelled in size and danger, and my own competence felt undependable. After a few hours of scrambling I reached the first limestone band that required actual climbing. To make it safe enough for my comfort, I would have to improvise a self-belaying system, which I'd never done. I paused there for a long time, trying to figure out how to belay myself, how hard the climbing would be, how serious the mackerel skies were, how much nerve and skill

I actually had under my veneer of ambition. After about an hour, I decided the weather was too iffy for me to commit to this next bit of climbing, which looked significantly harder than I'd anticipated. At least that's the excuse I settled on as I hiked back down the mountain.

The weather wasn't changing that day, so Chuck and I decided to have a go at the smaller nearby peak, Mount Whitehorn, the next. Dawn broke as we approached the glacier, revealing thick clouds where our peak should be. It was the first unpleasant weather I'd seen since arriving in the Rockies, and we were glad to have called off the Wishbone. Someone mentioned pizza in Chuck's apartment, and immediately we turned tail for Jasper.

In just over a week, Chuck and I had become best friends. I loved his intelligence and enthusiasm, and it seemed we could talk forever or not at all, as the mood struck us. We made plans that he would drive back to Colorado with me, where we'd continue our climbing rampage. Chuck's skills were not up to mine, but experience would change that. I'd always based my partnerships on friendship, nothing else. I just loved being with Chuck, and there was so much more we could do together. I couldn't wait to introduce him to Adele, and vice versa.

By the time we got back to Jasper the sky was blue and the forecast good. The next morning Chuck felt a shift in mood and declared himself ready for the big climb. We bought more food and drove back to Robson. The limestone band that had stopped me went easily with the courage of a rope on my waist, and the rest of the day consisted mostly of roped scrambling on loose shale. Chuck and I had so far been climbing mostly-ice routes together, and the Wishbone's stacked dinner plates of rotten limestone shale was not to Chuck's liking. We were very glad to finally reach the big terrace almost halfway up, where we pulled out the bivouac gear. Squeezing into my one-man bivouac sack, we spooned to fit the cramped quarters.

The next day would be the big one. There was supposed to be

some 5.6 climbing and then lots of ice to the summit. Light breezes ruffling the bivy sack and a brilliantly clear sky added to the cold, but most of our chill came from apprehension of what the morrow would bring. Chuck slept poorly, and I not much better given the cramped arrangements.

We reached the crux rock climbing not long after daybreak, and kept moving upward at a steady but slow pace. Almost the entire mountain seemed to be a consistency halfway between scree and rock, with runnels of rotten ice for diversity. We moved together and continuously, with me ahead placing occasional bits of protection when the opportunity arose, and Chuck cleaning the gear as he passed it. As we got higher Chuck's pace slowed even more. He'd complain of the bad climbing and I'd respond, half joking and half to encourage him to suck it up, "You'll live." A little while later he'd complain about being tired and I'd respond again, "You'll live." He'd complain about how much farther we still had to go and I'd respond as usual, "You'll live." It's not that I didn't care; in fact, we stopped for a while to brew up and to give Chuck a good rest. It's just that I didn't have much use for complaining. In climbing as in life one must get on with what needs doing; in the end we'll look back on the small sufferings and laugh and feel proud of having overcome them.

Finally we got high enough that the rubbled ridge had gathered a permanent coating of glassy ice. At last we'd found something worth climbing! The upper Wishbone had many of the *gendarmes* of ice that made the Emperor Ridge so famous, and for nine ropelengths we wove among them. Sometimes I'd try turning an ice pinnacle on the right and find my passage blocked by vertical ice, so I'd sneak back around to the left where a 70-degree funnel led to the next *gendarme*. That one in turn might block me on the left but go on the right. The route finding was devious, and the quality of the ice superb. It seemed like we'd spent a day and a half on a scruffy approach to finally reach the actual climbing route. But even from here it was a long ways to the summit, and we weren't moving fast enough, so when the opportunity presented itself just below the summit to traverse right to the ridge I'd climbed two weeks earlier, I took it. An hour later we were high-fiving each other on the summit. Chuck beamed with pride at having climbed the mountain; I couldn't quite believe I'd done it twice in two weeks. We had only one concern in the world: getting down. The perfect weather hadn't broken in any way, but the sun insisted on keeping its own schedule. We had to get on with the descent, and fast.

We were headed to the Forster Hut for the night, but there were two ways to get there. The obvious way was to retrace my route of two weeks before, the standard Schwarz Ledges south-face route. The other option was to take the Hourglass Route down. The Hourglass had the advantage of being more direct. It had the disadvantage of passing under a long ice cliff, and the guidebook warned of falling seracs as bits of the hanging glacier calve off. We decided that the Hourglass would be more likely to get us down before dark. We would use the standard mountaineer's trick in realms of falling rock and ice: speed. The goal is to spend the minimum amount of time in the danger zone. We needed to speed up anyway to avoid another night in the open.

Two rappels took us down the upper couloir, and then the terrain became less steep in a web of ledges and snow patches that required weaving through to find the best line. I left Chuck to pull the rope from the last rappel while I struck out to scout the route. I planned to stop if anything required another rappel. I kept moving slowly downward as Chuck followed, frequently directing him to go left or right to stay on the track I'd chosen. The sun had dropped below the horizon and dusk cloaked the valley below. I kept looking up nervously to the wall of ice above us, the underside of Robson's summit glacier. Just two weeks earlier I'd watched the avalanche that had washed over me plunge down this very ice cliff; there was debris all around from more recent slides and icefalls.

"C'mon, Chuck! We've got to keep moving!"

An eight- or ten-foot band of steep rock crossed below. I waited on top for a bit, then faced inward and climbed down it to see how it would go. The holds were solid and secure and led to a snowy ledge about five feet wide. I walked along the ledge briefly and could see that it led to a snowfield, which in turn led to the glacier below. This was it, the end of difficulties. From here it could turn dark and we could just shuffle along until we reached the hut. I returned to where I'd descended the little cliff band and directed Chuck toward me.

His crampons were ten feet above me as he studied the problem.

"There's a good foothold just down there," I said, pointing. "And good handholds at about knee level."

He found those, and then started pawing for more handholds in the deepening dusk.

"The handhold is right there," I said. "Can't you feel it?"

"No, I can't!" he whimpered.

And then panic gripped his voice as he moaned "Oh no!" and fell backward. I lunged at him and touched his coat but couldn't get my fingers on it. I thought he'd stop on the ledge I was standing on, but instead he bounced right off.

"Ohmygod, ohmygod, ohmygod!" I screamed as sparks flew into the dusk each time Chuck's crampons hit rock. I heard whimpering noises through my screams, then nothing more as Chuck was swallowed by darkness.

In stunned disbelief I ran along the ledge to the snowfield, ran down the forty-five-degree slope, and ran along the bottom of the cliff. There was a dark mass on the snow and I ran to it. Chuck lay face up. His face was dark blue. He was dead. I just knew it. He'd fallen more than 500 feet. I knew he'd be dead before I even reached him. And then his lifeless body stared up all blue, confirming my belief. I should have checked for vital signs just in case, but it didn't even cross my mind. Instead, I freaked. I was filled with a great swirl of empty numb nothingness, wild anxious dread, and horrific grief for the person who in a mere two weeks had become my best friend, whom I'd come to love like a younger brother. I had to move, to get out of there, to get to people, to escape, to get away. I ran across the glacier to the ridge that would lead to the hut.

The glacier held crevasses, but I wasn't thinking rationally. My legs popped through the snow and I felt my feet waving in empty space. I pulled out and kept running. I wasn't a thinking, reasoning human, I was an animal in panic heedlessly dashing across a busy road.

I could see lights in the hut below and used them to help guide me once I'd reached dirt on the other side of the glacier. Two people were brewing tea or dinner when I burst into their cocoon. After quickly telling them that my partner had fallen, I crawled into a bunk to wrestle with my demons. Eventually I wrote something in the hut log, a short passage that tried to distill what had just happened. Twenty-five years later the president of the Alpine Club of Canada sent me a copy of the journal pages. After describing the event and praising Chuck as the kindest and most considerate person I had ever known, the account concluded:

> Having lost my father on a 4,000 ft fall, and now watching Chuck die, I think I am coming to the conclusion that climbing is a bit too serious a game. Chuck was the most safety conscious and careful climber I knew. Were it not for my superior skill and impatience, I am sure that he would have been roped. But then with a rope we might have been slow enough to fall victim to one of the icefalls an earlier party mentioned [in this logbook]. I think too many people are dying in the mountains, are they worth it?

I left the hut quietly before dawn, before the others were up. First I went to the ranger station, and they sent me to the British Columbia police, where I was interviewed in depth about the accident. They then flew me in a helicopter to point out the body's location, and minutes later a ranger was dangling from a long line under the helicopter on his way to the mountain to pick up Chuck. I stopped by the weather station to tell Chuck's friend, whom I'd first met just two and a half weeks before—a lifetime, another world. And then I was out of there, driving south to Colorado, still in a daze, thinking only of escape, replaying those final moments over and over in my head.

After a few hours of driving I called Mom. I remember gasping, crying, and the feeling that if it had been me who had fallen she might not have survived the news.

Adele wondered why I'd arrived at her dorm in Fort Collins a day early, and where was Chuck, who was supposed to come down with me? I said I'd explain later. She asked if I'd seen a hailstorm a few hours before and I said yeah, it was amazing. Then she pulled a baseball-sized hailstone out of the freezer, and showed me the broken windows and dented cars, which revealed a storm far worse than what I'd driven through. Finally, after all the reunion rituals were over, I lay in her arms and sobbed out the story.

I hung around Fort Collins for a few days, wondering what to do. What I should have done was call Chuck's parents, but I didn't. Chuck had told me that his parents were divorced and he felt estranged from them. Twenty-eight years later, and a parent myself, I know that feelings of estrangement come and go, and love from parents lasts forever. I should have called. Ten months later Chuck's father reached me by phone in Paris. I wrote him a long letter and we talked about meeting when I returned to America. It was the last we spoke.

Adele's work for the Youth Conservation Corps took her almost daily to Estes Park, the town at the entrance to Rocky Mountain National Park. One day I dropped in at Komito Boots, headquarters for the local climbing scene. Despite my protestations about climbing, I was already making the distinction between the Alpine world—where one is forced to do things like move fast and unroped under ice cliffs—and the rock world, where one has more control over the variables and can choose to stay safe. My Alpine climbing dreams had crumbled, and in particular my dream for the Eiger. Paiju Peak in Pakistan was out, too. I vowed to stick to safe rock, and maybe some protectable ice. To a certain extent I managed to keep those vows for twenty years, despite a few exceptions, mostly on skis.

When I wandered into Komito Boots in early August I had no idea how much this place would change my life. It started when Michael Covington offered me a job teaching and guiding in Rocky Mountain National Park. Michael's Fantasy Ridge Mountain Guides was headquartered on the upstairs floor of Komito Boots, and nearly all the serious local climbers worked for Michael or Komito off and on, depending on seasonal business (on one side of the relationship) and need for money (on the other side). Timing didn't always work out between the two, as the clients came in the middle of summer, which is exactly when the climbing is too good to miss. So Michael needed a guide-in-training, and there I was. I explained to him about the recent death of my partner, and how I had given up on Alpine mountaineering. From Michael's perspective, this would only make me a better guide, more sensitive to the safety of my clients. Michael was one of the leading American Alpine climbers of that time, and losing friends in the mountains came with the territory for him. So I moved into a gear storage room/bedroom next to the Fantasy Ridge office, and fell in love with the entire ambience of the place, from the smell of oiled leather and grinding rubber downstairs, to the wood rafters and comfortable atmosphere upstairs after the clients had returned to their hotels. Mostly, though, it was the employees both upstairs and downstairs that I fell in love with, and after work and on days off we'd go climbing—almost every single day, and usually until dark. At night we'd drink beer, smoke pot, and go to bed early to prepare for the next early morning, whether it would be to climb with clients or with friends. And my new friends were the elite of Colorado's climbing community, the people I was reading about in magazines and books—including my precious *Climbing in North America.*

This was the good life, the best I'd ever had, and soon I saw how to harness it. At the time there was no guide certification program in America (unlike Europe), but Michael had instituted his own version. At first, an aspirant guide apprenticed under more experienced guides, and after five seasons of work (summers and winters mostly), one could become a full guide. This usually took two to three years. The pay scale increased as a full guide, but that didn't motivate me. I viewed full guide status as akin to getting a college degree: the symbolic completion of a process, after which I could move on. It was the perfect excuse to delay graduate school by yet another year.

The more I circulated among climbers, the more it turned out that people knew my name before meeting me. One day a local climbing ranger gave me a ride in his car. When I introduced myself, he responded, "Back from the dead, I see." His crimson blush when he found out that it was my dad he was thinking of revealed the innocence of his joke. The line that bothered me more, except that I was growing increasingly used to hearing it, was the completely straight question: "Are you any relation to the *real* John Harlin?" Ah, well, yes, the real one would be my father. It stung doubly because now I'd fallen in with a crowd that was replete with *real* names, and they knew that Dad had been one of their ilk. I felt the burn of judgment from these rock stars, though in hindsight I realize that to them my name didn't matter all that much—either I climbed well or I didn't, whatever my heritage. The judgment mattered a great deal to me, though. I felt that my name opened the door to their expectations, but my performance could slam it back in my face. Because my return to climbing had come fairly recently and had been far from full-time, I still had a ways to go before reaching their standard. Two or three more years while earning Full Guide status should just about do it, or so I thought.

FIFTEEN

THE LESSONS OF WADD

" S O , John Harlin, have you come to climb the Eiger?" The question rang out over the din of a German beer garden packed full of climbers taking shelter from the drizzle outside. I was climbing with Reinhard Karl in the Pfalz, a collection of sandstone towers near the French border, and my name had apparently drifted from table to table until someone finally stood up to shout the question from the other side of the room. It felt like a blow to my gut. Climbing the Eiger was exactly what I had planned to do. My ego desperately wanted to call back, "Damn right I'm here to climb the Eiger." It was clear that this person—and in my mind, all these people—were wondering, "Is he man enough to fill his father's shoes, or is he not?" But all I could do was feel my face flush, look down into my beer, and mumble, "No."

This was my first return to Europe since we'd packed our bags in 1966, thirteen years earlier. Because I'd ruled out climbing in the Alps, there had been no need to arrive in time for the autumn Eiger window. Instead I let Adele ground herself in her junior-year-abroad program, which spent the first half of the school year in southern France and the second half in Paris. I had stayed with my mother in Rhode Island for a couple of months before joining Adele at the Université de Pau. Her small apartments in Pau and later in Paris became my primary home bases, while my secondary bases were with Reinhard and his wife, Eva Altmeier, in Heidelberg and at their weekend cottage near the Pfalz.

I'd met Reinhard in Estes Park just after the guiding season ended. He was the star German alpinist of his day, with a budding Himalayan career, but my overwhelming impression of Reinhard was of his unquenchable enthusiasm. He simply loved the world, especially the steep-sided parts of it, with more passion than anyone I'd known. I think his greatest secret for climbing hard was sheer fervor: not even a mountain could resist his zeal. The fact that he could crank sets of one-armed pull-ups didn't hurt, nor that his mind could grasp any situation between heartbeats. Reinhard had grown up under cars in a mechanic's shop thinking the world was small. Then he discovered the mountains and he swelled to fill them. He never repaired a car again, not even his own. Against all the odds, he was making a good living as a writer and photographer, sharing his vision with others.

Reinhard had climbed the Eiger, as had nearly every serious alpinist; it was, after all, a rite of passage for the budding hardcore—a ticket to being treated seriously. He understood the brakes I'd put on my mountain goals, though he wouldn't consider making the same decision. Losing friends in the mountains is also a rite of passage; it simply comes with the territory, and Reinhard had lost several. I was the only person I knew who had quit—or even altered his goals—for a parent's sake; in fact, I hadn't met a climber who thought much about someone else's apprehensions, family or otherwise. I'm sure Reinhard found my self-imposed restrictions a little incomprehensible, but he was too considerate to rub my nose in them.

One day in the Pfalz we were joined by Reinhard's best friend, Nico Mailänder, a graduate student in philosophy, and his American wife, Liz Klobusicky. Nico had recently spent a hellish two months worrying about Liz. She had been on a team attempting Annapurna as the first all-female team to climb an 8,000-

meter peak, and Nico thought the route (a new one) was far too avalanche-prone and that her teammates were insufficiently skilled for the task at hand. Liz returned home before the team placed two women on the summit—and before two others died in an avalanche. Nico himself had an on-again, off-again relationship with risk, sometimes trusting himself and sometimes not. He wanted to climb the Eiger—maybe someday. He didn't have Reinhard's always-on persona, but instead was more mercurial and questioning; I sensed that he fully understood my situation. We hit it off so well that soon I was also basing out of Nico and Liz's apartment, and traveling with him to limestone cliffs in southern France.

Adele was undoubtedly relieved that I wasn't spending all my time hanging around her apartments waiting for her to come home, as this was perhaps the formative year of her rapidly expanding world. She had arrived with basic classroom French spoken in an American accent, and in a few months of intense effort strangers were confusing her for a Francophone of mysterious origin. She was having the time of her life.

That spring of 1980, when Adele and I made a pilgrimage to Grindelwald and stared up 10,000 vertical feet to the summit of the Eiger, I felt like a religious devotee at a sacred shrine. Here at last was the mountain that had played such a pivotal role in my family's life and in my recent ambition. The north face towered in the clouds—the place where so many epic campaigns of climbing history had been fought. There was no reason for me to fear the mountain: it couldn't hurt me because I knew I wasn't going to touch it. And yet, I wondered—strictly to myself—how would I do up there? How would it feel to have climbed it?

Adele returned to Santa Barbara in the autumn for her final year of school. I guided both summer and winter seasons in Colorado, and traveled to climbing areas researching a coffee-table book that I wanted to write and photograph. I was calling it *Sand, Surf, and Storm* to embrace the desert, the coast, and the mountains of the Lower 48. I hadn't found a publisher, but *Climbing* magazine had agreed to a series of articles profiling different areas. Ensconced in the attic of Komito Boots I could write in the evening after climbing all day, allowing me to save just enough money to live out of my truck when on the road. I was as happy as I'd ever been. Michael was going to make me "chief guide" the coming summer despite my relative inexperience, and Adele was planning to move in with me as soon as she graduated. If my luck held and she didn't get cold feet, we'd marry at the end of the summer.

On October 3, 1981, we tied the knot in an aspen grove above the cabin we'd moved in to. Adele was twenty-two, and I twenty-five. Reinhard and Eva stood in the gently falling snow as Steve Komito handed me Adele's ring, and our wolf-hybrid puppy, Lupine, dug a hole at our feet. People asked us about children, and we said we'd think about that when Lupine died of old age.

Then we set about trying to make a living in Estes Park. It was a hard year. That summer while Michael was guiding on De-nali, my fellow guides and I had talked about buying the Rocky Mountain National Park guiding concession from him. We even drew up articles of incorporation for a nonprofit Mountain Guides Association as an umbrella business, while some of us would run individual components. I was named president of the Association, and I'd be in charge of developing a ski-mountaineering branch of the company. But the whole thing fell apart when one of the key players, a born-and-raised local, decided to make an end-run and buy the concession and Michael's business for himself. I felt deeply wounded; a friend had betrayed something all of us had worked hard to pull off together. I probably could have worked for him, but I was too embittered for that. Suddenly the Park was off limits to my guiding, and the whole communal feeling of the town's climbing community fell apart for me. I wrote to Peter Boardman, who had taken over Dad's climbing school after Dougal's death— now renamed the International School of Mountaineering, or ISM. I was hoping that he might be interested in having the founder's son work for him, but he wrote back that the school now required guides to be fully certified as per European rules, something that wasn't available in the States. Not long after, Peter left on expedition to Everest, where he disappeared doing a new route on its northeast ridge.

It would have been the logical time to apply to graduate school and begin the life in science I still expected for myself. But I still had unfinished business in the climbing world, which now included business itself. I wasn't about to give up on this new world without accomplishing some kind of goal. The Park wasn't actually that good for skiing anyway—it was too cold and windy, and the snow too sparse—and the ideas I had for my ski business included the Alps and other mountain ranges as much as they did the Rockies, let alone Rocky Mountain National Park. A friend and I talked the Warren Miller ski film company into shooting us skiing Orizaba that winter, an 18,500-foot volcano in Mexico that's the third highest peak in North America. It was an easy ski, merely high, but the drive up remote dirt roads in Mexico felt exotic. Warren Miller used the footage for his movie *SnoWonder,* but the deal for me was that I would get a copy of the raw film and splice it together into something I could take on a lecture tour, earning some money and promoting my new company, Ski-Mountaineering Unlimited. I had also been approached by Chockstone Press and we'd talked about turning the *Sand, Surf, and Storm* idea into a multivolume series of guidebooks that we'd call *The Climber's Guide to North America.* So there were projects to resolve, and I still had time. After all, I thought, Mom had been thirty-six when she got her Ph.D. That gave me a decade to wrap up mine. I knew I would enjoy having built a business and written some books before I submerged myself in academia.

Adele's sights were firmly set on being a working artist, and her watercolors already graced a Colorado gallery. But selling paintings was no more lucrative than my writing or my dreams of a ski-guiding business; to make ends meet, Adele waitressed. But not even that was working, as Estes Park in winter had few residents outside the graveyard, and no tourists. We moved to Boulder in the spring, where I took odd jobs to fit around my guiding, writing, traveling, and lecturing. We converted a Quonset hut into Adele's studio and my office, and we pieced our finances together as best we could.

In addition to my articles about diverse climbing areas, *Climbing* magazine reprinted Dad's *American Alpine Journal* story about the Dru with Royal. In response to my introduction, many people wrote to tell me they'd love to see a book of Dad's writing. But when I sent *Introspection Through Adventure* to a publisher—the manuscript that Mom had worked so hard to pull together in 1966—I was told that Dad's writings were too brief and disjointed; they needed the author's hand to bring it into shape, not his son's. At about that time, in 1982, Dad's friend who had helped with the audio recordings during the 1966 climb came to my lecture for the American Alpine Club in New York. David Swanson said he had a copy of those recordings as well as a copy of Dad's film from the Direct, which he'd had blown up from Super 8 to 16mm. David soon mailed me those materials, and I combined them with Dad's slides, some of his writing, and my own historical research to make a lecture on the Eiger Direct that I also took on tour around the country. Night after night I would hear Dad's final words over the radio, "We're going to be working awfully hard and I don't know if we're going to be able to make that broadcast." Sometimes I choked up; sometimes I just swallowed hard and went on with the talk. But I always felt a connection to his voice issuing from the auditorium's speakers while images of the Eiger filled the screen.

I was at my computer in Boulder when Liz Klobusicky called. A serac had fallen onto Reinhard's tent on Cho Oyu in Tibet, crushing him in his sleep. Adele and I hugged each other and cried. Reinhard, of all people, was the most impossible to imagine dead. It seemed absurd that such vitality could vanish. So utterly wrong—so devastatingly heartless. So much like a mountain.

Not long after, an Italian alpinist stopped by our studio-office. Renato Casarotto had already established himself as one of the premier solo climbers in the Alps, and he was now applying his same high style to the Himalaya. British-Canadian climber Roger Marshall stopped by, too, brimming with enthusiasm. Both men caught me in deadline crunches and I couldn't go climbing with them. Both were dead five years later—one on K2 and the other on Everest, alone and without bottled oxygen, true purists.

These people sought me out, I realized, not so much to climb with *me* as to meet the son of the "real" John Harlin. I didn't mind too much, as I still felt honored, and I was glad that Dad was being recognized. Arthur J. Roth's book *Eiger: Wall of Death* was released that year (1982), with a half dozen chapters devoted to Dad ("The Blond God from the Valley"). The British filmmaker Leo Dickinson was in the process of making a movie, *Eiger Solo,* in which he staged an elaborate reenactment of Dad's fall using a flailing person dropped out of a helicopter to simulate Dad's last minutes. A friend of mine from Estes Park made the first American winter ascent during the filming, and he was hired to throw a dummy in Dad's clothing off the mountain for another shot—an unnerving experience for him. It seemed I couldn't get away from the Eiger. Not that I was trying to.

I was still sticking to my vows about Alpine *climbing,* but I hadn't said anything about Alpine *skiing.* I preferred to not think of my adventures as extreme skiing, which had been accurately defined as "If you fall, you die." I preferred the term "steep skiing." And yet, more often than not, I was just a bungled turn away from an unstoppable slide. A Utah telemark skier named Jimmy Katz had heard that I was making some first ski descents in Rocky Mountain National Park and he wondered if he might come over to ski with me. He arrived in May of 1984, and we proceeded to tick off some virgin lines that I'd had my eye on. For me the joy of this type of skiing was in bringing a climber's eye to the sport of skiing—I was much less attracted to a smooth open bowl of good snow than I was to an improbable face where I had to weave around cliffs, places where one had to think about each turn before making it. This was a new concept to Jimmy, as he was not a climber, though he was one of the best skiers I'd ever seen. The first time we climbed up the Notch Couloir on the east face of Longs Peak, Jimmy became so intimidated by the unfamiliar vertical environment (we were hemmed in by cliffs) that we climbed right back down. But after a night back in Boulder, and after my explanation of how we could use a climbing rope to safeguard the most dangerous sections, he was game and we pulled it off.

I knew that this sort of skiing wasn't right, that it violated the spirit of the quiet vow I'd made about alpinism. I told myself that overall I was being a good boy; I was being as careful as I could, and occasional transgressions would have to be forgiven. Mom saw the photos on my lecture circuit and didn't like them one bit, but I assured her these were rare, isolated descents, which they were. Inside I knew this skiing was hypocritical. I had to watch myself, maybe even stop.

Colorado felt perfect to me, but not to Adele. She'd grown up there and left on purpose. Colorado was dead for art as far as she was concerned. For my sake she'd returned temporarily, but our time had run out. New York was the place to be. Accepted into a master of fine arts program at the School of Visual Arts, Adele left at the end of the summer of 1984. I would follow a couple of months later after I'd completed the research for the second volume of my climber's guide, on the Rocky Mountain region. The third volume, conveniently enough, was for the East Coast, so I didn't really mind going back for the two years of her graduate school. Despite my best efforts, I hadn't found enough clients for my ski-guiding business and I let it fizzle.

Starting late in college I often made schedules for upcoming years—how one thing would lead to another, eventually leading to graduate school. Every six months or so I'd revise them to incorporate the new reality. By the time I drove our overloaded pickup truck east (the truck I'd bought while logging in Washington), I'd given up on outlining future years. It seemed pointless, almost ludicrous.

Two years later I'd telemarked the highest peak in Peru (22,205-foot Huascarán), skied a minor peak in Bolivia, and published the first three volumes of my guidebook—all 1,200 pages. There were four more volumes on my list, but I had burned out on poverty. Adele made more money working on the side during graduate school than I had with my writing, lecturing, and occasional guiding. She graduated in 1986 but wasn't willing to leave the New York area until she felt established as an artist; in the meantime, she was working a day job as an artist's studio manager.

I felt lost. I needed to make money, but I didn't know how. Again I thought of my own graduate school, but that would be West, and Adele wanted to be East, and we had no money, and . . . and maybe I'd lost the drive? It bothered me to even think about not becoming a scientist. It was what I'd always known I would be. How could I be thirty-one years old and understand myself less than ever? I'd been working as hard as I could, writing about climbing but climbing little, and it felt like I'd been on a treadmill without a payoff. A friend wanted to raise venture capital for me to start an adventure-travel mail-order clothing company, and I was half tempted if there was a paycheck in it, but that seemed like just another distracting direction. I didn't really know what felt like *me,* only that writing was most of what I'd been doing, albeit with little return.

That's when Eric Perlman telephoned. I'd briefly climbed with Eric a few years earlier in Joshua Tree, California, while I was researching the West Coast volume of my series. He worked part-time as a writer for *Backpacker* magazine, and he told me that one of their editors had just left. He told me that no one on staff actually did the activities in the magazine—backpacking mainly, but also all the other aspects of wilderness travel, including mountaineering, canoeing, skiing, and adventure travel in general. *Backpacker* was the flagship magazine of a little "Wilderness Travel Group" that also included *Ski X-C* and *Adventure Travel* magazines. It was based in New York City. Would I please interview with *Backpacker* so that he'd have someone on staff he could relate to?

I got the job as the new associate editor, and suddenly made twice as much money as I ever had in a year. What's more, I discovered that I loved working with other people, thinking creatively together about the entire range of wilderness activities that had defined my life. *Backpacker* felt like a half step toward the naturalist I had planned to become. Editors were encouraged to write as well, and my first story for the magazine was a sentimental essay on the miserable lives of caribou—much romanticized animals who in fact live desperate lives plagued by every ill the Arctic can throw their way. The essay connected me to my brief foray in after-college fiction, when in addition to my climbing stories I'd written several pieces contrasting the beauty we find in nature with its underlying heartlessness—not as denigration, but as a fuller appreciation of reality versus interpretation.

The most fascinating thing of all was that I was making these wilderness connections from a windowless office on the eleventh floor of a skyscraper above Times Square. The Wilderness Travel Group was owned by CBS Magazines, and the editor in chief enforced a coat-and-tie policy. He himself was partial to three-piece suits. It felt almost surreal to ride the train from Connecticut, where Adele and I lived, to Grand Central Station and then walk across town in my newly bought jacket and tie to ride the elevator to a glorified closet where I edited stories about wilderness. This was the strangest adventure I'd ever had.

Unfortunately, most of the building's inhabitants were not enjoying their own adventures. No sooner had I arrived at *Backpacker* than the president of CBS Magazines made a leveraged buyout of his division, named the new enterprise after himself, and started to sell off or outright dispose of its assets, otherwise known as people. My elevator partners as often as not had tears on their cheeks and pink slips in their briefcases. The main talk among Wilderness Travel Group employees was whether we were small enough to slip under the radar screen of the corporate moguls, and thus be spared the axe.

One day the mail delivered an article manuscript about Colin Fletcher—author of the backpacker's how-to bible *The Complete Walker,* and *The Man Who Walked Through Time.* This article was by far the best piece of writing that had crossed my desk. I called the author, Mark Jenkins, and over the next months we talked about writing, climbing, and the meaning of life. He lived in Laramie, and I discovered that he'd helped to organize a lecture I gave to the University of Wyoming six years earlier. I didn't remember meeting Mark, but I certainly remembered the lecture, as it had been the most successful I'd ever given—maybe three hundred people. Shortly before calling me at *Backpacker,* Mark had spent seventy-seven days without bathing while trying a new route on the north face of Everest, a statistic that never failed to impress. He then sent me a brilliant story he'd written using his experiences on Everest to contrast the gray world of ordinary days against the unlimited horizons of the adventurous life.

One day I exited the elevator to find that the Wilderness Travel Group had not been too small to escape corporate notice after all; we'd been bought by Rodale Press, in Pennsylvania. Soon John Viehman arrived to see which of us he'd want to hire. John edited Rodale's magazine *Practical Homeowner,* but he'd formerly been the editor/publisher of *Canoe* and he in fact did know something about the outdoors. We hit it off immediately, and in February, after a mere seven months perched above Times Square, I became the only employee to move to nearby Pennsylvania. Adele didn't mind because we were still within commuting distance of New York, and besides, we discovered that Pennsylvania was full of old barns. For the last year we'd talked about finding a derelict church or barn to restore into our home—it just had to be within striking distance of the city and cheap, a tough combination. Now the opportunity had been dropped into our laps.

We found a seventy-foot-long, two hundred-year-old stone-ender barn with a tree growing out the roof and moved into it six months later, after devoting every nonworking minute of our lives to making it habitable. Mark's article about Colin Fletcher became the cover story of the first issue of *Backpacker* from the new staff at Rodale, and six months later he'd moved to Pennsylvania to edit *Adventure Travel* and *Cross Country Skier* magazines (Rodale already owned the competitor to *Ski X-C*). Our friendship in person was as strong as it had been over the phone, but we had our differences. He simply couldn't understand my immersion in homebuilding (the work was far from finished when we moved into it), and when Adele pulled out a box marked "special mantel objects" he guffawed out loud. Mark was a Puritan: he believed one should never own more than could fit into a Volkswagen microbus. Anything additional is just that much bigger a ball and chain. Mark lasted less than a year in cubicle-world before packing his microbus and returning west, where he met his partners for the first-ever bicycle crossing of Russia, a seven-thousand-mile odyssey he chronicled in his first book, *Off the Map*.

A few months before Mark left, I fielded a call from *Summit* magazine, the country's oldest commercial climbing magazine. *Summit* was for sale, I was told; did I know anyone who might be interested? I called David Swanson, who was now a successful businessman, because I knew he wanted to buy a climbing magazine. I told him the price and on the spot he said, "I'll buy it." And then he asked me to run it for him. Taking on a magazine of my own was too much too soon, as I felt I still had a lot to learn about the business; but it was also too good an opportunity to pass up. I left *Backpacker* with excited trepidation. My old friend Craig Sabina (my ski partner on Orizaba) was the East Coast ad director for *Outside* magazine at the time, but we talked him into leaving his lucrative job for the long-run potential of managing our business. I would run the editorial side, and we would share responsibility for business strategy. Thirty-five years earlier *Summit* had been launched as a ski and general-interest mountain magazine; in the 1960s it turned into the nation's only climbing publication, and the likes of Royal Robbins had been part-time editors. After *Climbing* magazine emerged as a competitor in 1971, *Summit* metamorphosed into a humble, low-key mountaineering magazine that hard-core climbers didn't take seriously. Our plan was to put it back on the map as a glossy, literary magazine about all things mountainous. We wanted to bring the spirit of mountains to everyone who loved high places, whether they were hikers, climbers, skiers, or traveled by cog railway. Our goal was to inspire, not to serve up practical where-to-go or how-to-do-it information. To provide the artistic look we craved, we hired Adele to design the magazine, something she'd never done before.

The first order of business was to muck out the ground floor of the barn and turn it into offices for six employees. In the spring of 1990 we brought out the premiere issue of our new/old quarterly magazine. Each issue was to include a "Classic Reprint" of one of the greatest mountain tales previously told, and for the premiere we chose "The Tragedy of Toni Kurz," from Heinrich Harrer's *The White Spider*. The *Summit* relaunch attracted some attention in the mountain world, and I was invited to Zermatt for the 125th anniversary celebration of the first ascent of the Matterhorn. Journalists were promised a guided ascent of the Matterhorn itself.

After all these years I still believed that the Matterhorn was the most beautiful mountain in the world. Its chiseled shape rising to a spectacular point, the steepness and scale of all of its flanks, and the way it dominates the valley below, all conspire to make the Matterhorn the worthy symbol of mountain perfection, at least from a distance—you don't notice that it's a pile of rubble until you grab a handhold. And I'd never forgotten that Dad had promised to take me up the mountain when I was fourteen, nor the last line of *Straight Up*, about my own eye being on the Matterhorn. It had not been a rhetorical flourish.

It took the blink of an eye for me to respond to Switzerland Tourism and sign up for the whole package. It felt odd to let myself be guided, but this was an easy way to get myself off the mental hook of climbing in the Alps. Tied to a guide on the tourist route hardly counted as alpinism—at least that's the way I rationalized it.

On the eve of the climb, a large squadron of journalists slept side by side on giant bunks in the Hörnli Hut. We were told to rise at 3:30 a.m., or so I thought, but someone got up at 3:00 and started a stampede. I was so cranky at having lost the extra half hour of sleep that I stayed in the bunk until everyone had moved to the restaurant, then joined them at the appointed time: 3:30. The trouble was, by then everyone else had been assigned his guide and had started up the mountain. My guide was waiting for me impatiently. Thirty-four years old, I'd been climbing longer than he'd been living, and I'd been a guide longer than he'd been climbing. Now he was tapping his toes wishing his client wasn't so lazy. Embarrassed, I grabbed my gear as quickly as I could, and we raced to catch up with the others. Above us a long line of headlights weaved up the mountain, looking like a busy road on a dark night. After trudging slowly at the tail of the traffic jam, I finally let my guide know that I didn't mind going a little faster whenever the opportunity arose to pass people. We were the second team to reach the summit.

Along the way I remembered how much I loved moving fast up a mountain, even something as technically easy as the Hörnli Ridge (Whymper's line on the first ascent). And the summit itself was every bit as spectacular as I'd imagined it from below. Not a perfect point, it was nevertheless a knife-edge slicing through the sky. We hiked over to the Italian summit as well, where stands a tall metal cross, and we peered down the steeper wall where Whymper's Italian competitors had fled when he rolled boulders down to claim his victory.

I returned to Zermatt thoroughly happy. Now *that* had been fun, the most fun I'd had in a long time. The climbing itself hadn't been very interesting, but the speed had added luster, and the location was everything. Boy did I love being in these mountains. There was nothing more beautiful than this.

My magazine was beautiful, too. Adele's artistry brought such a fresh look to *Summit* that after our first year we were nominated for a National Magazine Award in design, the most prestigious design accolade in the publishing world—short of actually winning. That fall I was invited to judge the Banff Mountain Film Festival in Canada—I'd already judged twice at the Telluride Mountainfilm Festival—and the next spring I flew to the Trento festival as a panelist for a debate on how guidebooks affected the mountain world. During an Italian film Bernadette McDonald—the director at Banff—and I whispered ideas to each other about a traveling film festival, and soon she made our ideas one of the keystones of her festival. I was also invited to a future-of-mountains conference at Sundance, in Utah, where the reigning king of alpinism himself—Reinhold Messner—held up a copy of *Summit* magazine and told his audience that this was the first and only magazine to capture the true spirit of what he called the "White Wilderness"—those few places where real adventure could still take place. I'd been working on the barn and *Backpacker* and *Summit* and traveling to conferences so much in the last years that I hadn't actually done much climbing, but I felt like these were temporary dues, and that even if I was talking, judging, and editing more than I was actually *doing,* at least I was making a mark of my own. I felt almost smug when I did an interview with my old friend Nico, who had come to the States a few times since we'd met under Reinhard's wing. We'd climbed together at a number of American crags while I was researching my guidebooks, and had become ever-closer friends. He was now an editor at the German mountain magazine *Alpin.*

Then I received a copy of his story, titled (in German): "Yes, he was my father." It knocked the wind out of my sails. I had already outlived Dad in years. I also had hoped that, at least among my friends, I might by now have emerged from his shadow—it really felt like momentum was on *my* side. And yet there in headline-sized type was how the world still defined me: Dad's son.

Even as the years went by, Dad's name had stayed familiar among climbers. Out of the blue I'd get letters proclaiming the impact he'd had on people who'd only barely made his acquaintance but remembered every detail vividly. I'd meet someone who, upon hearing my name, would tell me how he began climbing after reading *Straight Up,* or how he recently made a pilgrimage to Dad's grave in Leysin. I'd get letters from his high school students who remembered "the shock and sadness that descended on Leysin at the time of your dad's death. He was the *uberman.* The guy that one could aspire to be, but never quite reach." "Yes," I would respond, "Dad certainly was inspiring." "No," I would continue when prodded, "I will not be climbing the Eiger myself."

That was also the year that Heinrich Harrer came to the States to lecture about the many adventurous twists in his life, including his famous seven years in Tibet. Harrer described his first ascent of the north face of the Eiger before going on to praise the north wall's second route, the John Harlin Route, and the man who had made it happen. Afterward we had lunch together, and Harrer described to Adele and me the major unfulfilled dream of his life: to publish his photographs of Lhasa in the 1940s. Apparently he had thousands of them, all shot on a roll of 35mm black-and-white movie film that had been left in Lhasa by one of the ultrarare expeditions to reach the forbidden capital. I spoke to David Swanson, who spoke to his friend at Abrams Books, and soon I became the editor/ghostwriter and Adele the photo editor/designer of a coffee-table book, *Lost Lhasa: Heinrich Harrer's Tibet,* copublished by Summit Publications and Abrams Books.

Meanwhile we were selling the barn and packing the home and office—the moving van literally took the table out from under Adele while she was proofing *Lost Lhasa* and the latest issue of *Summit.* At the end of April, 1992, we drove across the country to our new home in Oregon. The business seemed to be going well enough to move it to where we actually wanted to live, where I'd always figured I would return: the Pacific Northwest. We picked

Hood River for its beauty, environment, community, and proximity to an international airport and city culture (Portland). Adele hadn't achieved her goal of a gallery in Manhattan, but she was feeling relatively fulfilled with her work at the magazine and doing her art on the side. We had bought land in Hood River the year before, complete with a run-down farmhouse, and within days of our arrival we were working on making the place habitable. There was little time for climbing, but when friends flew in for the Fourth of July weekend, we telemarked our backyard volcanoes— Mounts Adams and Hood—from their summits. Later Craig and I telemarked Mount Rainier from the summit, and Mount Saint Helens as well, now 2,000 feet shorter than it had been when I'd last skied it with my team as a twelve-year-old.

What a change it was to have mountains so accessible. I could ski a volcano in the morning and be at my computer in the office in the afternoon. But the dream felt short-lived. The vast majority of my time and energy was spent at the computer's monitor, just as before, working the business and editing stories by other people who were actually traveling the world, going on expeditions, seeing new cultures, climbing their peaks. By contrast, I struggled to take half a weekend off of work, and most of those went to maintaining the property. I worked every evening unless a ditch needed digging by headlamp to repair a broken waterline. By 1994 I felt so despondent about the never-ending treadmill of work and the climbing vacuum in my life that I agreed to take a week off to climb the Salathé Wall on Yosemite's El Capitan with my friend Jeff Bowman. I'd guided the Nose thirteen years earlier, but hadn't climbed in the Valley since. I remember attacking the first pitch of the Salathé with an urgency that could only have been pent-up ardor unleashed. The feeling lasted for all 3,000 vertical feet, and for almost a week after my return to the office.

We decided to sell the farmhouse with twenty acres so that we could afford to build a new house above the river bluff on the remaining forty acres. But in order to do that, we had to turn a run-down shack on a far corner of the property into something we could stand to live in temporarily. Between keystrokes at work and hammer blows at home, I'd sometimes pause to remember the feeling of jumaring 2,500 feet up on the Roof of the Salathé Wall, spinning in space, and realizing that I wasn't afraid of dangling from a rope anymore. I remembered looking down and thinking that Dad had fallen twice that far. But his rope had been too thin, whereas mine was thick and safe. The Valley in October was so beautiful.

Lupine, the puppy at our wedding, now walked on unsteady legs. Where she had accompanied me into the most improbable of places during my research for *The Climber's Guide to North America*, she now tripped over steps on the way to the office. We usually left her in the house when we walked the bluff on our property, but one day she snuck out the door to follow us. Shortcutting a switchback, her hind legs gave out and she tumbled into the river 200 feet below. She died in my arms fifteen minutes later. Adele and I were devastated, as Lupine had been our child these last thirteen years. We took the day off of work to grieve, and to talk about family and future. We'd been trying to conceive for the last few months. Adele was now in her midthirties, and we knew it was now or never. We would be happy either way. But whenever I thought back to my own childhood in the mountains, I realized how much I would like to share that feeling with a child of my own. Adele was less certain, but she did know that if we were to have a baby, it couldn't wait much longer.

One gray Oregon office morning there was an e-mail from Mark Jenkins: "You and me. Waddington. New route. May." I stared at the message for days while the stress of work whirlpooled around me. Then the office manager took a phone message, also from Mark. He told her to write down the same words, nothing more.

Though Mark didn't realize it, Waddington was the North American mountain I craved above all others—the one I would dream about while editing other people's tales of Nepal and the

Andes. The highest peak in British Columbia's Coast Range, this 13,186-foot summit lies some 25 miles inland from the head of Knight Inlet, an 85-mile saltwater fiord. These days climbers generally reach Waddington by air. I'd been wanting to go by land from the sea, bushwhacking, river-fording, and glacier-navigating to the famous "south face" route established by Fritz Wiessner and Bill House in 1936. My goal was a journey wherein the summit was mostly the pretext for a grand wilderness escape. I hadn't planned to go soon; I didn't have time. But a *new* route? I gave in and returned Mark's call. He had discovered that an entire face—the true south face—had never been climbed. A collection of palisades and couloirs some 3,000 feet tall and at least that wide, the face had killed its only known assailant, Alec Dalgleish, who fell to his death two years before Wiessner's arrival. Wiessner's route, actually on the south*west* flank of the mountain, became a classic, and Dalgleish's true south face, which lies at the head of a separate glacier, was forgotten. Mark rediscovered it in a photo. I agreed that it had to be climbed. That spring. By us.

In the last days of April we bushwhacked, river-forded, and glacier-navigated to a high camp at 9,000 feet, all under crushing packs loaded with two weeks' worth of food, climbing gear, and skis. We left our tent, food, and extra gear there so we could climb fast up a steep snow face followed by an ice couloir. Three thousand feet above camp I popped over Waddington's big shoulder, just beneath the 900-foot summit pinnacle. It was like stepping into the jet stream. Instead of stopping to belay Mark up, I simply leaned into the wind and postholed in soft, fresh snow toward the summit pinnacle. Mark had gained the shoulder and was also hunched into the wind when a deep roar seemed to shake the mountain. It grew stronger, racing invisibly at us. Avalanche? Then a four-propeller military plane burst directly over our shoulders and roared across the mountain, well beneath the summit.

Our composures recovered, we resumed postholing, when the plane suddenly screamed straight at us, flying low enough that we almost ducked. Just when we thought the joke had gone too far a cylinder tumbled out, trailed by a red streamer. The plane bellowed by and vanished around the mountain.

We did a clod-footed dash to where the cylinder had fallen into a *bergschrund*. I jumped down into the soft snow, grabbed the bubble-wrapped cylinder, and Mark tensioned me back out. My ice axe slid through the tape, and I reached inside the bubble wrap. It held a bottle of Captain Morgan rum. Mark and I stared at each other dumbfounded. Beneath the image of a grinning pirate, the label read: "For Captain Morgan adventure was the spice of life and rum was the spirit of the adventurous." I reached into the cylinder again and pulled out a copy of *Penthouse International,* a special "Girls of the World" edition. These Canadians are right friendly folks, we thought, but why us? One last look inside the cylinder revealed a note: "To Jim and the boys, good luck." A case of mistaken identity, and now we had poor Jim's wine and women.

Unfortunately, those would have to wait. It was already afternoon, and the summit pinnacle looked much more intimidating than we'd expected. We thought our new route would end here and we could join the standard summit finish, which was said to follow a ramp. But we couldn't find the ramp. Instead we tackled the cliff above, and I scratched up one of the trickiest, most poorly protected mixed-rock-and-ice passages of my life. When Mark followed that section he yelled up, "John, you're a hardman!"

A warm shock of emotion pulsed in my heart. I savored the feeling, basking in its glow as Mark drew nearer. It wasn't vanity, or at least I didn't think it was. No. I felt like I was a boy hearing his father's praise. Did I really do well?

We made the summit and got back to the tent in the middle of the night, twenty-two hours after we'd left it. Mark and I talked ourselves to sleep, as we had each night. The Lessons of Wadd, we called our philosophical ramblings. In the week gone by we had transcended the strange, infuriating tyranny of our so-called civilized lives. On Waddington we'd found true life again, rediscovered what made us whole. We had known it the moment we started walking. Felt it grow stronger each day. Felt the world pour into us until now we were as big as it was. This was real. This was where we belonged. The workaday scene at home would have to change, would change, would never be more important than life again. We convinced ourselves this would be true.

Summit magazine alone was not keeping the business afloat, but combined with side projects—catalogs and corporate vanity magazines—Summit Publications looked like it would work. Then, early in the summer, our biggest client canceled their project. *Summit* went into a death spiral. Each day the office tried to tear me apart. It was surreal to watch Adele calmly sitting at her computer putting together the last issue of the magazine, a relaxed smile on her face. Nothing seemed to faze her. She was pregnant.

I spent the rest of the fall building a barn where we could move our household possessions (including many more boxes of special mantel objects) while we moved in to the cottage (formerly the shack) so that we could build the new house. *Backpacker* had agreed to take me back starting in January, this time as its Northwest Field Editor. Our daughter Siena was born one glorious day in April, 1996, and a month later I turned forty.

This time my job at *Backpacker* was primarily writing, and the job would take me to deep corners of North America and occasionally even abroad. It was the good life of travel, wilderness adventure, gear testing, and writing the best stories I could. That satisfied at first, but then the same old patterns crept in. I took my trips—always as rushed as possible—and returned to more work than I could manage, including the never-ending house building. I still wasn't climbing, and now that I was traveling so much for work, I didn't think I could leave Adele and our baby for recreation. Somewhere in the midst of my angst a new Hood River friend—someone who had been a hero in the 1970s for his extreme rock climbs—approached me at a party and asked point-blank, "What have you ever done besides being born to a famous father?"

I tried to make "Nothing" sound ironic, but in fact it was how I felt inside. My guiding business had failed, *Summit* had failed, my climbing ambitions had never gotten off the ground, and I endlessly pounded the keyboard when I wasn't digging ditches to divert water from flooding our new basement. Not only would defending my limited accomplishments sound defensive, it didn't fit what I felt. I changed the subject.

Mark knew of my internal struggle, as did Nico, but to others I only revealed it in my writing. Somehow thoughts that seemed too private for conversation kept coming out in my articles. In a 1997 *Backpacker* story I compared Dad to Mount Saint Helens, a volcano that had made the earth shake. I, by contrast, was "less volatile"—and by implication, less interesting. I had built my life in the "sedimentary" fashion: "a gradual layering of days." In an article for *Ascent,* I concluded that our "Lessons of Wadd" had been only half true:

> There are also toddlers taking their first steps wearing nothing but an angel smile and a very crooked halo. There's fatigue from overwork and too little sleep. There are warm homes built with hard labor. There are falls in ski races, and missing fathers. You do not escape to adventure. You do not escape from it. You live it each and every day.

Intellectually I believed those last words, which were intended to show that daily life was in fact as vital and interesting as what we find in the mountains. But the heart is not as clean as reason. The adventure of daily—sedimentary—life was not in fact making me feel like I'd "done" something to rise above merely being born to a famous father. If the biological clock had been running out on having a child, it certainly wasn't going to slow down while the kid grew up. Should I continue to cast off my dreams of difficult mountains—in particular my secret, buried urge to climb THE mountain, the Eiger—because it was inappropriate to my new status as father? In the *Backpacker* article I pointed to Dad's example, how he had met with a wealthy businessman while looking for funding. After the two had spoken for a couple of hours Dad's host said to him, "Of course you'll be giving all this up when you have a family." Dad led him out to the car in the street where my mother, sister, and I had been waiting. That had taken place in 1963, while our home was a tent in Chamonix.

I don't remember when exactly I started talking about the Eiger again. I think it was somewhere in here, not long after Siena was born, maybe it was earlier. I served on the board of the Polartec Performance Challenge with Stephen Venables, who had climbed the north face. Stephen had lost the toes on one foot to frostbite on a new route on the north side of Everest, and while he padded up a New Hampshire cliff in his custom-made climbing shoes, I peppered him with questions about the Traverse of the Gods. Nico was also on the PPC board, and we started talking about climbing the Eiger together. Nico was with me once when someone asked if I would climb the Eiger. Nico answered for me: "He has to." This wasn't a dare, or a provocation, or anything except a deep understanding of what made me tick. I felt grateful for Nico's response—it validated my feelings. We talked about my trying to keep my schedule and checkbook open so that he could call when the face came into shape and I would jump on a plane immediately. The problem with that—in addition to schedule (a.k.a. deadlines) and checkbook (all spent on the house)—was that I needed to be in climbing shape, and I wasn't climbing.

Mark and I spoke often of the Eiger as well. He knew that I really wanted to climb it with Nico, one of my oldest friends. This climb would be a pilgrimage for me, not simply a route, and Nico and I went way back. But Mark and I were by now best friends as well, and we talked about perhaps a team of three, so that I could climb it with my closest partners. And then Nico started drifting away from the idea. Five years older than I, he was questioning whether he wanted to climb such a wall—this wall in particular— just as I was fixating ever more on actually doing it.

These conversations drifted through the years, and I never spoke about it with anyone else. I didn't want to worry my family, and with others I didn't want to talk about things undone. So we kept it to ourselves, my semisecret dream.

SIXTEEN

FACING THE EIGER

IN AUGUST of 1999 I found myself pacing the Lausanne train station, tears streaming down my face, and quietly sobbing. When I couldn't stand it any longer I ran back to give three-year-old Siena a final hug before the train pulled out of the station.

"What's wrong?" Adele asked when I found them on their bench seat. My face was contorted in grief and wet from the tears.

"Nothing," I lied. "I just need to hug Siena one last time."

The truth was that I felt like I was saying good-bye forever, as if I would never see her again. We had been traveling Europe together for three weeks, first on a *Backpacker* assignment, then visiting various of my old haunts, and we had just descended from a pilgrimage to Dad's grave in Leysin. It was Siena's first connection to her grandfather and to the continent of my youth. That whole trip we watched her revel in the new experiences and languages; Adele and I joked that we could hear the synapses in her brain crackle as they formed fresh connections. And now I was putting her on a train that would take them back to the airport in Paris and then home to Oregon. I would take the car to Zermatt, where I was to meet Mark to climb the north face of the Matterhorn. After that we were headed to the Eiger to see if conditions were suitable.

What really caught me off guard there in the Lausanne train station was the sudden transition from doting parent to daring alpinist. The latter felt like a complete violation of the former. Instead of being excited about the climbing to come, I felt like a foot soldier handing off his child before heading to the front line where battle raged. It wasn't so much guilt that I felt, but loss. I was saying good-bye to the most precious thing in my life, and my tears were less for the difficulties my death would cause Siena than they were for the possibility that I might not be able to watch her grow up. I just couldn't bear that idea: to miss out on her life. Mine was a selfish misery caused by a selfish activity that could be called off at any time. And yet I felt I had to go.

A few hours later Mark asked what was wrong. I told him I didn't know if I could climb. At least not what Mark wanted to climb. He craved the Matterhorn's north face, which is famously loose and unprotectable in the best of conditions—exactly what I had sworn off. When I arrived, the Matterhorn had lots of fresh summer snow and the local guides thought the north face was in terrible condition. This sort of talk doesn't scare Mark off, but it does me. Finally I came up with an alternative plan that would be interesting enough for Mark and hopefully safe enough for me. We could hike over to the Italian side of the Matterhorn and traverse the mountain, ending up back in Zermatt. We'd go up the route that was being climbed by his Italian rivals when Whymper finally made it up from the Swiss side. And then we'd go down Whymper's own Hörnli Ridge. It was a long and interesting way to climb the mountain, full of history. Because the routes aren't difficult, I could feel safe.

But what an illusion, this feeling of safety. We spent five days hiking, climbing, and waiting out bad weather during our traverse from Zermatt to Zermatt. And during that time five people fell to their deaths on the Matterhorn. We saw one body being helicoptered off as we hiked up to a bivouac hut on our first day. The last victim solo-climbed past us on our descent on the fifth day (we learned of his fall, and the victims that came between, when we got back to Zermatt). Still, climbing is a psychological game as much as a physical sport, and as long as we feel in control we feel safe. These climbers all must have made mistakes; that's why they died. I wasn't going to make a mistake; that's why I'd be safe. In order to continue believing this, all I had to do was ignore all the mistakes I'd ever made, and the mistakes better climbers than I had made, too. Being perennial optimists as well as egotists, it's easy for climbers to keep themselves deluded.

Every time Mark and I get together we debate about risk. I argue that the only way I can rationalize Alpine climbing is by building my skills in relatively safe environments on good rock and solid ice before applying those skills to more dangerous environments. Even more important, I insist, is to enter those dangerous situations only infrequently, and to pass through them as quickly as possible. Then chance is in my favor. Mark cries bullshit. He points to coin-flipping, where the odds of the next flip coming up tails are fifty-fifty no matter how many times you flip. You could just as easily get the chop on your next climb, no matter how many you do. And then I'll retort that the odds of flipping at least one tail in the next ten flips are a lot higher than fifty-fifty. In fact, the more times you flip, the more tails you're going to get. And if the climbing equivalent of a tail is death, you only get to flip it once.

All of which sidesteps the central problem: I'd be just as dead if I fell on the next mountain I attempt as on the tenth mountain, and my family would be just as wounded, statistics and me be damned. When I look down and see bad protection and look up and see scary climbing, or when stones start falling or avalanches roar by, suddenly the bottom drops out of my stomach and the whole climbing enterprise looks like the selfish, foolish, absurd, and potentially destructive activity it really is. Condemning Siena to grow up fatherless and my mother to live through her son's death becomes an unforgivable sin, never mind the effect my death would have on me, or for that matter, Adele. What can justify this? Nothing. Certainly not personal whimsy. I can only pretend that this pursuit is irresistible, that what I get out of it is worth the risk I place upon others, and that I'll be wise enough to keep on doing it until I die of old age.

These concerns faded as we traversed the Matterhorn. That's another thing about climbing: you grow comfortable with a dangerous environment. If you're suddenly confronted with a great abyss, it's terrifying; but climb gradually until you reach the same exposure and you don't even notice it. I went to the Matterhorn fresh from a family vacation and afraid of the mountains. And I came off it adjusted to the environment and comfortable with its risks, which now felt manageable, as if I had control over them. I was ready for almost anything.

Except the Eiger. At least not in the condition we found it in. It was my first time to the mountain since 1980, when I'd come with Adele to look, not to climb. Now there were clouds drifting in and out of the face, which was whitewashed with a fresh coat of summer slush—just like what we'd been advised to stay clear of on the north face of the Matterhorn. Mark was champing at the bit. Never mind the recent snowfall. Never mind the dripping icefields. Never mind the fact that the wall looks twice as tall when you're thinking of climbing it than when you're merely taking pictures. Mark thought the conditions were good enough to at least have a go at it. I thought the conditions sucked. It was like we were back in Zermatt when I first arrived, with Mark eager and me a wreck; once again I was way out of my comfort zone without even putting crampon to mountain. Fortunately, Mark knew my mental state, and he accepted the current version of my old vow: that I would only climb this face when conditions were right—on the mountain, in my head, and in my body. Conditions on the mountain and in my head were all wrong.

Mark paced while I spent a day at the telescope. I needed to break the mountain down into pieces in my mind. The old elephant-eating trick: one bite at a time. If I could grow comfortable with each ropelength individually, then I could simply put all those ropelengths together. I scanned the lower 1,500 feet quickly, knowing that it was dangerous but easy. That much was like the Matterhorn, which now fit into my frame of reference, my comfort zone. Then I examined the other components of the classic 1938 Route in detail: the Difficult Crack, the Hinterstoisser Traverse, the First Icefield, the Ice Hose, the Second Icefield, the Flatiron, the Death Bivouac where Dad spent his last days, the Third Icefield, the Ramp, the Waterfall Pitch, the Brittle Ledges and Crack, the Traverse of the Gods, the Spider (under which Dad's rope broke), the Quartz Crack, the Corti Bivouac, the Exit Cracks, the Summit Icefield. I could put all the pieces together from memory of books. I knew why each was named, and the names of a few of the people who had died there. But I wasn't an observer looking curiously at someone else's world; I was now intending to put myself into harm's way. There was no controlling the dread, the despair, the fear of destiny. I didn't even know if I *wanted* to control my moods—nor in which direction to push them if I could. So I broke the mountain down into bite-sized portions in the telescope, trying to decide piece by piece whether I could climb from each belay to the next.

By the time we hiked back to Grindelwald I'd climbed the route in my head and had convinced myself that I really could climb the Eiger when conditions improved. Strangely enough, I felt a kind of liberation. It seemed like I'd processed all the emotions and historical baggage that led me to want to climb the Eiger. I had visually climbed the wall, which meant I *could* climb it. Having proved that I could climb it, I no longer *needed* to climb it. My burden had been lifted. I really believed this. Or at least it felt like I really believed it. And by some miracle the next day the mountain disappeared into a mass of dripping clouds and we never saw the face again.

I thought I should write this up and be done with it. But I didn't, and I wasn't.

SEVENTEEN

MONT BLANC

―――――――――――

WHEN I flew out of the Arctic National Wildlife Range in 1974, I would have been appalled to know that it would be twenty-six years before I returned. In 1974 our group on the Kongakut had split at a place nicknamed "Caribou Pass." Two people stayed behind for the expected migration to pass through, and six of us continued downstream because we'd run out of time. We later learned that two hours after we'd kayaked off, 40,000 caribou had passed through camp, tripping over the remaining tent's guylines. At the turn of the millennium *Backpacker* decided to send me back to see the big herd for myself.

But I had another agenda as well. When Mark had been the editor of *Cross Country Skier* he'd asked a few prominent skiers about their dream trips. Mine was to paddle the Hulahula River from the crest of the Brooks Range to the Arctic Ocean with skis lashed to the sides of my kayak. Along the way I would make the first ski descent of Mount Michelson—the third-highest peak in the range. Since *Backpacker* was sending me to the neighborhood to see the caribou, I decided to fulfill my skiing dream as well.

I invited Konrad to come along. Over the years, Dad's old friend had become one of Adele's and my closest friends, too, along with his wife, Joëlle. We had been visiting regularly since remeeting in 1980 during Adele's year in France, and we'd even climbed occasional rock routes together in Europe. Now it was my chance to share an old stamping ground with an even older friend. We found good white water, terrible snow—but skied from the summit anyway—one grizzly in the distance, two wolves, and only a scattering of caribou. But we reveled in the Arctic, and in the joys of long-lasting friendship.

The magazine continued to be good to me, and I was learning to piggyback climbing onto assignments, whether to Baffin Island, Europe, or finally, Tibet. Mark was an old Tibet hand, with many explorations under his belt, most of them clandestine. He'd invited me every few years to join him while he tried to sneak through Tibet illegally, usually on his way to Burma, where he wanted to make the first ascent of the country's highest peak without the knowledge of its vicious rulers. He was arrested numerous times, had snuck out of jail at least once, and his stories terrified me. Being savaged by nature was one thing; being brutalized by prison guards was quite another. I resisted Mark's overtures until 2002, when he broke down and agreed to let us get trekking permits to reach a range of virgin mountains, though it was still illegal to climb them. Mark knew these mountains merely from an American pilots' map (with 1,000-foot contour line intervals) and having passed nearby years earlier while hiding under a tarp on the back of a truck that he'd bribed his way onto.

We'd reached just over 17,000 feet on our 21,000-foot virgin peak when continuing snowfalls made us fear a trap. To reach the harder climbing we'd had to ascend a long gully exposed to avalanches on both sides; if the slopes built up with enough snow, they would cut loose and fill the gully, burying anyone caught inside. We could keep on climbing in relative safety, maybe even to the summit, but what about the descent? As darkness fell and the heavy snowfall continued, we decided that staying high was not worth the risk. We packed up the tent and reached base camp at midnight. During the next ten days we hiked in the neighboring valleys, always looking over our shoulders, ready to jump back on the peak if the weather cleared long enough for the snow to settle. It never did.

It had been an interesting test, and we discussed it a lot. We had stopped ourselves based purely on an intellectual judgment— a calculated evaluation of unseen risks. After flying halfway around the world and devoting a month of our lives expecting to attain an ultimate climber's dream—bagging a spectacular virgin peak by a beautiful line—we backed off because of what might be lurking in future snow layers. We felt frustrated, disappointed, and yet pleased that wisdom had prevailed over ambition.

Though *Backpacker* had sent me to Tibet, just before leaving I'd received a call from the American Alpine Club asking if I'd take over the editorship of the *American Alpine Journal*. The *AAJ* was seventy-three years old, and its editors did not turn over rapidly— H. Adams Carter had served for thirty-five years, and his successor had been in the post for six years. The *AAJ* was like the Bible to the Alpine climbing world, or maybe the Bible and the *Encyclopedia Britannica* combined, for its purpose was to present the prophetic new routes of the year in its first two hundred pages, and all the new mountain routes worldwide in the remaining three hundred pages. It served as the world's journal of record for mountain exploration. I'd often thumbed through editions from the 1960s, where all of Dad's published writing had appeared. And I had known Ad Carter—and his hallowed status among exploratory mountaineers. Though the *AAJ* wouldn't develop me as a writer, nor did it have the breadth of wilderness interest that *Backpacker* did, it felt like the culmination of my life's experiences. And it seemed that the publication would allow me several months off each year to take trips of my own choosing, without regard to publication. I signed the contract immediately.

In 2003, during my first glorious summer of total freedom since college, I had an epiphany. We were descending a steep glacier after traversing the Barre des Écrins, a long but moderate climb in the Dauphiné Alps, when suddenly I realized that the person roped just before me was exactly ten years my senior, at age fifty-seven. And the person in front of him was ten years *his* senior, at age sixty-seven. The latter was Konrad. Seeing those decadelong age increments arranged in front of me made tangible what I'd been trying to convince myself of, which was to appreciate all the mountains in my future, rather than to beat myself up about un-climbed mountains in my past. Mark and I had been talking about this for some time, but the sight of these men in front of me was like a revelation. Though I had never confessed to it, inside I had always wanted to be not just any climber, not even a good climber, but a great climber—one of those who made the visionary ascents that grace the front of the *American Alpine Journal.* Dad had been one of them. I wanted to be one, too. Life didn't turn out that way, and I will never know whether I could have reached that goal. Mark and I talked about this almost every time we got together, until finally I blurted out, "Okay, I'll never be a great climber, but I can still do some great climbs." Watching Konrad lead us down the glacier made me feel better about life's choices. It felt like I was, at least for the moment, transforming a rational, intellectual acceptance into something visceral.

Adele and Siena were waiting in the valley below, and we spent a relaxing few weeks together before Mark flew in. Mark's and my plan once again spanned two summits. In these days of ever-warming weather, the Eiger in August wasn't even worth considering. So we planned a new route on Mont Blanc first—something in the neighborhood of Dad's two routes—and then we'd move to the Eiger in September.

It is very hard to find new routes in the Alps these days. The range swarms with young climbers far more skilled and daring than we, and Dad's prediction had come true that even the Cha-monix area would become "a climbing playground like the Dolomites, with routes on the needles of Chamonix criss-crossing each other." But the southern flank of Mont Blanc was another story. The 15,780-foot summit is 11,000 vertical feet above the parking lot, and no ski lifts ease the strain—its wildness is protected by what the great mountaineer Kurt Diemberger calls "the barrier of effort."

Mark and I grunted up to the Eccles bivouac hut at 13,000 feet, groaning under rucksacks overstuffed with ten days of food and fuel and a rack of climbing hardware big enough to handle anything we might find up there. The weather forecast called for a storm, but we had a plan. We would have a look at the Frêney and Brouillard faces to see what ground we might stake for ourselves. We'd then acclimatize to the altitude during the storm by lying on our backs and reading a book. When the weather cleared, we'd go over the top and down the French side of the mountain.

Scrambling up the lower Innominata Ridge gave me plenty of time to remember Dad's three experiences with this side of the mountain. First there had been the terrible disaster in 1961—Mark and I climbed up the same rotten gully to the Col de l'Innominata on which Dad and Gary had left the rope Konrad rappeled. Then there had been the Hidden Pillar of Frêney with Tom Frost in 1963, which Dad had called the hardest climb on Mont Blanc. And finally his ascent of the Brouillard Pillar with Chris Bonington in '65. Dad had titled his story about that ascent "Thumbing a Nose at the Weather." He reported that on the way to the Eccles bivouac hut they had "seen every known bad-weather sign. . . . We had been warned!" But they climbed on anyway. Mark and I were not thumbing our noses at the weather. We were nearly twenty years older than Dad and his friends had been, and we would wait out the storm in the hut.

The morning after we reached the Eccles hut we eagerly scrambled up the Punta Eccles for a view of the faces before the weather changed. The glaciers below both walls were covered in a black blanket of fallen stones. The sound of sliding rocks was almost continuous, and occasionally we'd witness massive pillars of rock spontaneously breaking loose and crashing down the mountain in giant billows of dust. Setting foot anywhere on the Frêney or the Brouillard faces would have been suicidal. Neither of us had witnessed a mountain decaying like this. We knew that the Matterhorn had already been closed this summer due to melting permafrost causing massive rockslides, and that the glaciered faces of Mont Blanc had also been officially closed for a while because of the heat. But we hadn't expected to observe granite walls spontaneously crumbling.

Our plight seemed hopeless at first, but as we watched the mountain decompose we noticed a safe, seemingly virgin line rising out of the wreckage like a vision. Not only was it beautiful, it was the only rockfall-free space on the entire visible sweep of granite and ice, and it rose directly above us. The line was the crest of the Innominata Arête, a faint ridgeline that divides the southern aspect of Mont Blanc into its two famous faces: the Brouillard and the Frêney.

There is already a route called the Innominata Arête—it was the first route on the south flank of the mountain, and it is still the most popular. But it is an old-school route that wanders off the actual arête as soon as the climbing becomes difficult. At that point the route crosses what used to be a snowfield and continues up a different ridge. In August of 2003, the "snowfield" was just another river of tumbling rocks. There is also an Innominata "Direct" route. But this quickly slips to the right-hand side of the ridge and climbs hidden gullies before rejoining the crest to ascend the upper buttress with the help of some aid-climbing. Between these two "Innominata" routes lies the actual ridge. Where the Innominata route moves left and the "Direct" route cuts right, a perfect 250-foot dihedral splits the solid granite. Mark and I could scarcely believe this had not been climbed. The only trouble we foresaw was a ten-foot icicle that hung from the first of two overhangs.

That warm and sunny afternoon we had with us a rack, one pair of rock shoes between us, and time to kill, so we decided to see how difficult the dihedral might be. Mark led up to the roof's icicle while I cowered under a shallow overhang waiting for the dagger to drop. While pulling hard moves under the roof, Mark knocked the icicle with his shoulder and sent it shattering over my shelter. Then he powered free through the suddenly exposed jam crack to a belay above the roof. I followed in boots and had to rest on the rope in the icy roof crack. Because Mark had the rock-climbing shoes on, he led through the next roof as well and belayed on top of the buttress. It had been superb rock climbing on fantastic solid granite—a climber's dream. In splendid spirits, we yelled our joy to the empty landscape and rappeled, leaving most of our gear and one rope below the dihedral at an elevation of about 14,000 feet, awaiting our return after the storm blew through.

The wind hit around midnight, shaking our tenuously perched hut so violently that we feared it would be blown off the mountain. Several times during the night we debated leaving the dwelling and anchoring ourselves directly to the rock, but that prospect seemed so unpleasant that we decided to take our chances inside. The stronger gusts sent spindrift between the roof's metal panels, coating us with an inch of rime. In the afternoon during a lull we rappeled to the lower hut, which was drier and better anchored to granite. Three days later nearly three feet of snow had fallen. During these days we read a good chunk of *From Dawn to Decadence: 500 Years of Western Cultural Life* and we decided that if we made it up this route we'd call it From Dawn to Decadence. But as our food and fuel dwindled, we fretted that instead of naming the route, we'd be lucky to even find our expensive equipment.

Finally the sun came out and in the afternoon we climbed up to Punta Eccles to survey the new world. It looked perfect: all the loose rock was now anchored by fresh snow, and the dihedral's icicle had not returned. We left the hut at 3 a.m. to blast over the mountain, and by 6 a.m. we had reached the gear near the base of the dihedral. But as dawn lightened the sky we noticed a sheet of thin gray clouds and a wind that snatched our breaths away. We screamed at each other about this being the front of another storm, and we recalled our various hut-bound conversations about how frightening and miserable and dangerous it would have been if we'd been trapped in bivouac sacks on Mont Blanc's summit ridge. The clincher was that Mark couldn't feel his toes in his summer boots, which were inadequate in our winterlike conditions. Mark yelled that he'd still go on if I wanted to. But that was just Mark. Instead we clicked off our headlamps and rappeled toward a rapidly building layer of clouds below. We had to descend almost 10,000 vertical feet to reach the car, much of time groping through fog so thick we didn't know where we were going. But when we finally cracked open our stashed beers a brilliant blue sky framed the summit, which now glittered dazzlingly in the sun. Disgusted with ourselves, we drove to the Dolomites to climb off our frustrations. A few days later all the Alps were soaking in rain. Our bodies were fit, our minds were ready, but the Eiger was out.

My next window of opportunity for both Mont Blanc and the Eiger arrived a year later. Mark was traveling for work, but Roger Payne—a British resident of Leysin who had climbed the Eiger years before—agreed to join me, and we persuaded his wife, Julie-Ann Clyma, that traversing Mont Blanc yet again would be worth the effort. They had long ago climbed the standard Innominata Arête and also the Central Pillar of Frêney, which made them ideal partners with whom to wrap up From Dawn to Decadence. My plan was to climb this route before someone else finished it for me, and then I would head to the Eiger with the German climber Robert Jasper, who lived near Grindelwald. Robert and I had met a few years earlier and he had told me that the Eiger was his favorite mountain. I had been amazed—as far as I knew, only Dad had felt that way. Robert had climbed the north face a dozen times by different routes, some of them new. He told me that there were now some twenty-five routes on the wall, including pure rock-climbs that ascend pillars on the far-right side of the face and don't come near the summit. Times had certainly changed. As one of the best Alpine climbers in the world, Robert seemed like the perfect Eiger partner. I would still have chosen Mark because of our friendship, but I felt I was reaching the stage where if I were ever to make my dream real, I had to take advantage of any safe opportunity. Robert would make any opportunity safe.

But first I had to finish the Mont Blanc route—the Eiger would always be there, but my new route on Mont Blanc would surely fall to someone else if I didn't finish it quickly. On September 17, 2004, Roger, Julie-Ann, and I reached the Eccles hut via the easier glacier access, rather than the tricky ridge Mark and I had scrambled on our approach the year before. On the 18th we arrived at the dihedral shortly after the sun had warmed its jam crack. Instead of one long icicle, this time two short icicles hung from the roof 120 feet up. I climbed to them with an ice tool in my holster, hung from my protection to knock the icicles off and chip out the crack with my axe, and then I lowered to a belay stance. I really wanted to free-climb over the roof as Mark had, but the icy crack got the best of me and I ended up having to hang and rest once again. A few hours later we reached a tight little col at the base of the upper buttress, where we expected to discover a comfortable bivouac spot. Instead all we could find was a skinny patch of ice from which we chopped a ledge that left our feet dangling off the edge. We sat side by side, with Roger and Julie-Ann leaning against each other and me resting my helmet against the ledge. As we watched two climbers being helicoptered off the Frêney we worried that maybe they'd heard a bad-weather forecast and were taking the quick way out. We never learned what had happened to them, but the sky stayed clear as the stars emerged.

Around 2 a.m., during one of several sessions devoted to brewing tea to warm ourselves and pass the time, we discussed the sensual pleasures of middle-aging bodies on cramped bivouac ledges. It seemed, somehow, less charming than it used to. An eternity later, once the morning sun had warmed us, a semblance of youthful spirit returned, and soon we were locking jams with a splendid crack in the buttress. The route felt like it was leading straight to heaven. After we reached snow, endless traversing and ridge scrambling led off to the mountain's distant summit. Because we still had so many hours to go before reaching the Cosmique hut on the other side of the mountain, we traversed the icy slopes without protection. It was easy going, but only a slip away from being fatal. Roger marched along the steep slope confidently, as if he were hiking a trail. Julie-Ann turned into the slope for security, plunging her ice-axe picks in with every step and using the front points of her crampons; this slowed her, and she lagged behind. I generally followed Roger's example, because self-confidence is all it takes to walk quickly and safely on such slopes. But sometimes my nerve would give out and I'd slam in a pick to secure myself. The thing is that traipsing across such a slope really is as simple as Roger made it look. But a single misstep from any cause (including a patch of unseen snow caught in the crampons, or a frontpoint hooked in a pant leg) could lead to an ever-accelerating ride down many thousands of feet of steep glacier. So Julie-Ann's cautious approach made as much sense as Roger's confident one. It's the alpinist's conundrum, the one I'd vowed to avoid and that now I was vowing just to think about carefully and proceed through cautiously—and quickly.

We reached the summit at 6 p.m. and the Cosmique hut well after dark but just in time for dinner's final call. This was no little bivouac hut, but a mountain hotel built to hold a hundred and with a restaurant to match. The next morning we crossed the glacier and ascended to the top of the Aiguille du Midi aerial tram. I remembered that Dad had once finished a climb here just in time to catch the last lift down to Chamonix with Mom, who had been waiting at the platform. And then Roger and Julie-Ann and I climbed into a little six-person gondola that swept southeastward, back to Italy, where we had started our journey five days earlier.

As the gondola slid over the Mer de Glace glacier, it glided through my past. I could just make out where the Envers des

Aiguilles hut clings to granite under the Fou. Further down-glacier rose the Dru. Across from and above our gondola stood the massive Shroud and Walker Spur on the Grandes Jorasses. And then we swept past the Grand Capucin, a gorgeous 1,000-foot spire that Dad had climbed with Gary. Finally we came into view of the Col de Peuterey and the Central Pillar of Frêney, and then our own Innominata Arête, on the other side of which stood the Brouillard face. All around us orange- and gray-granite fins and pillars sliced the peaks, like Olympian jewelry set in beds of ice and snow. The sky's blue looked as if it could be bottled for pigment. This world could fill a lifetime. No wonder Dad loved it so.

We drove the two hours back to Leysin, just as Dad so often had, and from there I called Robert Jasper. Robert said that the weather had not been as kind to the Bernese Oberland as it had to the Mont Blanc Massif. A storm had blanketed the Eiger with fresh snow, and the few days remaining in my trip would not be enough time for the face to come into condition. My reaction split in multiple directions, as ever when it came to the Eiger. On the one hand, I breathed a sigh of relief. Though I wanted to climb the mountain, I remained very much afraid of it. Still, I wanted to get it over with, to have this climb finally behind me, not looming above like a specter. And this had seemed like my best chance yet. In Robert I would have had a partner so strong and so experienced that my confidence level was far higher than it had ever been. Coming down from Mont Blanc, I felt as fit and tuned as I would likely ever be. I was forty-eight years old now, and while age wasn't taking too much of a toll yet, I wasn't going to get any younger.

I was wrestling with these feelings when I called Stephen Venables in England. Stephen had left a message on Roger and Julie-Ann's machine. He half apologetically said that I could tell him to get lost if I wanted to, that he meant no offense by this, but he needed to know quickly if I might consider climbing the Eiger for a movie. Not just any movie, but an IMAX-theater film, the

EIGHTEEN

FROM ONE LIFE INTO ANOTHER

THE PHONE in Kleine Scheidegg rang at 9 p.m. on September 21, 2005, two days before I had planned to start climbing the Eiger. It was Robert. It seemed the weather forecast was changing again, and instead of five more days of clear skies, we could expect only three. Robert proposed that we begin first thing in the morning. Butterflies poured into my stomach. The serenity that I'd carefully affected these last two weeks while days of sunshine played tag with days of snow squalls suddenly crumbled through my gut like the delicately crafted fiction it had been. I gulped a tepid "Okay, tomorrow it is, then," and put down the phone. After all these years, the time had come. I had to sit for a moment to absorb that troubled dreams were about to turn into facts, and that I didn't know what the facts would end up being, only that they would take place on a very real Eiger.

I took a few deep breaths, and told myself that this was what I wanted, something I could do, that I would come back from it, and then it would be done. The butterflies' wings moved slower, settled into a gentle quivering. I breathed slowly and carefully, so as not to disturb them.

Everyone was staring at me—Adele, Siena, and the others.

Adele reached out her hand and gave mine a concerned squeeze. We had been waiting two weeks together, watching the mountain, watching the clouds, watching the snow, talking, drinking at night, and filming by day. Always the filming.

There had been filmed interviews, and filmed running in the fog, and filmed scenes by the train talking about the weather and how it was affecting our plans. We had filmed sorting our gear, and filmed Siena running around Adele and me hiking up a ridge with clouds drifting past the Eiger behind us. Nothing about the filming was supposed to interfere with the climb. That was my condition. We would start no sooner and no later than we thought right for safety. There would be no cameras climbing with us, other than the little digital spy cams on our helmets and whatever they put in position for us to climb past. My time on the Eiger would be my own, my climb every bit as real as it would have been without a movie. Before and after we set foot on the face, however, was a different matter. Our time was theirs, and they used it fully.

The film's concept, Stephen had explained to me, was to convey the power, beauty, and drama of the Swiss Alps to an audience that knows and cares little about mountaineering. I investigated the company, MacGillivray Freeman Films, and learned that they were the best in the giant-screen business—what the IMAX-theater industry calls itself. MFF had filmed on the top of Mount Everest and in the depths of the sea, deep inside Mexican caves and down the entire length of the Nile. They understood the priorities of serious adventure, and they respected that my priority was the integrity of this climb. They offered to buy me the time to come to the foot of Eiger and wait, however long it took.

I had thought a lot about this last point while stewing the idea of a movie. Over the previous decades the Eiger had never been off my mind. Conditions had to be just right on the mountain, in my training, and in my head, but there was one other issue. I had to be there when all these came together. Ninety-nine percent of the time, that meant I needed to fly across a continent and an ocean first. Even if I happened to already be in Europe, as I was every few years, getting to the Eiger itself required dumping Adele and Siena if they were with me, as they usually were, and having the right climbing partner available and in the same state of mind and fitness as I was. Between one thing and another, this matrix had gone on for a quarter century of talk (mostly inside my own head) with precious little action. I'd never even touched the face. Committing to this film would be truly committing to the climb—it would actually happen, no excuses.

I also thought about Dad during this time. Surely by climbing this mountain I was trying to make a connection. I would be on the wall that had meant so much to him, and I would somehow be with him. It wasn't a rational process. It was deep and personal, a craving inside me that hadn't gone away despite the passage of decades. Did I really want to *film* this? The unequivocal answer was "No." I wanted my privacy. I didn't want to be poked and prodded, nor distracted by people and cameras trying to get inside my head. But then I thought more deeply about Dad, and about where he had been going and how proud he would have been to be the heart of such a film forty years after his death. It would bring him back to life for a while. How could I deny him this opportunity?

The giant-screen format—projected as tall as many modern rock-climbing routes—seemed to me like not only the best, but perhaps the *only* way to convey the scale of these Alpine peaks that I loved so much. Of all the Alpine faces, the grandest by far is the Eiger. How could one capture it better than on an eighty-foot screen? I'd taken Siena to many an IMAX Theatre show in Portland, and I could imagine the incredible legacy this would leave for her, and her children.

By the time I'd returned to Oregon and presented the idea to Adele, it simply made sense. Adele agreed completely. The next question I offered was whether she and Siena would want to participate, as that was something that MFF also wanted. I couldn't recall Adele coming on a climbing trip since we'd been married.

Sure, I'd gone off for a day climb every now and then during our travels together, and there had been a couple of overnight climbs with Konrad. But she hated feeling like a tagalong, and that's how she reacted when I was distracted by climbing.

Adele's own mother had died from breast cancer twenty years earlier, so my mother is Siena's only remaining grandmother. Mom retired to Portland, just an hour from our home in Hood River. Doing this movie meant I would have to bring my secret dream into the open with her. She had suspicions already. While I had never brought up the Eiger with her, or even let an allusion slip into my writing, Mark had. He had written about most of the things we'd done together. His *Outside* articles about the Matterhorn and Mont Blanc climbs both mentioned our follow-up plan, the real prize we'd been warming up for: the Eiger. Each time Mom had asked me about it. And each time I'd told her an even softer version of what I'd told Adele: "Ah, well, you know, if the conditions had been perfect on the Eiger, I suppose we might have had a look, but you know how Mark needs to tell a good story." And while I was at it I'd point out how Mark always emphasized the dramatic parts of our climbs together, and really they'd been tamer overall than he let on.

Mom was not amused to learn that I really did have my sights on the Eiger, that down under it wasn't simply a literary construction of Mark's. And even less did she like fixing a date that she could worry toward. But neither she nor Adele ever tried to stop me, in part because I told them that my partner on the attempt was the best that there was, and that we would only climb it under the safest of conditions, and that this was a family movie and the film company cared for my safety nearly as much as I did, if for different reasons. She understood that if I was going to attempt this climb, which by now she realized was nearly inevitable, the best circumstance would be for the movie to give me the patience to wait for the right conditions with the right partner. In the end, it seemed, Mom and Adele had more faith in my judgment than I had in my own. I had their blessings, and cooperation. Siena was simply happy for another trip to Switzerland.

My sister made no comment at all when I announced the project at Thanksgiving dinner. She had married a Rhode Islander, Gene Cilento, in 1978 and had moved to the countryside near Olympia not long thereafter, where they had four children. Everyone was at the table, including the oldest child's husband. I nervously told them about the film and my plan to climb the Eiger, and the conversation immediately moved on. My mother, Adele, and I just looked at one another dumbfounded and dropped the subject. Though Andréa has photos of Dad on the wall, and framed newspaper articles in French about his climbs, she never discusses him, and never approved of my climbing, either, especially after Siena was born. She has had abandonment nightmares her entire life. To her the sport is an unacceptable risk, and the lifelong pain she has suffered from her father's death was unforgivable. She would not forgive me, either.

On September 22, the morning after Robert's phone call, he and his wife, Daniela, arrived on the first train from Grindelwald. They live in Thun, a half hour away, and that night would be the first that Daniela had ever spent apart from her two-and-a-half-year-old son, Stefan, and her one-year-old daughter, Amelie. Robert spends months away on expeditions each year, and while Daniela was a top-flight climber—mostly of very difficult bolt-protected rock-and-ice sport climbs, but also occasional mountains with Robert—she would be relying mostly on reserves of skill and experience, as the children had prevented her from climbing like she used to. The film company very much wanted a woman along, and her partnership on and off the rocks with Robert seemed the perfect opportunity. This would be her first climb up the main wall on the Eiger, though they had together climbed a shorter, steeper rock buttress that led to the west ridge.

Adele, Siena, and I hopped on the connecting train to join them, and headed up to the last stop before it entered the Eiger tunnel on its way to the Jungfraujoch. At the Eigergletscher station, Adele gave me a tight hug and wished me "Good luck, sweetie," as tears gently rolled down her cheeks. Siena didn't understand the fuss, as I was only going away for a couple of nights, but she returned my own hard squeeze.

The approach from the station to the start of the route is short, about twenty minutes on a good trail. I needed that time to begin switching mental gears. This had been a first for me: saying good-bye to my family so close to a big climb. And the climb to come felt like nothing I'd ever done, even though individual pieces should be much like those I'd been doing my whole life. I was headed into unknown territory and I didn't know how it would affect me. For three days this world would be mine, or rather, I would belong to it. Would it be as intimidating as the stories I'd read? Would I be able to find protection when I needed it, or would I be reduced to a quivering mass of gelatin eighty feet past my last piton with crampons scraping on a thin glazing of decomposing ice? My greatest fear was falling a long distance. That is always my fear, but the Eiger is infamous for its lack of protection, and I was infinitely more afraid than I usually am.

At least the lower face would offer a transition. For nearly 1,500 feet the climbing would be easy, allowing us to move together and me to adjust to a new mental state that could handle the 4,500 feet of harder climbing to come. So I breathed deeply and softly and calmed myself down, hoping that those butterflies would soon be replaced with the focus of climbing.

THE COLD Eiger rock feels good against my bare hands. There's nothing like actually touching the mountain to complete the connection. I pull down lightly on the handholds as my feet step onto ledges. My body is awakening, and it likes what it's doing. The pack on my back feels light; I barely even notice it. We move steadily, rhythmically, continuously, weaving from one small obstacle to another, each rapidly dropping into the distance below us. This is exactly what I have loved since seemingly forever. It feels like a homecoming.

But it's still different from normal. A couple of weeks ago when I first arrived at their house, Robert, Daniela, and I did a climb together to see how we'd be as a team. Daniela, ever cheerful, talked and joked like a continuously percolating coffee machine, promising good cheer with every sip. We bantered, feeding off one another's joy in the mountains, while Robert joined in when his quieter disposition was moved to. Robert is a professional climber, and it's a rare day that he doesn't have rock in his hands. For Daniela and me getting out is a special treat, and we behaved accordingly. But it's not like that here on the Eiger. I'm quiet, inwardly focused, with a tense calmness slowly spreading over me. The climbing down here is easy enough that I can think about where I am, and how long it has taken me to get here. As the rubbly rock alternates with solid bands and all of it glides past to the next small obstacle, I'm growing increasingly comfortable with the bigger challenges to come. This is my element.

The three of us have been moving simultaneously, with Robert in the lead because he's been here several times before. The only difficulty on this lower section is choosing the simplest way among too many options. That's why we decided to climb this section in the daylight rather than in the darkness as Dad and Konrad had done it. It's nice to see where you're going, and we know we can easily reach a good bivouac ledge at the base of the Rote Flüh—just before the Hinterstoisser Traverse—by early afternoon, allowing a long, comfortable rest before a predawn start tomorrow. Robert makes sure that there are at least one or two pieces of protection clipped to the rope at all times, just in case someone makes a mistake, and I remove the protection as we follow. Our rope system for this climb is the modern standard for three people: the first person leads on two ropes, each of which is tied to an individual partner. Daniela has the pink rope, and I the green. She climbs about ten feet above me, and I try not to crowd her, nor to lag behind. The system allows for plenty of talking between the two people following, but we climb almost silently.

The first hard bit is the Difficult Crack, famous as the entry gate to the main wall above, in combination with the Hinterstoisser. I've asked for the honor of leading the Difficult Crack. We switch the ropes around so that I'm dragging both.

Steep rock, tricky moves, enough protection, fast climbing . . . the Difficult Crack itself and the rest of the rock above seem to pass in a blur of joyful movement. I almost feel cheated when I hear a shout from below that the rope is running out and I need to search for belay anchors. All I can find at first are two rusty pitons stuffed with weather-beaten slings. I try to open enough space in a piton to clip my carabiner directly into the metal, but it's too jammed up with old cord. Rather than waste time cutting out slings I don't trust, I move off to a freestanding pillar of rock that I can loop a big sling around. I yell down at the top of my voice, "Off belay!" and then soon after, "Climb on!" And then I settle into my giddiness. That pitch went so well that I'm fairly bouncing. My metamorphosis on the lower 1,500 feet climbing— gradually replacing my fears of a myth with my love of an actual mountain—just took a flying leap into the beautiful real world. I feel like a climber climbing, not an abandoned son obsessing, and even here I must shout my joy to the world. I wish I could yodel like Dad did, but I can't, so I yell a huge "Yaaahooo!" to the sunlit world below. I wave to Siena and Adele, just knowing they're there. I feel on top of the world.

In no time, it seems, Daniela and Robert arrive, but they stop at the rusty pins with the old slings. "These are fine!" they say, and perhaps it's true. Europeans put a lot more faith in old fixed slings than Americans generally do. I climb back to them before grabbing the gear and leading up the last ropelength to our bivouac site at what's known as the Japanese Ledge. This pitch makes the transition from rock to snow, and from here on we expect to climb in our crampons. But the snow is soft enough at this time of day that I can kick steps all the way to the ledge just in my boots.

There's a camera pointing at me when I arrive. A small crew had come out the train tunnel window and climbed up fixed ropes well off to the side, where we wouldn't see them. That had been one of my conditions—that any fixed ropes be well away from the route—as I wanted nothing to intrude on my climbing.

"So, John, how does it feel to finally be on the Eiger?" Jochen Schmoll, a German filmmaker, asks from behind the camera.

"It feels great!" I burst, still on an emotional surge. "This is just beautiful!"

He films while I set up the belay and bring the rope up while Daniela and Robert are climbing. The camera turns to Daniela when she arrives, and Jochen asks her the same question. She launches into a tirade against me. Adele's tears this morning had shocked and disturbed her. She rages against my quietness this morning, so different from the enthusiasm I'd shown on our getting-acquainted climb two weeks before. She is appalled that I'd spoken to the microphone on my helmet camera, identifying features to the filmmakers to help them understand what the camera was seeing. My last belay had been unsafe—I'm not competent enough to use the obvious pitons. The climb, in her mind, is a wreck, all thanks to me.

I sink onto the ledge, dumbfounded, my legs kicked out from under. This can't be happening. Not here, not on this climb. It doesn't even make sense.

I'm too despondent to argue, and we can't afford the emotions of battle. There must be some underlying stress that's triggering all this, maybe thoughts of her children. Robert quietly assures her that my belay had been fine. I tell her that if it bothers her that I sometimes tell the camera what it's seeing, I'll stop doing that.

This climb is a big deal to me, and that's why I seem serious. We can resolve her concerns; all will be fine.

As we prepare our thin bivouac ledge and pull out our sleeping bags, I do what I can to pretend nothing happened. Apparently Daniela is doing the same, for I hear nothing more of it, at least not in English. She and Robert talk quite a bit in German, but that is a language I forgot exactly forty-two years ago.

It was forty-three years and two months ago that Dad passed by this spot on his way to the Hinterstoisser Traverse with Konrad. The Japanese had not yet excavated the ledge, and he passed by at 7 a.m., after six hours of climbing. He was headed to the Death Bivouac on his first day, a different strategy from ours. We plan to make it up the Ramp tomorrow and to bivouac at the Brittle Ledges near the start of the Traverse of the Gods. Tomorrow is our biggest day of climbing, and despite my happy feelings a couple of hours ago, I'm again having to breathe deeply to soothe the restless butterflies. I think of Adele and Siena below. I can see the hotel lights twinkling, and perhaps even identify their room. But they won't be there now. Dinners in Kleine Scheidegg continue late into the evening. Our freeze-dried food, cooked in bags, involves few courses, little conversation, and less wine. Now I have my head propped on a rock, softened by my helmet, which I never take off. The ledge is flat and full-length, a wonderful treat on steep mountains. It's just wide enough that I've been able to place a flat rock under my right shoulder to prevent me from rolling off. If the rock slides an inch, it will fall down 1,500 feet, though it might also stop on a snowy ledge along the way. A sling runs from my harness, which I never take off, either, to a piton on the wall at my left shoulder. Physically, I'm comfortable. Mentally, I'm okay.

I'm looking for ghosts. I don't actually believe in real ghosts, but I'm told that it takes a traumatic death to make one, so if ever there were a place for them, this should be it. We're trying to sleep perhaps 100 yards from where Toni Kurz met his drawn-out fate while his three companions went more quickly. That team accounts for almost 10 percent of the fatalities within a mile of where I'm resting.

But I don't seem to be able to call up even my own father's spirit, much though I try. My mind keeps drifting to Siena instead, and wondering about her future. A few months ago we moved to Oaxaca, Mexico, for a couple of years so that she could experience what it was like to live in a foreign culture. I had proposed Switzerland, but Adele thought Europeans are too much like us. And Spanish is the most useful language Siena can learn, so Mexico made sense. Siena is not yet happy about learning the language, and her first weeks of Mexican school were the most difficult of her young life. We had to pull her out of school to come here just when she was starting to accept it. But it's good to see her flourish again in the mountains.

I pull my mind back to the Eiger. This is where I'm supposed to be. I try to think again about Dad, but the thoughts keep drifting away. My own world seems more real these days. When my friend in Hood River asked what I'd ever done besides being born to a famous father, he probably only meant it as a joke about my climbing, or a prop for his own. But I've gradually been letting that failed ambition go. Every year I realize better that other things mean more to me, from the family that has guided me these past decades, to what I might contribute to the rest of the world in future years.

I was thinking about death not long ago when I was running in the hills above Oaxaca, and what it would mean if mine came soon—if perhaps I stepped on a coral snake alone in the back of beyond, as I almost did once. The thought saddened me. Not so much for the loss of my life, though that bothers me, too, but because it would happen before I'd had a chance to move on to new projects that mean more than the ones I've already lived through. For years I've been building stacks of notes on things I want to do, mostly in the field of sustainable development, which I see as the great need of all life on this planet. These thoughts and notes and ambitions have become my new secret life, filling far more than the space I once reserved for the Eiger or being a great climber. I keep thinking about this bigger world that I should enter, though I'm confused about my path for reaching it. Instead it seems life just pulls me along, day by day, and I've been unwilling to rock the comfort and security I've been able to craft for my family. But if I were to die, I've started wondering, what would I leave? A sad family, and some stories. I can't bear the thought of leaving my family. But I can't tolerate the fact that I haven't done more for a world that needs so much fixing.

THE STARS in the black night are nearly as bright as the lights of Grindelwald when our wrist-alarms announce the new day. We're allowing an hour for breakfast and packing, and another hour or so to reach and then cross the Hinterstoisser before daylight arrives. This next section of the mountain—from the First through the Third icefields—is the most subject to rockfall, and by climbing early we should be able to avoid much of the danger.

By the light of his headlamp, Robert lowers himself off the rock ledge to unseen footholds and then traverses far across the snow until we just see the occasional stab of his headlamp and hear his crampons scraping on rock. When he yells that he has us on belay, I gingerly lower over the edge; it's a surprisingly long ways down to the next foothold. The rope disappears into the darkness, and there's no evidence of protection. A slip here would mean a pendulum fall of at least 100 feet, probably more. Since both "seconds" climb together in our roping system, Daniela is coming down off the ledge just after I am. But her legs are short, and she's having a great deal of difficulty finding something to step on. This move off the bivouac ledge has blindsided us with its difficulty and danger. What a rude awakening; could this be a portent of the day? I maneuver back toward the ledge, where I use my ice axes to set up a snow anchor to become a belay point on Daniela's rope. Now if she falls she'd only pendulum about 40 feet, while dropping 20. She doesn't fall—she's too good a climber. But her nerves are rattled. I let her pass me by and then I follow the beam of her headlamp across the steep crunchy snow-ice.

Before reaching Robert we find the steep rock where we'd heard his crampons. I wait for Daniela to climb it, and then follow with a mixture of rock climbing and ice-tool placements in frozen cracks, with feet alternating between frontpoints on little rock edges and kicking delicately into thin ice so that it doesn't break off. When I reach the belay I gush about how good the climbing is—this mixture of snow, rock, and ice is my favorite kind.

Two Austrians are in the Swallows' Nest bivouac at the far side of the Hinterstoisser, preparing to start their day's climbing. They had passed us at the Japanese Ledge just at dusk as we were cooking dinner. It is daylight now, and my inclination is to pause a few minutes to let the Austrians get going. But it seems things are done differently in the Alps. Robert plows right through their arrangements and starts up above them. Soon one of the Austrians is climbing as well, with ropes crossing each other. It's now a race to see who reaches the Ice Hose first, our next major obstacle. When I get a moment to think about more than what I'm doing, I recall that it was right around here that Dad was struck by a rock on the side of his head in 1962. We haven't seen a single falling rock, nor even evidence of newly fallen stones caught in the snow. Instead everything is caked in a sheet of hard névé, a snow that's halfway to ice. It is like a skin over the mountain, trapping all the loose rubble and rotten rock—and indeed, all the low-angle rock no matter how solid. It's providing us with an unbelievably good climbing surface. Dad had said that just before the Ice Hose he encountered the most rotten and dangerous bit of climbing he had ever had the misfortune to come across. Two weeks after his climb a German had fallen to his death here. But for us it is a technical walk. It appears that our timing is perfect: just as Tobin Sorenson had told me, and Dad had known, too, the early fall offers a narrow window of opportunity, when the first wet-snow of autumn freezes to the wall before the extreme cold of winter changes the dynamic yet again. As long as the temperature doesn't rise—in which case this skin will melt into a cascade of snow-and-rock avalanches—we will have ideal conditions.

Even the notorious Ice Hose is in perfect shape. Where many have written of ice that's too thin or too rotten to climb, for us it's deep, soft, and strong. I can see the same bottleneck formations that Dad had pinched with his bare hands, but my modern tools sink into it as if it were Styrofoam. Above that, where Dad had encountered slablike rock with only friction for holds and nothing for protection—one of the passages I dreaded—we instead encounter a thick layer of hard snow. The Second Icefield that Dad had painstakingly chopped steps across because his crampons were dull—where he dropped his own axe and Konrad continued—this we kick steps up with our boots and could climb without crampons. All three of us move simultaneously straight up the Second Icefield and then traverse along its upper edge. Still not a sign of falling rock anywhere.

We reach the Death Bivouac in the late morning. The snow here has pulled away from the slightly overhanging rock above, leaving a gap where spindrift has created a ledge. I try to imagine Dad, Chris, Layton, and Dougal digging four hours to craft a tight snow hole—and Dad's week here with a pile of feces growing on the inside of the sealed doorway, and bronchitis building in his lungs. I try to remember how I'd spoken to Dad here by walkie-talkie from Kleine Scheidegg, and how I had believed him when he said all was well on the wall. Here is where he'd scribbled the last he would write, hoping that Topolino had been fun and that my exams not too miserable. He had written, "We are hoping to make the top in a few days but we are being very safe so don't worry."

I'd like to reflect more on these things, but we can see the Austrians we passed this morning as they cross the top of the Second Icefield in our footsteps—and rapidly gaining on them is a party of two. On the far side of them are moving specs that imply even more people. This is the way of the Eiger. For long spells the face is too dangerous to climb. Everyone who wants to climb it this season monitors the weather reports and calls his friends to learn the latest conditions. When the stars finally align, we all pounce on the same opportunity. It had happened on Heinrich Harrer's ascent, on Dad's, and on many more right up to today.

It's my turn to lead, and I tear off across the Third Icefield. This is the steepest icefield by far, and normally subject to rockfall from the Spider above. But still we haven't seen a falling rock on the climb. I need to keep moving, just in case, but there's no reason to rush in conditions like these. I pause every now and then to appreciate the fact that I'm truly alone—I can't see any climbers at the moment, not even my partners—and this fact helps to set my mind free. I stop to look up toward the Spider's legs and make out the Central Pillar. I think I can pick out the overhang where Dad's rope broke. If I'm right, he would have struck the wall right around here, maybe touched the ice that my frontpoints are standing on.

What did you think about, Dad? What was it like to feel the rope go slack and see this icefield coming up on you fast? Were you the hero you—and we—thought you'd be? Did you reach for the movie camera to film your ultimate experience? Or were you savoring the vivid moment of truth? Did you think about us? Is it possible that in the end you were terrified and sad and sorry, like I would be? How much time did you have to decide?

I wonder these things while I look up toward the Spider. But it's strange. I'm in my world, not Dad's. In my world my frontpoints are stabbing the ice and my ice axes are holding me tight. The rope drapes horizontally twenty or thirty feet to an ice screw, and a similar distance to the next. The ice I shatter slides down until it disappears off an edge. And it feels good. It's beautiful here, though cold and utterly heartless. I have to keep moving.

Reaching the Ramp, I first look up at the obvious snow line above, and then over to where tracks lead leftward to an alternative start. Foolishly, I assume that the people who'd left those tracks knew that their line was better than the obvious one above. A pitch later I can see that the obvious line would have been faster, but this doesn't become relevant until another pitch higher when I see the fast party from the Second Icefield racing up the line I'd avoided. They are climbing simultaneously, whereas we're belaying each ropelength, and when they reach me I wave them through.

Robert and Daniela know the lead climber. Michael Wärthl is a very strong German guide with a client in tow. He's racing to pass us, and as he speeds by, Daniela comments that he looks something like Dad. She reminds me that MFF is looking for someone to play my father in the movie and we should remember to mention him. As fate turns out, Michael will become the one jumaring a 7mm rope when an unseen hand above cuts his rope for the film. He will also dress in old clothes to ski with the boy they find to play me in my childhood. But here on the Ramp there is just Daniela's short comment to hint at the future. I hadn't even noticed a resemblance.

And now it's our turn to wait. Michael led the crux Waterfall Chimney pitch quickly, but his client is thrashing. It's a very steep, intimidating pitch with a bit of ice squeezing through the narrow upper section and maybe 100 feet of vertical rock below. The client does okay for a while and then alternates between hanging on the rope and knocking the remaining ice off the wall as he slowly hacks his way up. He's making it look scary. He's also taking a long time. We can hear the Austrians gaining on us from below. I had planned to lead this, but now I'm thinking that it would be faster if Robert does, as I don't want the Austrians to be tapping their toes if I don't climb it quickly. Robert, of course, is only too eager to get back in the lead. He starts up while the client is still hanging on the rope near the top of the pitch.

Robert is smooth, as ever, and makes it look easy, as always, but when Daniela and I follow we find out how hard it really is. They are both world-class masters in the modern art of climbing rock using crampons and ice tools, hooking their picks on the most improbable of edges. I do this, too, but am much more used to using my hands than my ice tools. Still, I follow their example, kicking crampons and knocking the tools into ice whenever it presents itself, but mostly hooking gently on bare rock. This is where Dad had placed several pitons into a solution hole and packed ice chips to hold them in place before affixing a sling that he stood on. We manage to climb it all free using a type of ice axe that hadn't been invented in Dad's day.

I want to get back in the lead, but the way the belay is set up would make this transition difficult. It is much more efficient for Robert to keep going and for Daniela and me to keep following. The next pitch provides a short crux called the Ice Bulge—a few moves past a slightly overhanging mixture of rock and ice. From below I had watched Michael pull with his hands on a series of fixed pitons just left of the ice, but Robert climbs it free with his tools hooking the rock instead. When it's our turn I try to free it like Robert. The hooking moves are thin and steep, but my rope runs safely up so I decide to keep trying the rock. Suddenly my picks pop off and I drop about five feet to the steep snow below. I laugh at my weakness on this type of climbing, and then slam my picks into real ice to the right, more on the Bulge, pulling strenuously over it without incident. Little do I know that Adele had put her eye to the telescope just moments before my little fall. She saw me drop and gasped. She held Siena and walked away from the telescope, unable to watch.

A few ropelengths of easy climbing take us to the Brittle Ledges, where we'll climb up to the Traverse of the Gods. While I'm stomping ledges where the steep snow meets overhanging rock, Daniela belays Robert as he puts a rope up the next pitch to save us time in the morning. Not long after he's done, two climbers file by. I can't keep track of who is who anymore, but I think they're the Austrians. Apparently the distant party we'd seen starting up the Second Icefield is just below. The Austrians, if that's who they are, clip into the rope Robert left and haul themselves up hand over hand. Dusk has nearly turned to dark by now, and they want to quickly reach the next bivouac at the start of the Traverse of the Gods. A short while later, after complete darkness, we hear voices below. The others, whoever they are, have cleared the Ice Bulge and are yelling up to ask us in German about bivouac options. We scan the wall on the other side of the Ramp with our headlamps and see what appears to be a good option under a rock sticking out of the snow. With our lights held on the rock we direct them to it.

It's been a good day overall, and I'm happy as I settle onto my skinny snow platform. My ledge is just barely shoulder width, so I've rigged a circular sling to help hold me in position. Our bivouacs on the Eiger have been nothing short of luxurious compared to the cramped little butt-ledge that Roger, Julie-Ann, and I shared on Mont Blanc.

We don't see stars because in the final hours of daylight gentle clouds condensed out of thin air around us before drifting off, only to materialize again and slowly drift off in another direction, and then materialize yet again. Just before sunset we had briefly caught the sun's reflection coming off the wall where the other climbers are now rattling their cooking pot, but we've not actually felt the sun's rays since the day before yesterday. It's been cold enough to keep the snow frozen, but warm enough that we're comfortable in our light sleeping bags. It's peaceful as I lie down on my ledge. This is an extraordinary place up here: huge, dark, and awesome, but magnificent in its scale and its views. I can see why Dad liked it so much. I know that I'm having a different experience from his thanks to the superb conditions we've encountered and our modern gear. In many ways I'm on a different mountain, and it feels a bit unreal to be climbing it this way. But it's okay. Safety is good. This is how I'd always promised myself I would do the climb: under the best of conditions, and only then. It seems that I've stuck with my vow after all. Or that one, at least.

Mom thinks we're starting the climb tomorrow. I so much want to call her and say that we're done before she can enter the crux stages of her worrying. This has been hard on her. After I told her about my Eiger plans she dreamed that I fell off a cliff and hit my head on a rock; she heard the loud crack but woke up before learning my fate. And I've been asking her a lot of questions about Dad recently. She slipped once and said, "You had a mother, too, you know!" I'm starting to see how much I've taken that fact for granted. Dad came and went, but Mom never left other than, as she once put it, to move into the background when I had a change of women in my life, first to my wife, and then adding my daughter. I remember how much Grandpa George meant to me when I was Siena's age, and I'm so glad that Siena has a grandparent she's close to.

I've been constantly asked why I'm not climbing the Direct, or whether I'll return for that route after this one. Even Siena asked me why I wasn't on Dad's route. I chose the original route, I told her, because it's the one that Dad succeeded on and the one I could most likely accomplish. And also because the John Harlin Route would worry Mom ten times as much. She wrote me in Oaxaca, "I've been asked whether you intend to return to the Eiger for the Direct. And I have said emphatically, NO! He will NOT put us through that again. The North Face classic route will serve quite nicely, thank you. So glad that part will be OVER!" During the last weeks I've seen Adele interviewed and felt her tension even as she strove to salve mine. Siena recently asked her what they would do if I died; Adele responded that it's not going to happen. As I rest here on my snow-ledge, I know that there's only one thing I must do, and that's to climb out from this specter so we can get on with our lives.

The morning dusk is already brightening as we stuff our sleeping bags into rucksacks. We expect today to pass quickly. At the Traverse of the Gods we adopt a new trick for safety. Robert crosses first, heading straight horizontal and placing a couple of pieces of protection. When he reaches the end of the rope I stay put at the anchor so that Daniela can clip into my rope with a carabiner at her waist. That way she has a safety line and doesn't face the risk of a huge pendulum. It's not that she needs the protection any more than I do, just that we might as well make one of us safe when the option presents—and that should be the mother. When she reaches Robert's belay, I come across, removing the gear. It's an unnerving feeling to take out protection and then see the rope loop unattached fifty feet horizontal—especially when crossing the most spectacular section of the Eiger, with more than 4,000 feet of space under my crampons. It's immediately obvious why this is called the Traverse of the Gods: up here you feel apart from the world, on a mountain without end. I can look down to the Central Pillar where Dad's rope broke, and occasionally I pause to sweep my eyes lower. But I can't let myself think about that; action will purge me. We have a lot more climbing left to do— thanks to storms and a tangle of other climbers bunched up in the Exit Cracks, Dad had spent two days getting from here to the summit.

When Dad and Konrad climbed the Spider, it had been hissing with avalanches. For us it is crusted with firm névé and perfectly silent. We glide up the icefield and are entering a couloir when a head-sized rock arcs through the sky from 400 feet above, knocked loose by a climber in the upper Exit Cracks. We watch and hear it whop-whop-whop through the air and then notice with a shock that it's headed straight toward two climbers below us, the ones who had bivouacked nearby. My heart is a drum when the rock slams into the snow right next to their rope. It takes a few minutes for my pulse to calm down.

We have been moving simultaneously since the Traverse of the Gods, but when Robert stops at the rock above I insist on taking over the lead. I want terribly to lead the famous sections at the Quartz Crack and then on out the Exit Cracks, the final diffi-culties of the route. As a climber I haven't been comfortable with the amount of time I've been spending at the back of the rope instead of the sharp end—the front—especially after having turned over the Waterfall Chimney pitch, a decision that has been nagging me. Leading us out will restore my sense of having contributed my share—and maybe quench my doubts about courage.

Before I can climb we must wait for a bottleneck of climbers struggling with the difficult pitch ahead, just as Dad had had to do, but we're spared his epic. By now I've lost any sense of intimi-dation; instead I'm filled with a burning itch to launch up the rock. The guidebook describes this pitch as a 130-foot overhang, but in fact it's a funny hybrid between a sometimes-overhanging prow on one side and a smooth slab of ice less than an inch thick on the other. When I reach it I find I can usually stem between the two, with one foot on each side, and move back and forth as need dictates. I feel like I'm flying up the pitch, perhaps because I'm on fire this close to our goal. I'm ecstatically proud and happy as I set up the belay anchors. When Daniela and Robert arrive, I leap into action on the next pitch, traversing and climbing to a lowering point where I pendulum over to the final pitches of the exit gully. I throw in an anchor to bring Daniela and Robert over quickly. We've gained on the other climbers, and I want to maintain the momentum. While they follow I steal looks up the wide groove above. It's amazingly smooth and there's not a crack in sight, but it's not too steep. Here and there is a little ice to mix with the rock—ice that's coming down in crumbly bits from crampon scratching.

When Daniela and Robert arrive I start sorting gear for the next pitch. They exchange glances, and then she apologizes. I raise my eyes. Robert looks like he's feeling awkward as Daniela tells me that they want him to lead up to the cameras that will be waiting at the top of the Exit Cracks. They have to think about how he'll look in the film; it wouldn't be right for him to be seen coming up second again, like at the Japanese Ledge.

I collapse into a silent rage, a toxic brew of anger, frustration, and disappointment more intense than I've ever felt—the great moment of my life feels like it's being ripped out of my heart. I can't, or won't, even speak. While Daniela belays Robert I hang from my slings pouting, deliberating exposing myself to a rain of ice coming down the crack and bouncing off my helmet. I don't give a damn what falls on me; I almost dare a rock to hit me.

And then gradually a little voice of reason starts working its way through my all-consuming anger. I start thinking of Siena when she occasionally throws tantrums, and how Adele and I tell her that her mood is standing between her and her goals—and that only she can control her emotions. As I start looking at myself that way, from the outside looking in, I see the absurdity of what I'm doing to myself. Just imagining Siena starts to slowly, gropingly pull me back to what I'm on the verge of accomplishing. I look over at the steep ledge that Daniela is standing on and I realize that we are at *exactly* the place where Dad and Konrad had spent the night holding a burning candle in their hands to keep from falling asleep. That had been a *real* struggle, and they never gave in. Me not leading the next two pitches will not exactly shake the world. Soon I am going to be climbing to the top of the Eiger, damn it, *the Eiger!*

When Daniela and I start up the pitch we find it every bit as tricky and unprotected as it looked. My mood is far from where I want it to be, but the climbing requires most of my focus—my balance, both inside and out. Still, because I'm not leading, there's some room for distractions, like thinking. I've often said how we never defeat a mountain—instead we defeat the things that prevent us from climbing the mountain, and most of those are inside us. On this climb it seems that my internal battles are coming from unexpected sources. Where I had prepared my head for sketchy climbing, falling stones, and maybe a storm, instead we found excellent conditions. Where I'd expected to wrestle with fear and emotional ghosts, instead I'd felt a transcendent love of climbing and mountain. In Robert I've seen the climber I always wanted to become, and yet I don't feel the envy I might have when I was his age. No, the battle I ended up facing was to relearn a child's lesson: that ultimately we are in charge of ourselves and our happiness.

When we reach him, Robert turns over the lead so I can take us up the Summit Icefield. It's clear that he's seen and maybe even understood my struggle; my face does not hide emotion well. I thank him—no ill had been meant toward me—and I shift partially back into my earlier leader's headspace, this time racing up toward the sunshine. Two hundred feet above us the sun cuts a diagonal swath across the ice slope, and when I get there the unexpected brightness nearly blinds me. We have at last escaped the Eiger's shadow. The light is a balm for my soul.

On the knife-edged summit ridge we coil the ropes in our hands and walk together about twenty feet apart. Robert calls this "jumping rope," because if someone slips, your job is to jump down the other side so that the rope straddles the edge. In this case the left side—south—plunges 3,000 feet to a huge glacier; on the right, where we've come, it's 6,000 feet to the talus.

Physically, this ridge is a variation on the Matterhorn's theme. Emotionally, I'm on another planet. It's the most spectacular place I've ever been. Every step is a gift, a dream being fulfilled, a new life revealed. I can see the terrifying slabs where Dougal fought his way to the summit while Dad was being lowered into his grave. But I can't think about graves here, nor titanic struggles, not even fear or heroism or victory or things that could have been or that weren't meant to be. None of those can break through the euphoria that swells inexorably inside me, leaving room for nothing less. For the moment I have arrived where I've always wanted to be; it feels like my journey is nearly complete.

The surrounding peaks are bathed in alpenglow when Adele

and Siena come running out of the Mönch hut to greet us. I scoop them up in my arms and we start spinning, around and around, when suddenly I realize that I'm still wearing crampons! I'm terrified of stepping on their toes. Like a drunken sailor I stagger holding them in the air until there's nothing for it but to collapse onto the snow, laughing like fools in love.

ACKNOWLEDGMENTS

I F   I T weren't for MacGillivray Freeman Films, my dream of climbing the Eiger might still be unfulfilled. Instead, I can look back with a sense of accomplishment, and look forward to a beautiful film, *The Alps,* that will be a legacy for my daughter. Perhaps the greatest joy I felt in this process was in watching Siena excel under the demands of long working days, which extended into a strenuous month of filming throughout Switzerland during the spring after I reached the Eiger's summit.

First at MFF I must thank Steve Judson, *The Alps's* director, writer, and editor, whose vision, sensitivity, and talents are the core of this film. Next is Greg MacGillivray, producer and everyone's boss, whose own vision long ago created a company with true heart and soul, and who was willing to gamble on my being able to climb such a monstrous wall if it ever stopped snowing. And Alex Biner, executive producer, who had the original dream of an IMAX-theater film about his beloved native-Swiss mountains, and whose long efforts finally made *The Alps* possible. I also thank Stephen Venables for inventing the notion that my ascent might be interesting.

On the Eiger and throughout Switzerland, we worked with an amazingly talented and dedicated crew, from whom I relearned the art of patience and the virtue of tirelessness. Rob Walker, assistant cameraman/associate editor, stands out for his indomitable cheerfulness and shoulders big enough to bear every burden. Brad Ohlund, director of photography, leavened many a tense moment with his special brand of good-hearted sarcasm. How Anne Marie

Hammers, line producer, managed to keep cool while fielding more cell phones than I have brain cells is utterly beyond me, and the same can be said for Mark Krenzien, producer, for whom fresh complications merely add spice to a day. Michael Brown, director of mountain photography, displayed his gifted combined vision as both adventurer and filmmaker, and endured my temper without snapping back. Jochen Schmoll, assistant cameraman, showed unflagging dedication to getting each shot no matter the obstacles. Mike O'Donnell, chief rigger and a climber's climber, displayed his enormous skills quietly while touching my heart by knowing Dad's story almost better than I did. Pasquale Scaturro, expedition leader, organized and kept safe the vast team on and around the mountain, a formidable challenge at times. Barbara MacGillivray hovered below the mountain, camera or sound system always in hand, making sure the background was being documented when she wasn't entertaining Siena. Also a princess with Siena and an invaluable Swiss-American cultural and logistical link was Bettina Wild, Alex Biner's associate at 4iS.

Protecting the camera crew on the Eiger and the Matterhorn, and occasionally doubling for climbers and skiers when we couldn't be in two places at once while filming on precious good-weather days, was a crew of Swiss, Austrian, and German guides who also happen to be among the most talented climbers in the world: Simon Anthamatten, Stephan Eder, Bruno Jelk, Kurt Lauber, Dorte Pietro, Roger Schaeli, and Michael Wärthl. Stefan Anthamatten was the film's avalanche explosive expert. Aerial photography by Ron Goodman and ground-supported by Jack Tankard was made possible by the expert flying of Gerold Biner and Robbie Andenmatten of Air Zermatt.

My colleagues in front of the camera, known in the industry as "talent" and in all cases more talented than I, included Beatrice and Bruno Messerli, whose good work, friendly humor, and lively conversation have my greatest admiration. I have a similar high regard for Christine Pielmeier, snow scientist, with whom I skied in

Zermatt. Michi Wärthl put up with multiple rope-cuttings while playing the role of my father, and the young Marco Just displayed tremendous good humor while playing my nine-year-old self. Robert Jasper showed mountain judgment as good as his formidable climbing talent, while Daniela warmly and graciously welcomed me into their home despite sleepless nights from restless infants. And finally I must thank my great friend Mark Jenkins for encouraging me to get out and climb and not just whine about not getting out and climbing, and also for stepping aside graciously when my timing for the Eiger didn't mesh with his.

The film was made possible by the generous contributions of Holcim and Switzerland Tourism—Roland Walker, Christian Birck, and Bjoern Kaelin of Holcim as well as Roland Baumgartner, Eva Brechtbühl, and Urs Eberhard of Switzerland Tourism, who worked endlessly to ensure that *The Alps* reflects the breadth of Swiss mountains.

Meanwhile, back in California, I must single out Kathy Almon for her generous warmth during the early days of the project; I felt like a lost child when Kathy finally had to let go of my hand. And Lori Rick, book publishing supervisor and director of public relations, has been patient as I try to swim through new worlds after the climb. Harrison Smith, general manager, keeps me in check with a smile. Most of the rest of the staff I've only begun to know at this stage, and it's probably fairest to just list them alphabetically while looking forward to knowing them better soon: Tim Amick, Chip Bartlett, Alice Casbara, Patty Collins, Mary Jane Dodge, Janna Emmel, Nadine Ferdousi, Kana Goto, Bob Harman, Jeff Horst, Jennifer Leininger, Mike Lutz, Shaun MacGillivray, Pat McBurney, Matthew Muller, Chris Palmer, Samantha Spaeth, Tori Stokes, and Susan Wilson.

I ALSO want to show profuse gratitude to my agent and friend Susan Golomb, who encouraged me to write my story long

ACKNOWLEDGMENTS

before I actually climbed the Eiger, and to Marysue Rucci at Simon & Schuster, who believed in this book and who edited my prose with great kindness and superb insight, making this a vastly better book than it otherwise would have been. Thank you so much.

I AM beyond indebted to my mother, Dr. Marilyn Miler Harlin, for fifty years of loving support, for leaving me with a treasure chest of letters from the 1960s, and for detailed critiques of every stage of this manuscript. Also my undying gratitude to Adele Hammond, my wife, for unflagging support and love, and to Siena, for patiently tolerating a Dad who has been too wrapped up in writing about himself to finish her tree house. Where did I leave the hammer and saw?

DAD'S BOOK *Introspection Through Adventure* and many more of his photos can be found at www.JohnHarlin.net.

INDEX

INDEX

PHOTO CREDITS